The
HEALER

A Guide to Spiritual Healing

Dr. Tamsyn Freeman ND

Howling Wolf Press
Grande Prairie, Alberta

Howling**W**olf books may be ordered through any bookseller or by contacting:

Howling**W**olf**P**ress
10024 107Ave.
Grande Prairie, Alberta
T8V 1L7
www.drfreemannd.ca
1-(780)-402-8098

ISBN 10: 1460993896
ISBN 13: 9781460993897

This book is a reference work based on the research by the author, her teachings and experience. The content of this book is for information purposes only and is not intended to be a substitute for professional medical, naturopathic or other health care advice (either directly or indirectly), nor is the content intended as a diagnosis, cure, treatment or prevention of any disease. The intent of the author is to provide information to assist you in your search for emotional and spiritual well-being. If you use any of the information in this book on or for yourself, which is your constitutional right, the author assumes no responsibility for your actions.

Names, locations and case details have been changed so as to protect privacy. The resulting case examples are therefore fictitious and written for instructional purposes only. Any resemblance to real persons, living or dead, is purely coincidental. Permission has been obtained whenever possible.

Third edition

Howling**W**olf**P**ress rev. date: 01/25/2013

Cover art © Tamsyn Freeman
Author photo © Madisyn Bishop

THE HEALER
A Guide to Spiritual Healing

child—'Someday I will be powerful!'
parent—'You will be more powerful than you can possibly imagine.'

Intention

This book is intended for the healer in all of us. It is for healers from all modalities, those in the process of healing and any student on the spiritual path. It is simply meant as a guideline for spiritual journeying and healing— your own way will be unique and Self-guided. Some generalities are explained here to help support and help you keep faith throughout some of the more challenging times you may encounter on your path and as a healer. There are many different spiritual outlooks, paths, modalities and ways. This is written without any particular way in mind so as to help you better apply it to your own journey.

There really is no word than can describe our concept of the divine Self. However, to point to the concept, the capitalized word 'Self' in this book is used as a reference to the Divine, Higher Self, You, Me, God, Soul, Spirit, Within, Oneness, Universe etc. The word 'self' is used to demarcate the ego, animal self, small self etc. The word 'karma' is used to denote inertia, propensity or tendency. She and He are used interchangeably.

You can also replace 'patient' with client or friend and 'practice' with business or work to better apply the information to your own life.

To best absorb the meaning of this work, find a place of meditation or stillness to read, reflect and contemplate. This is not a book to be read all at once as the content speaks to the soul and requires processing. Do not be discouraged if some things allude your understanding upon the first read. Be patient and allow this processing to occur and understanding will come in time.

I encourage you to make your own notes of trends you have noticed for you personally, for your patients, clients or in others in order to deepen collective understanding and change the world as we know it.

CONTENTS

Dedication

To all healers, those that are healing and all students of
the spiritual path—to You.

When I began to practice naturopathic medicine in 2001, I realized that I could only go so far in helping others find true cause of dis-ease with the albeit practical and useful tools and skills I had been taught. To leave healing at palliation when more was desired, became unacceptable to me. I had to go beyond just treating the physical which led me deeper into the mind and ultimately, into the spirit. I had to, for myself and those willing to take this journey, go further into the spiritual in order to access and treat the deepest and most crucial aspects of the human soul and psyche in order to be most effective as a healer. At this point, my life changed drastically and I literally saw a whole new world as I began to accept the innate powers of intuition that we all possess, and allow them to surface and be utilized on myself, within my practice and in the rest of my life. As this new Self immerged, so did my entire perception of health and healing and of life itself. My only guide at this point, was Within—so I started to write . . .

This book started off as a simple compilation of case examples and journals from my practice and my own life around the subject of spirituality and its impact on health, the mind and our state of being, from the perspective of my personal observations and intuitions. Over time, I was guided to share this work with others in a book form.

Although the book is now complete, I can say that our life's work is never done. We can only really take a snapshot in time when it comes to our awareness. In that sense, the book and my intention for it, are ever-revealing— it's meaning changes over time as does our own consciousness. I pray this book provides you with some guidance on your path and helps to lead you in the right direction for healing and for your own life.

Love and Blessings,

Tamsyn

Thanks

Thanks goes to each and every person that has crossed my path and taught me so much about Myself. Know that I thank you all each and every day.

Thanks to all the patients, teachers, healers, writers, students, family and friends, both past and present—I see your beauty and power and with it I know anything can and will be done. Thank you for reminding me of our true nature—of limitlessness.

Thanks to my partner Matthew—your love, support, humor and wisdom has kept me disciplined, sane and laughing.

Thanks to my girls who have taught me more than I thought possible with the wisdom that all children possess.

Thanks to my animals, to Mother Earth and all of her creatures for your grounding and unconditional love.

Thanks to my office manager, Terry. You have been my faithful assistant and loyal ally.

I am eternally grateful to my greatest Teacher, Self. In Your shadow and with Your unfailing guidance, I have come to Know MySelf. May I constantly pass on light and love to all as I surrender fully unto You.

I love you all. May you forever love YourSelves.

Prologue

Work, like any work, never exists alone on its own. It cannot. It is a reflection of each one of us. Of everyone we know—of our true connection to one another. This reflects the true work of what is possible, of hope . . . of limitlessness. It reflects the strength that lies in each one of us. It reflects and illustrates and encourages this, to show you it can, has and will be done.

No fear is too powerful, no dis-ease too terrible, no cure unobtainable. This we know. We merely need to remember. All that has ever existed, does exist and will ever exist

is love.

The Healer

I can only point the way to you.
The way will become you and through it, you will remember Who You Are.

The Definition of the Healer

A healer is simply one who is present. To be present is to be fully here in reality with all your senses fully engaged, with what's in front of you—to flow and be in full alignment with your surroundings—to share. Anyone can be a healer, doing anything. The only requirement is presence. No titles, schooling, experience or practice is necessary. Do not mistake a learned person or practitioner as necessarily being a healer. A healer can be a small child, your hairdresser, mechanic or grandmother. Do not mistake healing as something that occurs outside of you or that you yourself do not have the ability to heal or be healed. The only true healer for you is Yourself.

A patient is simply one you are sharing with. A patient is a healer as well.

Why Be the Healer?

In life it is seemingly easier to follow the paths set out for us by the world we know. To take this or that course, to educate ourselves that this means that and that causes this. We then automatically apply this 'knowledge' to what's in front of us without question or feeling—without intuiting what is correct. We simply go through the motions. Many of us will do so with very good intent and even with some effect. Our successes will be the products of hard work and our feelings around them limited to pride and reward. The soul becomes unsatisfied and hungry for something more—for Connection. It is only through this yearning that we become Healers. To set aside societal notions and expectations—even our learning from the past—and lay it all down to something deeper, something greater—to something limitless. The satisfaction and contentment gleaned from being a true Healer is greater than anything else and will sustain your soul for eternity.

What Is Healing?

Healing is presence itself. It can be anything from a moment of presence to a lifetime. Do not judge healing or what you think it is. It is true sharing. A moment of sharing can affect you forever. Do not think that if someone continues to be ill or even passes on that healing has not occurred. Healing is the awakening to the true Self. Be satisfied that you have done your job at that moment in time with what was required of you. There is nothing more to be said or done. You have set in motion something that will stay forever regardless of outer circumstances. Be still with this and you will see the blessing of this mutual encounter beyond the physical.

The Courage and Dedication
of the Healer

You are the ant. I the garden is your Home.
You have eternity to find It so you can't help but find It.

For anyone who's spent any time in introspection on the spiritual path, being present (being a healer) is not common or (seemingly) easy. Although it is certainly and thankfully gaining in popularity, it takes immense courage and personal power to sustain it. One must be dedicated to the pursuit of peace and presence to the extreme, wanting nothing else in one's life. This of course, is understandably rare. It seems simply too difficult to provide this much focus and intent at all times.

Students stop and start many times, some never to recover or to regain their faith, while for others it seems to make them stronger. It is fraught with risks and dangers and it's lonely. Self-sabotage is common and along with it, the extremes of frustration and other emotions.

Often a healer can be upset at the state of the world and at our collective lack of consciousness and presence. Apply compassion to this as it is viewed by most as all too difficult and only those who really want it have the endurance to pursue it. Be happy that you have at least pursued the journey. Pray/meditate for others that somewhere, sometime, they will be as fortunate as you.

With all this said, apply the extremes of gentleness to yourself. You must work at the very least at being kind to yourself (and therefore to others) rather than engaging in the all-to-common past-time of self-flagellation and self-hatred for not 'succeeding'. The journey is simple but not easy and you can never go back once you've raised your consciousness and evolved Yourself. Keep walking forward and you cannot fail – you are not given anything you cannot handle.

The Powers of the Healer

Through these things, you will heal.

A true healer is one who has ultimate faith the patient (self or other) can heal—without doubt. A true healer has the will to apply that faith with unwavering intent and the compassion to hold it there.

Whether the patient chooses to heal or not is up to them but the healer must maintain this utmost potential at all times that they can and that they will. A healer doesn't ask how the patient heals or when, she just knows that he does and can.

Love and compassion heal all. By extending unconditional love to a patient who accepts this love, they subsequently *must* heal at some point. Love is life force. Directed with will and faith, it can literally do anything. Love (which is another definition for sharing) is the only tool you really have.

A healer always heals him/herself first and foremost. This practice is ongoing, ever-revealing and attracts those also ready to heal, to you.

We are all potential healers. There is no one that cannot help heal or heal themselves—completely and permanently.

Both the healer and the patient must have will, faith and love. The patient must pick up these things from the healer (or from some other source) to be healed. Love (life force) must be accepted by the patient— a contract must be made on a soul level between the healer and the patient for healing to occur through them.

Love is the vibration above all vibrations that reminds us of our perfection. It's the reminder that figuratively gives your head a shake and says to you, remember Who You Really Are—back to your beginning when you first came into being—your true Self. A healer must see this in all patients and focus on it to help them heal. Ultimately, a healer 'holds' the highest vibration for the patient so that they can tune into it—so they can change their own vibrational frequency into that of love (sharing/life force/presence) again. The healer sets the 'reset' button so the patient can begin anew again through the sharing of their own faith, will and love.

Will

Will is the Spirit-deep desire to manifest. It is the Will of Self with no agenda other than that which is required and intuited of us and to us. There is no self or small will involved. Will is faith in action. For Will to function, there must be passion from the Self to fulfill it.

When a healer applies Will to a patient, it is a powerful force that commands healing to them. It is a knowing and the use of life force that comes through the healer, to do so. The Will must have unwavering faith backing it to be effective. Will requires confidence and therefore, faith—they work in unison. This faith must trump the mind and with assertion, that Will is applied. It is an act of finality as if the thing being healed is already unquestionably done.

Hand gestures or the use of hands-on energies, certain words and breath are important in applying Will—however, they need not always be overt or outward to be effective. Certain practices such as these can train the energies to go where they are commanded to by the Self. Practice the application of Will in whatever means you find most effective. The art of manifestation is important to learn here for Will to be effective.

Faith

Faith must be cultivated. Don't try to push faith—it must come of its own accord and it often doesn't happen overnight. With practice and the continued viewing of everyday miracles at home and at work, you will gain proof that intuition has served and then faith will strengthen. Many people overlook miracles that happen constantly. Why did that job come just as I lost the old one? Why did I see that person just after thinking about them? How did that plant survive the winter when I was sure it was dead? That book was the only one left—the one I needed . . . Meeting that person today lifted my spirits immensely just from her smile and thanks . . . The picture that child drew for me was of an angel . . .

We may look at them briefly and then dismiss them, not wanting to admit their immense power. With the continued viewing of these miracles all the time, you will build your faith. Watch your own life and others and you will see. It's constant, every day and usual. Watch how similar patients seem to come at the same time. How similar cases pop up at the same time. How something in your own private life continues to arise when treating your patients. All these things are more than just synchronicity. They are attractions and miracles of consciousness. Watch, listen and learn from them. Do not shuffle them away to deal with the toils of everyday life. Keep your sights on them at all times and your perceptions of this reality will rapidly shift. You cannot heal yourself or others using the mind and logic. Only *knowing* and truly seeing can heal.

Compassion

We are often told as healers to have compassion (which literally means 'with passion'). To approach healing with passion is correct but the passion must be from Self Will, not due to any other notion of sympathy or need. Compassion must be only applied in terms of empathy—to understand yet remain unaffected.

It is most difficult to be compassionate when you are irritated, annoyed or fearful. Compassion requires quiet observant understanding—coming from a higher place than any thoughts or feelings.

A patient who cannot seem to follow instructions, 'comply' or heal themselves, those asking only for palliation, those demanding or even lusting patients require the utmost attention in compassion. Although a patient of this kind is not seeking permanent healing or immediate healing, they are seeking healing on a more subtle level—through understanding. Although they may not seek to awaken and to heal, they must still be attended to with appropriateness. To palliate can also bring about healing eventually as the patient sees his/her potential and the mind allows for this change to gradually occur, sometimes taking years. For each patient, you must be patient and tolerant and always ask Yourself what role it is you are to play with them—how You fit into this relationship. Each visit, your role may be different. Forget the patient as you remembered them last so they may be renewed for you each time and compassion can more easily be applied through this freshness.

One such patient I had was under my palliative care for a long time. We worked through many layers but he could only commit to taking what remedies I gave him and not to diet, mind-body or any other self-healing or commitment. At first, I found this frustrating as I felt he should be 'out of my office' and healed. Upon the expression of my mild irritation toward him, he would become deeply hurt and no good would come out of it. Although I planted seeds with him whenever I could, I found myself at times, becoming impatient with his stubborn resistance to change. With any other patients that didn't want to heal, they were kindly and promptly let go of. Somehow, it was different with him as I knew I wasn't to let him go and I couldn't quite pinpoint why. It then dawned on me that I had judged his 'healing' as he was doing so on a different level. We were both learning from this relationship.

His health did improve vastly as my own faith with him did, and as he changed himself slowly over time. I soon learned that compassion, gentleness and inspiration were the only keys for him. Even if he were only inspired for a day or a moment to change, it was a start—it was now an energetic *possibility* for him, even if he only practiced it irregularly. He himself would start to see the possibilities of what he could do, how he could change and how it wasn't so scary after all. Even if he is never fully healed this lifetime, his karma has been set into a positive motion. *When* he achieves his full healing I realized, was not up to me. Perhaps just sharing and connecting with one another was enough for now.

I had to overcome my own feelings of non-performance (so called lack of success) with him, harshness, loss of control and boundary issues. I had to learn to become unthreatened by him in any way and just to allow. I had to become vulnerable in his presence to give him full compassion without becoming sympathetic or losing boundaries. It was a practice of discipline and patience for me—to constantly uphold faith in his presence.

Most patients that reach the threshold of healing and truth will rapidly decide to heal or not to heal. In his case, his decision was merely 'delayed' in time.

It seems dangerous for the mind to enter into this area of vulnerability and acceptance. There is only one place where true freedom and power lay—in the arms of Higher Self—the knowingness of Supreme Safety as One with All That Is. We must truly surrender to this Something that's greater than us and in doing so, we become safe in our vulnerability as It knows best somehow. I had to become vulnerable or lay down all my defenses and agendas because the more fearful I was, the more threatened I was and the more fear I attracted to myself. There can be no threat without fear.

How many times have we ourselves fallen back into old behaviors and habit? How many times does it take to learn something, to be truly at ease with something new? It could be a new way of eating, dropping an old habit or adopting a new outlook. It can take years to master and a lifetime to get used to. Only kindness, diligence and compassion bring us to it. Ultimately, it's not the diet, the habit or the outlook that matter—it's the underlying adoption of compassion toward oneself that does.

Certain practices can help lead us to compassion but they are merely practices. Sitting in compassion within all the fluctuations, suffering and changes of life is the mastery of it. When you can look upon a person, thing or situation in all its 'unpleasantness' and still feel acceptance, compassion is yours. Remember, in the end, nothing in and of itself, matters or actually *means* anything.

Knowing

Upon a trip to Sedona, Arizona, a favorite power spot for me, my office manager and I set off to the petroglyphs and cave drawings just outside the town. The interpreter there was speaking about the meaning of these drawings but we politely paid no attention as it did not resonate with us. We excitedly took many photos without judgment and left.

I did not look at the photos for some time but one night decided to pull them up on my computer to contemplate them. All at once, great messages of their meaning fled toward me. I understood them to be mostly a teaching aid for a master healer. They showed life cycles, DNA, cells both red and white, difficulties at birth and how the soul enters at birth, how to stand properly on the earth, how to meditate, how to listen and remain balanced in mind etc.

There is no need for digging, extensive mind-based logical research and 'proof'—all the answers are before you if you open up to listen. You have the very answers in your very cells. All the energy and memory of the entire Universe sits in your cells, in your very Being—even quantum physics shows us this now as we know consciousness is all there is and that it affects everything. With this knowing, all things can be revealed to you at any instant simply through listening and being present. It is not difficult to know all the secrets of the Universe let alone the secrets to healing. Simply allow yourself to be a pure channel. Practice disregarding the mind and its incessant and inane thoughts. When the mind uses logic or states something but the inner drive or feeling says something else, practice listening and following the heart even though it may seem irrational to the mind. Soon, with practice, your skills as a healer will sharpen as you go beyond the everyday expectations and venture deep within the soul. Knowing is intuition.

As you sit with faith, will and compassion, knowing comes easily and naturally. With these innate powers, there is nothing you cannot know or do in an instant.

Self-worth

Self-love is really self-worth. This is the often forgotten necessity for healing (and for other forms of manifestation and prayer etc.). Without it, we see no point in healing others, let alone ourselves as we have no sense of self-worth at all. Self-love and self-worth must be cultivated in order to be a true healer. Without it, you cannot possibly see that you are the same as all those around you – that you are just as worthy and just as important and that what you have to offer is as well.

I once knew a practitioner who had little self-worth. He was highly intelligent, capable, had a good sense of humour and was good with people. He had will, faith, compassion and knowing. He did not succeed in practice—simply no one would come to see him. After trying to succeed for several years, he eventually had to change careers. He told me it was due to all sorts of things—the economy, where he was practicing, etc. but my soul knew that he simply didn't love himself enough to allow any sort of success or abundance into his life at all.

The Tools of the Healer

You are not left without instruction.
Many tools are at hand for you.

Education

When it comes to taking courses and higher learning, use what tools you need to understand things in the world practically. Education was very valuable to me in this way. However, facts are only a starting point that wisdom can jump from. We need a baseline from which to understand. If I knew nothing about the body and it's functioning or disease, it would be difficult for me to understand the messages given to me from intuition and how to proceed because I have a limited reference.

Educate yourself as far as your intuition allows (as far as it feels right for you—not for ego, titles, pride or fear). Beyond that, you are simply reaching for more and more facts that at some point, will not serve you. Continue to educate yourself no matter what your awareness level, if you do not understand something or if something requires clarification. You are expected to do the groundwork and for Self to fill in the rest. This simply provides context from which to work.

Hands on Healing

With hands on healing of any kind, you may find your body will get quite hot, you may yawn etc. if a patient is drawing energy/healing energy i.e. when they are receiving. However, no matter how much you try, if a patient is not willing to heal or receive, you cannot get hot or feel the heat through the hands or body. Depending on the amount of healing they need, the temperature will rise. If they need a little, they get a little and you will just feel a little warmth. If they are ready for a miracle and total healing, you will feel all over body heat and even sweat. This is particularly the case during the beginnings of one's work. With years of practice and self-healing, the sensation eventually leaves entirely and only the patient may feel heat or other sensations.

The hands are simply an extension of the consciousness of the healer and they are used to direct will toward the patient. Eventually, as pure intent strengthens in the healer, even the use of hands are not necessary as all that's required is the intent of the healer.

Visions for clarity

It is easy to begin speculation and postulation upon the beginnings of the visit, however, it's important to silence the internal chatter by allowing inner knowing (intuition) or visions to occur. Simply closing the eyes and waiting for the intuition/vision to arrive allows one to know both the issue and what to do to help. When all the facts have been gathered, intuition will then pipe up when we are listening. Sometimes, this requires leaving the room for total silence for a few moments.

With practice, pure knowing or intuition will not require any formal exercise of shutting the eyes etc. as you will simply 'know'. Although intuition/visions may seem at times fantastic, they are either symbolic or actual and are correct every time. Only *interpretation* of them can be skewed by the mind, by fears or through poor communication. With regular practice in visualization, visions will come whenever asked for, giving concise answers to any question. One must practice knowing confidence with visions and only through their relay and sharing with others can this be accomplished.

I had one patient who was having trouble with faith and every time I closed my eyes to receive a vision or instruction around what to do with her, I saw her jumping around the room doing somersaults and dodging me and my attempts to 'get' her or see her. In this case, there was nothing I could do as she was not ready for the faith to heal. I had to let her go for a time until she was prepared to face the truth, at which time, she returned.

With despairing patients, I sometimes see them sitting on the floor crying and waving their hand at me to 'go away'. Through visions you will see their true nature, intentions and position. You will see exactly where the patient is at and what you're supposed to do for them.

In the past, I have been upset with myself for not seeing what I needed to do right away with a patient—sometimes their healing has eluded me for a time. However, the Universe always is perfect and it's not up to self when and how it occurs. Two scenarios, often in combination occur in these cases for the practicing healer:

1) the healer is having trouble listening i.e. mind gets in the way due to their own issues
2) the patient is not ready to heal quite yet

A combination of both means we both (patient and healer) need to learn. Patience, surrender to Self and faith pull you through.

Humor

Most people that come to see you are in a serious state and humor seems way down the list for them at this point. Some patients are naturally more light-hearted than others and you can use this to both of your advantages. Your work is supposed to be fun and 'light'. Some patients and visits are so much fun, that we actually look forward to seeing one another and delight in the humorous sharing that goes on. Don't take dis-ease too seriously and the patient won't either. Seriousness belongs in the realms of fear. Be content and serene if you must, but never serious—seriousness is literally deadly. For those more stern in their outlook, you can always inject humor here and there in creative, yet respectful ways. Be yourself with every patient using a lightness of heart. Show them by example that nothing's that bad and that all things can be healed. A twinkle in your eye, lightness in your step and a knowing that these are mere dreams, illusions and fallacies before you, will lead them to the same place—to limitlessness.

Parables

When you allow intuition to flow during a visit, stories, anecdotes, parables and lessons will come to you to share with the patient. If the subject is one where only a seed can be planted, parables and even stories from your own life can be very effective in relaying a deeper subconscious message. The message will still get across to the soul even though the patient may not be consciously aware of what you are relaying to them in terms of their own issues. Humor and humorous stories work well here as well. It is a clever form of healing that uses metaphoric access to the subconscious. A more aware patient may pick up right away the nuances of the conversation or 'play' you are acting out. This helps them to also learn to shift their consciousness to an indirect angle rather than always through the direct rationalizations of the mind. You essentially 'speak another language' to them while still getting the point across. This assists them in changing their viewpoint (that has kept them ill), to one that is advantageous to them and allows for their healing.

Most of us have had words that come out of our mouths 'unexpectedly', without forethought or preconception. These are the words of the soul and must not be suppressed as great wisdom is imparted through them. You may not even understand them at times yourself or even be 'shocked' by them but simply allowing them with trust allows a wisdom higher than intellect to work through you and the patient.

Sometimes, the Spirit will require a more direct approach. There are times when one can literally 'act out' the part the patient is playing to themselves. For example, if a patient has some degree of self-awareness and they always have issues with abundance, Spirit may drive you to say something like 'yes, that trip would be just too expensive for you to go on', using a serious tone. Such a direct approach must be used wisely. It will be lost on someone who is unaware (they will simply agree with you!) and insult someone if it's said in a sarcastic, mocking or derogatory tone. It is however, a very effective way to get a difficult point across by 'showing' the person how they talk, look and act—a direct and blatant reflection. This can be done in an even more subtle way by acting out a reflection of the patient within a story of yourself. In this case, you would shake your head and say something like 'yes, I would love to go there but it's just too expensive for me'. This interjection must be done skillfully—only at the right time and with the correct tone. The mind of the patient may not even pick it up—but the soul will. I have even used sighs and slight exaggerations to help this along.

None of this is premeditated however—one must only do what Spirit guides you to do in the moment without emotion or frustration and with the air of unaffectedness. It is simply a tool to provoke awareness of the ego and its habits. It cannot be preplanned.

With a very aware patient, you can exaggerate to the extreme because they are able now to laugh at themselves, a true sign of great wisdom. 'Sigh' 'Yes, I would really love to go but it's just too damn expensive for me. What a shame.' 'Sigh'.

The Spirit of the healer will often work in this type of reflection, depending on your personal tendencies. Over time, you will automatically display egoic reflections to others when Spirit finds it appropriate, with the aim of healing. I always found it interesting that I would adopt a certain tone, use certain words or language use and gestures with some patients that I wouldn't use with others, even to the point where more aware patients would notice the consistency of our conversation and eventually understand it as a reflection of themselves. Aligning oneself with the energies of the patient is called sharing and when done with awareness by the healer, it is a very powerful and valuable tool to bring another to healing and self-awareness.

Choosing remedies and therapies
The patient will tell you if you listen to intuition. Life force will speak to you. A certain remedy will simply stand out to you. A remedy may seem unconventional at times or mundane at others. Listen and

follow regardless. With practice, you will no longer question these intuitions. Use your background and training as a basis of course but follow intuition for the rest.

The remedies have their own life force energy about them. Their vibration when thought of or held matches the healing required by the patient. It could be just one. It could be a few. It's rarely many. It could be just a food that needs to be added or removed. Be precise and simple. No healing occurs through complication which only engenders fear. One example of this is with cancer. Healers often feel they need to apply a 'shot gun approach' to cancer and give many remedies and treatments. Never is this necessary and will lower faith and healing in both the patient and practitioner. Apply confidence that the patient can heal with precision and fine-tuned adjustments. Hold it in your mind as the same as any other dis-ease so its 'importance' is minimized. Dis-ease must be 'ignored' as being important and looked beyond, in order to be healed. It cannot take forefront attention—only health and joy must take this, our true and natural state and the one the system must be reset to.

Showing the patient how to heal themselves

Keep your faith high at all times. Practice this. When your faith falters, ask Higher Self to do it and carry it for you. In this way, you cannot fail.

The patient is always right—they will tell you what's wrong and how to fix it if you are truly listening. Some will tell you outright what it is as it has been their conscious suspicion, others will tell you only through subtle subconscious cues or you may need to go into meditation. Knowing how to read these cues and what they mean requires listening to your Self and experience.

Teach your patients to know their own vibrations and preferences for healing remedies and doses so they can tune into themselves, if they are able. Some people can hold remedies in their hands or minds and just know if it's right for them. If they are not ready for this, you can teach them simple kinesiology to help test. Your goal is to empower them to know nature's remedies, foods, attitudes and thoughts that are best for them.

Point out to them gently, how they are thinking and what they are saying. Observe them through seeing the bigger picture that surrounds and encompasses them and all becomes clear to you which you can then share with them. Their body is simply a reflection of the mind. Show them this. Sometimes you can only start with a small seed of awareness planted at the right time. Other times they come in ready for awareness and can be flooded with it. Trust they will never be the same not because of you but because they have accepted healing. Sometimes you will not be able to show them in words as this will inflame them. Simply observe them and listen, while being aware yourself of what they are saying to themselves. This awareness that *you* have seeps into them and grows without you saying a word simply because *someone* is aware of it. Your eyes and soul's understanding speak to theirs and if and when they are receptive, they will pick it up. Many patients may have revelations months or even years after your visit and sometimes in the most unlikely places and situations but always with the right timing.

Distance healing

It is no concern of yours if the patient is not physically present. Nor is it concerning if you do not obtain direct physical consent as consent will be given on a soul level if they contact you either through dreams, intuition or otherwise. Distance healing is as simple as faith. Meditate on the soul, going within and asking, not in words but through feeling, and vision will come to you. You will be shown the souls' torment and the remedy. Send it to them by your breath and your focus. Ask that all be released with the knowing that all is well and it will be done. Do not be restless thinking more is necessary. Stay in your faith. This is also a time when using assistance i.e. asking Creative Life Force, God, Universe, angels, Source, Self etc. to work through the patient, is tantamount to successful healing.

I was told by a distant relative about a baby that was born with epilepsy. The child lived far away and was being treated conventionally. The parents had no interest in alternative medicine. I felt there was nothing I could do for the child. Later that day, my partner came to me saying he felt desperate that I could help the child. He told me to meditate and 'send' him the remedy. I immediately went into meditation and saw the child in my mind asking for help. The remedy immediately came to mind. At the time, I was near my homeopathic remedies and chose the remedy through intuition. I held the antidote in my hands and 'sent' it to him. I felt a sort of peace come over me and left it. Days later, the relative notified me that they no longer needed my help because the child was miraculously healed!

The child asked and she received. I was only a channel, a vessel. If the faith is kept strong that she is permanently cured, she will remain that way. If faith falters within and around her, illness can return. Children are heavy reflectors of their surroundings and influences. Until she remembers that she creates her own reality, she will continue to suffer.

Even if you don't have anything physical on hand 'to hold', you can send anything via resonance of consciousness. The vibration will hit its target every time through the powerful flight of faith and love. Faith is confidence—the assurance and deep knowing that it is just so. There is no question.

Sometimes patients may call and ask for help and for whatever reason you just can't seem to physically connect with them either by phone, in written form or in person. Simply focus for a moment on the patient with the knowing and faith that they are healing and healed and it will become so as they align themselves with the healer—with Self. Often patients in these cases will say they started healing just after calling (they have elicited their own healing through the release created by calling) or after hearing even a recorded message of the healers' voice— they have healed without direct guidance or support from you but healed themselves through the reminder you provide by your healing presence.

This kind of distance healing can occur regardless of the patient's awareness level.

You are healing everyone you meet

People can't help but heal in the presence of those of us that are aware and connected to Self. Healing occurs in many ways and through many different forms but happens nonetheless, through no real conscious effort on your part. Continue to practice presence with love and humor and people will come into your life to heal, from all walks of life. No encounter is 'coincidental' for the healer. Your presence is required at that moment for reasons you may never understand.

They will also share with you aspects of your own self. Always keep one ear to them . . . and one to yourself.

Tuning In

The mind is like a radio transmitter and receiver. Its job is simply to receive messages and transmit them. It has no 'mind of its own' and cannot determine what's correct from what's incorrect. It simply reads messages. There are lots of messages out there flying around in the collective unconscious and we encounter them every moment. As you learn to see them simply as thoughts with no real meaning, you can dissociate from them, preventing them from becoming beliefs or pulling them into yourself and believing them to be true. The true mind sits in the heart—the knowing/intuitive place of you. It's here you must focus your utmost presence and attention. Only It knows best and what to do.

The mind can often take over when we're not present and provide all sorts of ideas, questions, doubts, criticisms and the like, that we 'tune' into, thinking they're ours. It can even lead to mental breakdown. You are trying to make sense of something that can never make sense— random thoughts. You must relearn to tune into something deeper and beyond these thoughts. These thoughts will always be floating around out there and they don't need to be pushed away. See these thoughts as habitual and not a definition of who you are. You must simply tune into another station—the heart station—the knowing station. Practice watching, thinking or feeling these random thoughts as impersonal—as outside of you and you will become truly unaffected.

Finding a reason for healing
It's so easy for us to fall back into bad habits. Our egos are lazy. There are no consequences it seems for remaining where we are. We may be able to be strict in some areas of our lives but when we are out of this context, we fall back into old behaviors easily. It's not that we can't or that we're just 'hard-wired' this way, it's that we've had no real motivation to stay changed.

A male patient once told me his wife was always telling him for years that she was tired of his harshness and constant criticism. Although he knew it was a problem and he tried to change, he just couldn't seem to do it (or believe he could) until she threatened to leave him one day. He said it was then, the easiest thing for him to do — to change. He then did it instantly and permanently.

Anything can provide us with this push—a loss of relationship, career, life or health, an accident, or a move—anything can provide the jolt into a new perspective. At this point, it becomes no longer a luxury or a game to stay ill in mind or body—it becomes serious and reality threatening. At this point, you can do anything. You can heal anything.

You don't have to have life or reality-threatening circumstances to create this for yourself but you must have a damn good reason. Ask for this reason and it will come to you.

Intuition
Although we all have it, intuition requires focus (presence) and practice to master. The deep sense of inner knowing beyond the mind is common with many healers but can be underutilized as we place too much trust in logic, protocol and the scientific method to reach diagnosis and healing. These tools although useful, can never replace the awesome power and certainty of intuition, of inner knowing.

Certain tools can help to sharpen intuition such as focused meditation (during practice visits and outside of them), visualization, divination or kinesiology to name a few. Intuition must ride above logic in all cases and this requires discipline, faith, practice and great courage. Intuition is the product of focus/presence and is literally your best guide and must be treated as such.

Focus

Focus is really the same as presence. Only through focus can we be excellent at anything we do. Focus requires unwavering silence, stillness and presence and takes practice. Through focus, you become the vessel through which all intuition and Higher information arrives. The vessel must be still and clear of noise and clutter for healing to occur. There are many ways to practice being focused and formal meditation is only one of many. You must 'meditate' at every moment with each patient using unwavering focus and silence of the mind to achieve clarity. Treat each patient as if they are the only one in the world and that they are in dire need of your help which no one else can give them at that moment. You don't have the luxury of rationalization, of wasting time listening to old thoughts, of engaging rote behaviors or doubting. This focus will channel you into the focus you require to heal with excellence. (In fact, this is why it helps us to help others—they force us to be present).

We must remember that the potential for death is always nearby and as morbid as this may sound, the real exercise here is to force one to stay present. The reminder of death creates a pungent reality that only this moment exists and that we cannot afford to pretend otherwise. It's usually easier to stay present while doing our life's work because death is closer—we must be present in order to keep our jobs, our careers and therefore, to survive. The thought of death then, becomes an ever-present friend keeping us on our toes. We must extend this practice over into everyday life where the seemingly mundane and non-threatening allows us to put our guard down and drift away from presence. The reminder of death is not an exercise to create constant anxiety but to keep us at peace. It helps us strip away the trivial and stay focused in joy, presence and reality right now.

Meditation

Although formal sitting meditation can be very helpful for many, it is only one way to meditate. Meditation is not a practice—it's a state of being. Meditation is focus—being present. Find your own unique way that allows for you to be present. Some find running or other sports puts them into a present state. Others find it doing surgery, yoga, taxes, nails or truck driving. It can be found in creative writing, art and music. There is no place that it does not exist. Find your meditation and expand it into your life so that it eventually encompasses all of it. Find the meditation in all you do. This is your only true practice.

Types of Healers

Use your uniqueness to your advantage.
You must know yourself intimately to know Me.

As healers, we usually know it's our calling—it's simply an innate pull or passion toward helping others. It does help to know your own particular tendencies as a healer so you can use your strengths to your advantage. It also helps to know what challenges you also possess within these tendencies so you may heal your own self. There are many systems and schools of thought around tendencies. Shamanic medicine uses the medicine wheel and its directions to know oneself. Eastern medicine uses chakras or energy centres that are dominant or weak in each of us. Chinese medicine uses the yin/yang system. Using a system of some kind that suits you can be an excellent tool for self-awareness.

What is your greatest challenge will also be your greatest strength. There is no good or bad here, it's simply a tendency. The great challenge we have as healers is to keep this strength and challenge in balance.

No two healers are ever alike. Accept your tendencies as they are. They provide your uniqueness. Once you accept what you perceive as the 'good, bad and the ugly', you can truly become at peace with Who You Are.

Dominant chakra

Although one can use any system to determine tendencies, for simplicity, we will use the chakra system here.

Chakras are energy centres located in the aura that deeply affect the body and mind. If a chakra is healthy or strong, the body and mind will be free of dis-ease that dominates that area. The chakras can also be too strong or too weak thus creating dis-ease.

You can discover your dominant chakra to determine your strengths/weaknesses as a healer and use this to your advantage in terms of how you practice and what tools you use. It is not meant to define you in any way but simply allow for you to use your strengths and challenges to your advantage. There are many ways to determine chakra dominance and it can also change over the course of a lifetime. Some simply know what they are; others have seen their own colours. Another way is to calculate it using birth dates. For example, my dominant chakra number is my birth date added all together and that answer separated and added again. If you come up with a double digit, add these together again to get your number: 6+6+1+9+7+3 = 32. 3+ 2 = 5. Although 5 is my dominant chakra, 3 and 2 will be very important as well in my abilities as a healer. Although the section here is more specific to healers, other books and references can provide more information about the life path numbers and chakras. (Please see Bibliography and Suggested Reading).

In general, the chakras mean the following for healers:

1 – Strong ability to stay present, focused and grounded with patients, strong connection to animals and nature and using earth tools to heal such as herbs, plants, animal medicine, shamanic medicine and rituals. Colours are red or earth tones. Relates to organs and systems below the navel and lower back. Healers with this dominant chakra must be aware of survival and financial fears/issues.

2 – Strong relating and relationship abilities. Knack for getting along with others and connecting with them. Healing is done through humor and lightheartedness. Stories and personal accounts assist greatly in healing. Ability to support others. Colours are orange and brown. Relates to organs and systems around the navel and upper lumbar area. Healers with this dominant chakra must be aware of boundary and relationship issues.

3 – Strong will and courage. Solid decision-making abilities and firm in commitment and faith. Physical strength and exercise are important as tools, like yoga, qi gong, martial arts and meditation. Excellent manifestation abilities. Colours are yellows. Relates to organs and systems in sternal areas. Healers with this dominant chakra must be aware of stubbornness, fears of change and difficulties making decisions.

4 – Strong compassionate abilities and ability to see others points of view easily with kind understanding and love. Listening is the main tool. Physical and personal contact is important and used often with tools like Reiki and hands-on healing, reflexology and massage. Colours are greens and pinks. Relates to organs and systems in chest, breast area and mid-spine. Healers with this dominant chakra must be aware of over-nurturing patients, over concern and not taking time and space for themselves first.

5 – Strong communication abilities both spoken, written and soul level. The word and vibration of tone and music are important. Writing and journaling are important healing tools along with music and talk/counseling therapies. Hand gesturing, Reiki and hands-on healing with a bend toward soul communication and movement. Colours are blues and turquoise. Relates to organs and systems in throat and neck areas. Healers with this dominant chakra must be aware of talking too much or too little to patients and exhaustion due to overexertion or 'trying too hard'.

6 – Strong natural intuitive and clairvoyant abilities. Strong sensory input and output to assist and assess others. See and feel deeper into this reality and into others as well. Crystals and divination tools, cards, sacred music and meditation are helpful tools. Colours are purple and indigo. Relates to head, face, occiput and forehead areas. Healers with this dominant chakra must be aware of too much inward journeying and thinking, imbalances between the metaphysical and physical worlds when dealing with pathology and patients. Depressions can ensue due to coming out of intuitive and higher consciousness states back into everyday life.

7 – Strong connection with the Big picture and overall view. Easily channel life force energies into the bodies and fields for self and others (7 and above have broader understanding and abilities to relate and see beyond this realm and into other realities). Toning and chakra clearing, Reiki and hands-on with a more spiritual focus are used. The power of gentleness is key with this chakra. Colours are gold or purples. Relates to top of head and head areas. Healers with this dominant chakra must be aware of challenges with staying grounded and centered in this reality, tendencies toward fantasy and feeling misunderstood. This chakra mirrors our understanding of the crystal and rainbow child energies.

8 – Strong compassionate abilities for all life and forms. Broad understanding comes easily. Meditation, clairsentience and hands-on healing are key. Colours are light purples. Relates to non-physical auras such as emotional and feeling bodies. Healers with this dominant chakra must be aware of feeling different from others and challenges with emotional balance.

9 – Strong will, courage and faith with the addition of broad and overall understanding of the bigger picture. Global, political, planetary and environmental interests are important tools along with yoga and martial arts. Colour is white. Relates to extended universal auras connecting to the All and Oneness of Spirit. Healers with this dominant chakra must be aware of challenges around using force and becoming involved with spiritual, environmental and political righteousness or elitism. This chakra closely mirrors our understanding of the indigo child energies.

Although these are general, it gives you a basic view of what to look for within your own chakra systems and that of your patients. Chakra numbers will also indicate tendencies toward challenges in these same areas that can be triggered during certain situations. For example, although my voice is a great tool, when fearful, I would overuse it and talk too much or when fearful of saying the wrong thing, I would lose my voice.

Staying present with awareness is key to using these strengths at all times to an advantage during practice.

The Mechanics of Healing

Healing has a way.
Know what it is to help yourself and others.

How the body heals

The body can only heal if the mind is healed. The mind heals by changing perception of the current situation and sees it a different way. The body is simply a biofeedback machine that responds to the mind. It has no consciousness in and of itself. Dis-ease is not random or 'genetic'—it is simply due to misperception. Our job as healers is to help change the mind, to alter perception so that healing can occur naturally. We can use whatever intuition guides us to in order to create the setting for this change in perception. If a patient arrives with a diagnosis of cancer or hepatitis, our job is to help alter the perception around these dis-eases. There is no dis-ease that is any 'worse' than any other, nor any better. Cancer is no different than the flu. Both can kill you. What makes the two seem different is simply perception. Fear is the only thing that can kill us in the end. We cannot afford to feed into that fear as practitioners regardless of the patient's perception of the matter. We must remain utmost in our knowing that all dis-ease can be overcome while remaining respectful of the patient's journey and how they choose to perceive the dis-ease.

The two types of healing

In general, there are two types of healing: palliation and true healing. Although palliation is not true healing, it can lead to it so it must be included. Palliation is simply support and provides a relieving of symptoms and signs, but does not address the deeper layers or core of the dis-ease. Palliation relies on placebo effect and only ever lasts for a time as long as the patient believes it is working. Most of modern medicine relies on palliation for effect. Both the patient and the practitioner believe this placebo effect and therefore, it can work as a palliation. Palliation at times can become permanent healing if the patient has changed his perception around the dis-ease and knows himself to be cured. How the cure comes about (through what remedies, medicines etc.) is irrelevant on a general basis but relevant on an individual basis. As mentioned above, each patient 'chooses' the remedy that works best for them in the mind.

Other times, palliation only lasts for a time as the underlying mind/body issues creep to the surface only to plague the patient again or to reappear as other symptoms. Sometimes new and different palliative care helps the patient once again, however, many times faith has been shaken and the patient can become despairing. The patient then reaches a threshold and a decision must be made. To suffer and eventually die or to surrender to the Spirit and tackle true awareness of the dis-ease and its true cause.

True healing occurs when the mind has changed perception completely and dis-ease simply no longer exists as the mind is no longer 'fueling' it. The patient has truly seen their predicament from a spiritual perspective and with this awareness, greater understanding ensues, creating stillness and therefore, healing. This healing can come as a great battle for awareness between our small and Big Selves or can come as an immediate miracle as the mind simply shifts to greater awareness and the body follows suite with little or no resistance. For example, if the mind knows it will heal the cut finger, the body does so without question within the 'recommended time frame' governed by the mind. Simple unfailing knowingness leads to healing. If the mind questions its ability to heal for whatever reason (I'm a sick person, my immune system is weak, I'm worthless etc.), the body battles to heal and healing can falter or take longer. If the mind has no concept of recommended time frames for healing the finger can heal instantly. The mind puts the broken parts back together again. In the Hawaiian Huna system of medicine, the Higher Self has a blueprint or mold of itself in Its perfect etheric form before dis-ease or injury. Through focused healing intent/prayer, life force is placed into this original blueprint or mold again so that new cells and entirely new organs can be created from this original . . . instantly.[1]

All cases you encounter are examples of miracles. Healing has occurred. How and when a healing occurs, however, is only *perceived* as more or less miraculous.

[1] Long, Max Freedom. *The Secret Science Behind Miracles*. Wildside Press. 2009: 119-120.

The 6 Roots of Dis-Ease

Use form to gain understanding.
It gives ground from which to grow.

The 6 roots of dis-ease

From a practical standpoint, there are only 6 dis-ease roots, meaning all dis-eases can be traced back to these roots:

1) **allergic** (usually to certain foods or environments)
2) **infectious** (parasite, bacteria, virus, fungus, yeast)
3) **structural** (orthopedics, spinal subluxations, past physical traumas, birth defects, genetic *tendencies*)
4) **nutritional** (deficiencies and toxicities)
5) **toxic** (heavy metal, chemical)
6) **mind/body** (subconscious, emotional, spiritual, mental habit, stress, karmic)

*hormonal, autoimmune diseases and other disease labels are not included as a disease root. However, these diseases can be caused by any of the disease roots.

Not all dis-ease roots may present themselves at once. There may be anywhere from one dis-ease root present to many within the patient. Mind-body is always present, even if it's not dealt with or looked at. Only those roots the patient is ready to heal from will appear at any given time. It is common to also have to work through several dis-ease roots before reaching the level of mind-body. In these cases, a patient must go through spiritual evolution and establish trust before addressing subconscious or mind-body issues.

Sometimes, patients arrive showing only the mind-body issues right away. In these cases, the patient has either reached a breaking point or they are simply prepared for deep work.

Most times, a patient will present showing two to three dis-ease roots at once and some mind-body issues. Work only with what you are given by the patient at any given moment. Even though you may suspect other roots or issues are present, pushing into these areas prematurely can worsen the condition.

Dis-ease layers

Dis-ease roots tend to layer on top of each other and must be worked through, sometimes one at a time, before all layers are addressed for the patient. Children usually come in with the least number of layers as they have less history or time to accumulate dis-ease in both mind and body. Sometimes, a patient will be ready to deal with many layers at once but this is not common. Deal with the layers that present themselves to you first and work your way through the other layers during future visits.

Here is an example of dis-ease layers that may be present in a patient throughout the course of their treatment:

Layer 3 or surface layer (presents on initial visit)—mental/adrenal stress and mercury amalgam toxicity (2 dis-ease roots; 1 in mind/body and 1 in toxins)

Layer 2 or a middle layer (second visit)—hypothyroidism (1 dis-ease root in nutritional deficiency)

Layer 1 or deepest layer (third visit)—past suppressed sexual trauma (1 dis-ease root in mind/body)

These layers tend to build one on top of the other and can literally reveal themselves as such during the course of treatments. Do not get discouraged if you 'miss' a layer on the first visit. Often the patient is not ready to heal from it yet. Patience and constant observation are paramount to success.

The procedure is self-revealing and inherently 'safe' as the practitioner and/or patient themselves will not become aware of deeper issues until the very time they are ready to be healed.

If the patient's body reveals only mind-body issues to start, this deeper healing work can begin right away. They may or may not need physical support at this time as well. Do not fall into the trap of thinking that simply because someone has achieved higher states of awareness and healing that they may not need additional physical support. People can often feel fantastic after a visit and then a few days later go through a challenging healing on all levels as fears are removed and perceptions changed. Additional support can come in any form (books, meditations, clearing tools, remedies, exercises, art therapy etc.). Allow intuition to guide you to the best tools for the patient.

The Process of Healing

Process allows for understanding.
Without it, you are lost in the bliss of oblivion or in the pain of suffering.

The decision to heal

As always, the patient must be asked in some way if they are ready or not to heal. This is not a flippant or redundant question but a serious spiritual question that must be asked when the time is right. At the point of every relationship with a patient, this question must be asked in some way or another. Depending on the response at this point, the relationship either carries on or it ends. For some patients this question is asked early on, for others much later. Timing and patient intent is everything. Sometimes, you will just know intuitively whether the patient is 'done' or does not want to heal. Other times you must ask outright. I usually look people in the eye and ask 'are you ready to heal'? This deep question comes from the Divine because to heal means to be present—to be made whole and at One. Even if they do not understand you on the mind level, the soul does always. If they look away or avoid the question, I have the answer. If they face me and answer they do, we can continue.

Many healers are naturally frightened of approaching this subject but like anything else, it simply takes practice to build confidence. For me, I had to set aside any personal agendas and allow the big picture of healing to take over. I had to see my purpose as 'dire' for the patient or we could have no effect and our time would be wasted. I could not spend future visits palliating the patient without asking this question. Many practitioners stop here or continue palliation but simply do not carry on further, go deeper with the patient or broach this question. The patient must be made aware at some point that the possibility for true healing exists otherwise, we have failed as healers and we become only palliators.

If the patient says no at this point and chooses palliation, we know where we stand and can work with this. They have taken responsibility 'not to take responsibility yet' and that's understood between healer and patient. Otherwise, the journey into true healing can begin.

Signs of awakening

Many times you may feel yourself wanting to yawn or the patient will yawn during the visit. This accompanies a sort of 'awakening' or revelation on some level. They are already in the process of healing. This can even happen when you have conscious awareness and you are in a public place—people in grocery stores may yawn just standing next to you. Animals will also yawn (usually as a reflection of our own healing in their presence and sometimes because of their own).

Release all personal expectations of the methods and timing of healing. Allow for it with space and time and it will come about. Always keep it simple and fresh and you will know what to do at each stage and step for the patient. Medicine and healing are not difficult or complicated. The body, mind and Spirit are meant to work properly and efficiently—in their natural state.

Healing crisis

A healing crisis is when the body is re-aligning itself with the mind—with a new way of perceiving the world. As this occurs, there can be a sort of battle occurring within both the mind and body as the physical and mental structures change to suit the new vibrations of the healed patient. New neural networks are created in the brain, different hormones and endorphins are released, cells are shed or grown—all this takes great change and massive energy. The old must be shed before the new can be made manifest. The more resistant and engrained the old patterns or perceptions have been, the more of a crisis it can be. Once this is accomplished, we see healing and renewal.

Let patients know beforehand of the possibilities of a healing crisis without scaring them. Handouts are helpful regarding what can be expected so the patient is somewhat prepared and doesn't give up on the treatment thinking they are worsening. Often your support is needed at this time and a few minutes on the phone for reassurance or a quick visit can relieve anxiety for the patient. Using awareness and acceptance techniques such as EFT®, counselling, clearing etc. can alleviate physical, mental and emotional upheaval.

Helping a patient deal with pain

Although difficult for the mind to believe, pain is a mental (thought) construct. Pain has no meaning in and of itself, it simply is. Suffering and pain are not the same thing. One can have pain but not suffer if there are no judgments around the pain itself. This is an important lesson to teach open patients and students. The whole concept of pain must be approached and its so-called meaning. Once, when I was in great physical pain, I thought I would die from it. In desperation, I went within and asked God for help. It said 'be patient, my child'. What?! Be patient? My panic and fear and impatience to 'get better right now' were creating most of the pain and I needed to accept God (not the pain which is a common misperception. One cannot accept pain because it's an illusion). Once I accepted God and was patient with this process of healing (rather than labeling it 'pain'), the pain subsided substantially and would actually improve further upon emotional release and insightful acceptance. I understood that I had 'mis-created' this pain through years of emotional suppression that was now surfacing. It took a few days for the pain to leave completely in this case but strangely, I was at peace with it. I stopped fighting it and allowed this 'release' to run its course.

Many times, patients will come to you that have chronic pain mostly due to suppressions (conscious desires to forget) or repressions (subconscious desires to forget). It is our job as healers to help them uncover the true cause of their pain so they have a chance to truly heal. Palliate as you must but never back down from the true cause for the patient. In this realization is their Self-salvation.

Pain is pain but there is no need to suffer. Suffering is always due to judgment.

Removing layers of repression

When a patient removes an overlying layer that has been repressed, we almost always see a healing crisis of more than just a physical nature. The patient will undergo sometimes longer than normal shifts in physical and emotional energy, revealing an underlying mind-body issue that has not yet been addressed. Often, a patient can become stuck in these issues for years. Therefore, bringing accurate attention to the underlying issues as the patient is ready, is essential and must be timely.

A common example is gaining weight after smoking cessation. Physiologically, we know smoking affects acidity in the body—involving blood, digestive, nervous and other systems. Smoking in a subconscious sense, replaces the need to eat or orally and spiritually fulfill oneself. It essentially represses an underlying sense of deprivation (which most of us have on some level subconsciously—seeking fulfillment through food, substances, drink, talking, relationships and on and on). A sense of deprivation sits in the stomach and relationship chakra. With smoking cessation, food now becomes the replacement filler. Even if no more food than usual is consumed, the mind still feels unfulfilled so weight gain occurs regardless as the body simply responds to messages to fill itself up somehow.

The real issue is never about the addiction we use to fulfill. The issue (or what's been suppressed) is seeking fulfillment in anything outside of us.

Sometimes people are unable to go off substances or foods—they simply aren't ready to commit. The true commitment is to Themselves and until they can achieve that, there is no use in pushing matters. I encourage people to continue on with their behaviors until they are finished with their suffering. Contrary to popular belief, suffering is a great tool for evolution and can launch one into great awareness and to the eventual release of all suffering. People are usually aware of what they need to give up or change and making them feel guilty or coercing them through fear does no good. Do not judge them or their suffering but be compassionate and allowing of it as necessary. People are often shocked by your release of judgment of them—that you actually accept their behavior without judgment. This compassionate stance alone can launch a patient into life-altering behaviors. Only through creating space and allowing can someone change in our presence.

The Manifestation of Healing

I will show you your power through Me and by Me.
There is nothing you cannot create.

The 'side effects' of healing

Healing in the present has interesting 'side effects'. Not all patients will experience these but they are common:

• *Loss of memory for the details of the visit*

As you both enter meditation, you are in an altered state of consciousness. Unless the patients' normal consciousness is close to this altered state, they may 'forget' large portions of the visit or at least the details of it. True healing only occurs in higher states of consciousness. Reassure them their forgetting is normal but their soul remembers which is all that matters. Sometimes a patient will want to write down or record parts of the visit so they can reenter that state. This is fine but also encourage them to find their own triggers for entering heightened states of awareness such as meditation, journaling, music, exercise, reading spiritual books, etc. As a healer, you may also 'forget' the contents of the visit. This is actually to your benefit as you do not want to see the patient on their subsequent visit, tainted by the last visit. They are fresh and new as the present moment commands, with no past. Only with these eyes, can you see their potential and allow for their full healing when you see them again.

I would find that any pertinent information or detail that I needed, would simply return to me during a subsequent visit, without the need to recall it with effort or dig it up somehow. I was sometimes amazed amidst the busi-ness of my life and the numerous people I saw, how accurately I could remember certain details without any props and completely forget others that were simply no longer relevant. Being present creates clarity.

• *The feeling of peace or elation after a visit*

This will sometimes last for hours or even days for a patient as they remain in that consciousness or vibration for a time. This can turn into a longing to see you again but as they become used to the new vibration, it may not be the same for them the next time. Remind them that they are simply tuning into a new and different tune/vibration/perception and their own system will now be set to this and be able to recall it anytime they like with the ultimate intent of remaining in that state permanently.

Intuitive passion

When you are 'told' by Within to do something, buy something, go somewhere, talk to someone, take a certain course etc., there is a passion or excitement that comes with it. To the unaware, it can seem that this passion only exists with truly 'exciting' events, trips, new toys or hobbies etc. that occur in one's life. We are only more accepting of these exciting things because it is 'normal' to get excited about going on a holiday or taking up a passionate hobby, rather than feeling you need to go over and see your neighbor or buy that vacuum cleaner or simply do the laundry! The passion exists—it's just been suppressed usually due to feelings of unworthiness or incapacity. Clear these issues and one's passion then becomes clear.

I describe passion as something that drives you from Within but it is not from wanting or lusting. It is a knowing that something must be done—it has an assuring quality to it. It can still be accompanied by actual excitement but the underlying feeling is sure and confident.

Sometimes passion occurs for only a few moments. This is the time to act. A healer must make his decision at this time and swiftly. If he hesitates, the moment passes and the passion is gone. Becoming in tune with the ebb and flow of passion is innate to the healer. Practice using it to its full potential, otherwise passion simply becomes fleeting with no outcome. *Passion is the parent of creativity.*

Sometimes passion will spur us to begin something but as time goes on, the passion wanes—or seems to. The passion is still there but our impatience or other fears, hides it—the Universe delivers but it has its own timing. As with the conception of a child, passion is there at the beginning but wanes until the birth of the child.

Often, a certain course, destination, job, person or item will keep crossing your mind or path somehow. Your head will keep turning toward it. These are the subtle messages we often miss. There is passion there to manifest but our minds keep blocking it out for whatever reason—'it's too expensive, I'm too busy, I don't need that, I can't just leave like that, what about the kids, what if I fail' etc. We make up quick and convenient excuses for ignoring the gifts that are coming to us or that we have been born with. Sometimes we miss opportunities because of our ignorance. I was once in a music store looking for a new guitar as I was intuited to do. I played some from all price ranges and found one I really liked. I couldn't believe it because the guitar was not that expensive and came with a case, a pick-up and tuner—surely I should look around some more. I hesitated but promised myself I'd sleep on it and come in the next day. I arrived just as the store opened and—it was gone! Although I ordered another one, I had literally passed up the perfect opportunity—it was a lesson for me in following my passion.

There are always other opportunities of course but we must work at not passing up yet another one so that joy and passion may be manifested in our lives constantly starting now. Listen and follow your passions and soon you will be able to hear them all the time, leading your every move. Even what meal to cook and clothes to wear can be inspired with practice with the ear toward listening to Self's guidance.

We are not used to living by passion. It requires fearlessness and courage. A good friend of mine once told me he always bought or did what he had passion for—for himself and others as he was very generous. I asked "what it if doesn't turn out or it wasn't right?" "I can always sell it or chalk it up to learning . . ." he said. "I work hard for it and I'm grateful to myself for what I do. I'm grateful to others as well. I'm allowed to show my gratitude by doing things or buying things that I've got passion for. I also know I'm capable of making more money!" Money and a bad time was never his concern—only gratitude was—so money was always there and he never had a bad time! He taught me many things about abundance. As long you give gratitude to yourself and others, know that you're capable, and discipline yourself to be enthusiastic about life—to pursue your passions—abundance is yours!

Passion, as mentioned above, is the necessary ingredient for effective prayer. It essentially 'pulls down' the energy from the etheric into this reality. When a patient would cross my mind and there was some passion there, I would quickly and immediately go into prayer for them.

Manifesting

Conscious manifestation can only ever effectively occur during high states of consciousness—joy, Oneness and peace—passion. When you are vibrating here, you are extremely attractive and will (and can) instantly attract anything to you. Apply your joy to everything you touch, look at and interact with. People and things will bend to you and reflect back your love. They will give you things and want to be near you. The Universe will work entirely in your favor and it does not care what you manifest or choose be it positive or negative. Things will just seem to 'happen' for you—we've all had these days when we were 'on top of the world' and the world was ours—we could do no wrong. Life becomes 'at your service'. Stay here and prolong it. Practice its sustainment. It's not just a one-time thing. Cultivate joy and these days will overflow into each other, making your life a heaven on earth. Animals and children will come to you and want to be near you and no vicious person or creature will enter your reality. When you are in this state for whatever reason it has been triggered, move your thoughts into the visualizations of what you desire to manifest—be it peace, a new home, a better career or relationship etc. so you can pull it in.

Two things are required for conscious manifestation: faith and will. It's interesting that the same rule applies for healing which is really just a positive manifestation.

There are two types of manifestation:

- *Unconscious manifestation*

Most people manifest things into their lives quite unconsciously. They don't fly because they have ultimate faith in gravity, they are still alive because they eat daily and have some basic requirements for life, they have a decent job because they are educated and capable etc. They are not aware that all these things, staying on the ground, staying alive, having a job are simply the application of pure intent—of faith and will.

We often manifest the negative into our lives much more easily than the positive simply because we are so used to negativity and lack. For instance, we'll rush into that store just for a minute and not pay the meter. We are already fearful of getting a ticket somewhere deep inside us (will) and the knowing that 'we always get screwed' (faith) brings about our manifestation—a ticket! At this point, we blame outside sources and carry on using this incident as fodder for the next one and on we go through life continuously manifesting negativity. Even when one is relatively consciously aware, we can still go about doing this form of self-sabotage or 'negative manifestation'—until we get sick or fed up. Once this comes about, we then 'put our foot down' and almost 'make it happen' in our favor. The trick is it doesn't have to come from a place of anger or fear but from a place of *commandment*—of assertion—of a dire need to do so. We must know we are capable and we must be resolute about what we desire—without passion there can be no manifestation. We only manifest the negative because we are afraid of what we might manifest if we are positive—absolute limitlessness.

- *Conscious manifestation*

Conscious manifestation is quite another matter and can take some time to master as it's quite an art. It requires unbending faith (the knowing of limitlessness within You) and a Will that is no longer ego driven by the negative (fear and survival motivators). The Higher Will (Self) and Lower Will (ego) must come together in full alignment to make something positively manifest in the physical world.

We can all dream and even listen to Higher Self with a full knowing of Its intentions for us. We may know we need to do this or that or that this or that is our destiny etc. but putting it into action is quite another matter. 'Convincing' the lower self (ego) that this is a good idea can be quite challenging. To truly master this, one must push all egoic fears and alternate arguments to the side and literally *command and surrender* the will to be taken over by Higher Self.

We are given these gifts constantly and we do many things with them:

- we cannot or refuse to hear the message (denial due to fear or habit)
- we hear the message but don't take it seriously (ignorance)
- we hear the message but don't think we can do it (incapacity) or have other fears around it
- we hear the message and know we can do it but we don't align our will with it (in other words, we simply 'allow' without any action—we get lazy thinking it'll be done *for* us)
- we hear the message and put it into action but apply too much force or control without any allowing or flexibility
- we hear the message but can't decide what to do (irresolute)

There is a gentle balance here with the will between:

command (the will for it)
allowing (with flexibility, listening and right timing)
action (the doing part)
faith (it will be told to us what to do at
each step and that it must come about)
self-worth

Often all we do is listen to the message having the full faith in it but never applying our will to it—never bringing little will up to meet Big Will. We just don't see how it can be done or how we can do it. This is

36

simply fear. All manifestation requires effort on the part of ego and Higher Self together. Action still must be applied. The action is not so much in the doing part but in the will part. We must *will it*. When one applies only egoic will (little will), it requires energy expenditure because it's usually based on fear and survival. If one allows Higher Will to take over, something greater than us supplies the Will or *passion* so no energy is expended on our part—it is already done for us. Let Self do the hard work but we still must be the willing participant and vessel through which it works and our will must match that of Self to make something manifest—which is not always what we *think* we desire. We may not like what we've been told but we *know* it's right. Finally, our sense of self-worth (deservedness) must be present to manifest anything. Worth must be present in order to attract the worthy thing to oneself.

This 'battle' always reminds me of the classic fairy tales when beast (ego) eventually becomes the prince (Higher Self). Life has become so horrible for the beast that it has no choice but death or to become the prince. So, the beast, through loving itself (symbolic outward love and compassion of the feminine aspect or 'princess' that comes along) after many trials and tests, becomes One with its Highest Will—good, kind and princely.

The ego often 'gets in the way' of positive manifestation because it has many, many underlying agendas based on survival that we tend to let override our true and Higher desires and intentions:

- **Self-sabotage** is most common, usually coming from fears of our own power. The need to experience pain or to be the sacrificial martyr is another, usually because we think we have to 'pay' for things or for our so-called mistakes.
- We also **repress** (listening but not following what we are told) as a way to control or feel in control—so we can dupe or trick Self (what ego sees as authority).
- We also **deprive** ourselves of abundance/love/nurturance because we need to prove to ourselves somehow that we are worthy of receiving.

All of it is sad and powerless. Adopt an attitude of Self-ishness—of birthright to abundance and you will see how not only is it easily made manifest but how unselfish it really is as you positively affect your own life and others along with it by default.

Spiritual students often have a great deal of difficulty with this one. We've spent a lot of our time listening and not much doing—years in meditation and not much action. We just can't seem to get selfish enough to reach for the stars and our full abundant potential. We never say, 'yes, this is mine' and grab it. We spend too much time being 'nice' and not enough time focusing our intent. A wealthy person knows this rule well. As 'selfish' as they may seem, they are often excellent manifestors as money and wealth they command into their lives with ruthless intent. As misdirected as some of our financial overlords and superstars may seem to be, they're darn good at manifesting! Simply use their examples of will as a starting point—you already have spiritual morals and Will to prevent you from being 'greedy' and all-consuming. Learn from them to apply ruthless intent to everything in your life from your own spiritual growth to the physical manifestation of abundance in your life. There is no room for pride, spiritual elitism and martyrdom as a healer. You are here to be an example of limitlessness and infinite possibility without judgment, in every way.

There are certain choices (your destiny) that lay before you. They feel right and they fit into your life. Spend as much time as you need to make the correct decision for yourself so you are absolutely sure of your choice. Be patient with this process because you cannot manifest in a hurry or without absolute assuredness. Then, like an arrow, you must never go back, applying your full unwavering intent on your target, using Will and full action. In other words, where you *point* your arrow is a choice and this you can take your time with. However, when the timing and the choice has been made, fire straight and true. This is your directed Will and it will, (in fact *it must*), be made manifest.

During the birth of my third child, I had asked/prayed for an easy, painless, short labor. As 12 hours rolled along with intense pain, a vision came to me in my angst of 'feeling betrayed'. An angel sat before me and said simply, 'it's your choice' and walked away. I became furious. Why didn't I get what I'd asked for? Wasn't I supposed to 'just allow'? Wasn't I 'looked after'? The truth of the matter is no. The Universe/Self does not care what you choose. It cannot apply faith and will *for* me—after all, I have free will. I had to learn to command what I desired to myself every moment of every day and settle for nothing less. The Universe is ruthless itself and cares not for our decisions and choices *because it has no judgment*. We have to learn to manipulate and master these forces of the Universe until they bend at our very notion. Then we become a master—Self made manifest.

The anger and pain I felt drove me to make a decision and 'fire'. Through my own choice and commandment, I simply decided to have the baby on the next contraction and lo and behold, I did. It was no longer a question of 'waiting' or 'allowing'—it was a question of Will. With directed Will using full faith, anything can happen.

This is a common notion that 'things are done for us by God' and belies one of power as we lay down our lives in waiting after our feeble prayers are said. God or Self must be commanded to your will. It has no sympathy for you as it is simply Isness—don't fool yourself into thinking Life Force is anything but Presence—it contains no judgment nor has sympathy. Take this Life Force then, and use it to your advantage and bring your life into full commandment with it—use this Force as your ally otherwise, it will consume you as you have allowed it to. No one and no thing can betray you—only you can betray yourself.

Karma

Karma is a term thrown around quite a bit in spiritual circles but is not well understood. Karma simply means inertia or movement—propensity. It does not mean your fate or something set in stone or something you have to settle for. It does not mean punishment for wrong-doing as there is no such thing because there is no such thing as judgment in the first place. Karma is constantly changing as *you* change and evolve in your consciousness. Karma does not wait but is instantaneous and changeable. You have the right to choose because you have been given the free will to do so. Enlightenment is not 'accepting' negative things and doing nothing about it. You have the choice to apply your limitlessness to heal or live anything. Life force does not care and will literally consume you if you do not use Its power and manifest Your heart's desires for Yourself—it is ruthless and so you must be for Yourself. You have permission and the right to live a life of full and complete abundance in every way. There is no place for dis-ease of the body of any kind in the fully enlightened mind—it literally cannot exist because the mind is fully at ease. There is no dis-ease in the present because all is well in this moment because there is no judgment in this moment. It is what it is.

Assisting others

Helping someone else achieve their manifestation of health is usually much easier for us to do than to manifest it for ourselves. There is no baggage we bring to the agreement as we care not about the outcome because it doesn't concern us. We also don't feel the need to sabotage or to be afraid of the power of it because it doesn't directly involve us. We can safely stand back and let it happen. If one applies the faith that another can heal and that they will heal, all the person must do now is realize this for themselves. It helps that they see the healer as an 'authority' not in a worldly or worshipping sense, but in the *spiritual sense* of hearing the Truth from the Self. With this kind of physical, vibrational and spiritual support, anything is possible.

Timing

A healer always waits patiently, for a long time if necessary, to apply intent at just the right moment. A patient may take years to slowly awaken to the powers of healing and they may have much to learn along the way. The healer, though at times may feel frustration at their supposed lack of movement, must apply patience and compassion. If you yourself are healed, you will only attract those ready to heal at some point, whether through you or not. If you are not healed, you will attract also those not ready to heal.

When the patient reaches their time, you will know. Then you must strike with power and intent. As a concrete example, I would sometimes see patients who would come in for a few visits without much improvement physically at all, even though we had worked through a couple of layers. At a certain point, a feeling of intensity would overcome me and I would proclaim, 'you must choose now' as it was their time. There was some 'force' to my intent at this point, with directed Will for their healing. It was up to them now to choose to manifest the healing or not. My faith and Will as always, remained strong. Oftentimes, they would come back with a 'miraculous healing', pinning it on whatever remedy or area of the body we targeted. As helpful as these things can be, they do not in and of themselves do the healing. The patient had decided to grasp the tools and finally used them to manifest their healing—they had made the choice.

Sometimes, a patient would not return. They simply could not commit to healing at that time.

In many cases of 'timing', fear, anger or impatience are motivating factors. If a patient's health has deteriorated or changed—they become fed up or frustrated. This is a great opportunity to use in their favor as excellent 'motivators' to overcome fear and make health manifest.

Reaching our 'limits'

A spiritual student reaches many illusory limits during his/her journey. The most formidable and challenging however, is the manifestation of permanent surrender to Self. We feel we can safely go along healing and learning without fully committing to Higher Self permanently. With the ego still intact as 'separate' from Self, we are still part of and connected to 'this world'—we still haven't released those around us and societies' expectations to the fullest. The ego at this point fears full abandonment/aloneness as its purpose becomes permanently aligned with Self Will—it can seem like a most real limitation.

I had succeeded in all ways in life. I had a beautiful, healthy family, a lovely home in the country, money, assets, and a successful career. I had met societal (and ancestral) expectations of success for me this lifetime. At this point, most of us simply sail along without truly challenging our limitations further and die years later in the same situation, as our life has passed us by. We can even move to a bigger house or make more money and travel more but in the end, it's the same. Of course, there's nothing 'wrong' with this either but we have only achieved a state of satisfaction in mediocrity—we have not gone out and 'tested' our dreams, inventions and limits. We have not listened and followed what Self has commanded of us to the fullest because at least at first, we often don't even *like* let alone understand what we are intuited to do!

I realized as I gave up my mind's dream of the perfect 'dream home' for a non-conventional cabin in the wilderness, doing non-conventional things and living out dreams and testing myself, that I was pushing beyond societal expectations and norms now. I was doing the questionable, 'the bizarre' and the confusing that the collective ego would never do let alone understand. I knew then, I had reached a formidable barrier beyond which lay my greatest freedom. Life is not meant to be 'comfortable'—we are meant to create and truly put that limitlessness into action. What is it that you *truly* desire?

Receiving

Manifestation also means allowing or receiving. As healers, it's most natural to give to others and it is part of what brings us joy. However, there's a balance here that often becomes thwarted. What we have failed to realize is that receiving is just as valuable, valid and important. Many times we are told from Within to do this or that, to go here or there, take this trip or do that course and many times we just don't listen—the mind *jumps* to excuses as to why we can't. If we'd only allow ourselves to receive everything that came to us without question, we'd see how this joy we now can share with others. If I'm told to go on a retreat or do something for myself, I can see it as selfish and costly or I can receive it and know I will grow, evolve, learn and change on this retreat and this in turn, I can give back to others I'm healing. Change receiving into 'investment' and your outlook will shift.

There is always a balance between giving and receiving and it's determined by Self. Sometimes we can get into chronic taking patterns (running away, too many retreats, too much indulgence) or chronic giving patterns (overwork, responsibility, worrying, emotional investments, giving too much away). It takes the practice of *listening* to master this. If we practice not questioning what we're told by Self, we come to this mastery.

The Nature of Healing

The earth is your home and lives within you.
To flow with Me you must flow with it.

The four elements and nature

It is helpful to have knowledge of at least the four elements of nature; water, earth, air and fire. They are consistent within our very physical makeup. It affects us in such profound ways that it must be paid attention to as it affects us not only in the physical but in all other aspects of the mental, emotional and spiritual. We cannot escape nature not matter how hard we try. We are a product of it and must flow with its cycles to be effective humans and healers. The seasons, temperatures, moon cycles, plants and animals, winds, waters, skies, clouds, sun, planets, stars and earth all affect us in varied and deep ways that must not be ignored. All these elements are ultimately healing and balancing as most ancient practices and modalities of medicine teach us. Learn where your energies are most prominent (at the moment) and balance them using the other three elements. For example, fire is calmed by earth and water and accelerated by air in Chinese medicine. Keep your practices in this area extremely simple and intuition-based for you and your patients. You can use the colors, materials, tools, directions and sensations born of each of these four groups to help with healing and balancing. Nature provides us with all the keys and healing tools. Using at least the four elements along with any healing modality only serves to enhance it.

Water

Water is a major part of body composition and air we breathe. It provides flow of movement and qi (energy). It is symbolic for Life force or God. Use spring water, water cleanses, hydrotherapies, baths, water fasts and vacations near water, swimming exercises, items such as rocks from rivers and moving water, water sounds and fountains to literally flush, purify and clear the mind, body and soul. Water allows for movement, release and flow.

Air

Air is the source of literal inspiration and intuition and connects us to Self. Use the breath and breathing to enhance meditation, focus and intuition. Use meditations techniques, breathing techniques, qi gong, martial arts, exercise and aromatherapies to enhance the relationship with air and inspiration. Air brings one to the present moment and allows for clarity of body and mind and the feeding of the entire system with oxygen. It cleanses, purifies, stimulates and silences the mind.

Earth

Earth is the carbon part of our composition. Nature and the Earth provide for ultimate grounding and reconnection to life and reality. Use nature and wilderness, nature retreats and adventures, travel, camping, forests, gardening, walking, parks, bare footing and simply getting outdoors to remind us of Who We Are—to settle the mind. The earth is quiet, grounding, nurturing, soft and feminine.

Fire

Electromagnetic, heat and light energies are emitted by the body. Fire literally provides passion and direction. It fuels us with the joy that uplifts us. Anything that encourages 'fire' or passion encourages movement and healing. Use candles, outdoor wood fires, fireplaces and woodstoves, safe sunbathing, natural light, full spectrum lighting, infrared saunas, heat therapies and bathing, sweat lodges and steaming, spicy food and warm soups to stimulate the fire within. Fire is noisy, consuming, upward and alive.

The gender of healers

Most of the Universe is made up of female energies according to the ancient knowledge of the Toltecs[2]. This implies that male energies are a rarity compared to the more abundant female energies. (This in no way implies superiority either way, but simply *uniqueness*). At one time, the goddess energy was a powerful presence upon this earth being both revered and feared. Our very population shows us that females dominate in sheer numbers alone and tend to outlive males. Female chromosomes show us the completeness of the XX chromosome compared to the more unique, XY. The universe itself is also mostly darkness which according to ancient Chinese medicine is yin or female—the great womb or void. As an observation, perhaps this is a reason why male and patriarchic energies have been attempting dominance for so long. Somewhere deep within us, we feel threatened by the more dominant, common female presence in the Universe. With this in mind, the male

---

[2] Castaneda, Carlos. *The Art of Dreaming*. New York: Harper Perennial. 1994. 188.

would certainly feel 'compromised' and need to assert his power.

The irony is that we are made up of both male and female energies and cannot exist one without the other. We are the balance of yin and yang. We are androgynous in the spiritual sense.

As women, we gave up our power somewhere along the line and forgot our maleness. As men, we did the same in a different way and forgot our femaleness.

As females, we backed away from the male and forgot our power, giving it up in favour of our strong desires—our egos wants, needs and to survival—symbolic to 'Eve's apple'. We gave it up to the false guise of weakness, unworthiness, being looked after and cared for. We cannot blame men. They simply followed their own egos and took up the space—and then ate of the apple as well.

A shaman once told me that the men need me to pray for them. I didn't understand what he meant at the time and it irritated me because I was thinking that he was being patriarchal. Now I know he meant 'pray for male *energy*'. Only through this knowing, through love and acceptance of power for all, will the balance between yin and yang return and both energies take their honoured place in the Universe.

The female healer

A new pattern must be set for females of this reality. Gender is never relevant but perceptions are.

Many female healers carry the labels of woman, wife, mother or daughter into their work. These labels must be diligently removed (as all labels must be) and released for the true power of the Spirit to shine through. The female is rapidly evolving now, with intuition and the feminine more accepted than ever. Do not blame, look to the past or buy into the so-called persecutions of females which serve only to empower these notions as being real. As women 'band together', they disempower themselves into weakness with the idea of a separate female collective. To be truly powerful she must release all labels and know herself only for Who She truly Is. A female is safe and free to pursue her destiny no matter what she has endured in the past, collectively and individually. She creates her own reality. She is not better or worse. Her domestic life must become a living example for all others. She must come and go as Self wills. She must be ultimately responsible only for Herself. She must remain kind, compassionate, neutral and unaffected. She must not succumb to the collective obsessions of worry and weakness, doting and nagging—she knows these are not Who She Is. She must treat all people with the same deep compassion, attention and focus. If she is truly present and joyful when she is with others, including friends and family, she will not regret leaving them to teach, heal and learn as she must. Presence will satisfy her longing and she will not yearn for them. If she truly follows her own destiny, she sets a pattern of strength and example for her sons, daughters, partners and others. She does not waver to societal expectations of the 'good mother'—she knows she will perish with pain, bitterness and sadness as her soul yearns for the fulfillment of its unique purpose this lifetime—to be Herself without rules and duty—to be free. She knows her duties are never to cares of this world—only to Herself. She trusts her family is well cared for by Self and that they learn not dependence, weakness, neediness or to look for love outside themselves—the modern sickness that rages throughout. She does not own her family. They are only *with* her for a time. She releases the lowest form of fear—guilt—and turns her head from it. She knows she only teaches her children guilt if she doesn't. She only teaches them slavery by enslaving her own life to her children and family. She shows them love and freedom as the individual souls they are, through the example she sets.

We have no more time or energy to waste deluding ourselves of our power—by raging against the male or cowering in guilt and weakness.

The balanced female healer sets the pattern for the Goddess that she is.

Teaching the female

Females are usually much better able to accept truths, get on with life after trauma and to heal, to accept mistakes, to be vulnerable in emotions and to recognize what needs to be done, when and how. This has nothing to do with any inherent ability, only social training. She has a strength of endurance and survival that allows the teacher to relay messages to her with love yet ruthlessness. Unlike the male, the female can be ruthless to the point of seeming cold or lacking gentleness—with herself and others. This can be a great advantage in pursuing the truth but can be damaging if gentleness and compassion are not applied appropriately.

The male healer

In some ways, the male healer must be extra diligent and courageous. The collective female allows for intuition, love, healing and softness whereas the male collective does not. He must have an unrelenting drive toward his destiny as a healer that surpasses all other goals that have been set for him—uncommon in the material success-seeking collective male. Female healers can often seek out their own kind and become somewhat accepted but this is rare amongst males except in certain and specific cultures or circumstances. Oftentimes a male healer will be seen in the presence of a female healer to support and assist him as she may be more acceptably unabashed in her intuitions.

The male healer must too remain diligent to the release of labels and let them fall away. There is no such thing as the 'man' just as there is no such thing as the 'woman'. He is safe to be fully powerful as Spirit alone. No man will question him as his love will become crushing to all fear and the seemingly meek and smallest of men can overcome all through this love. He does not distract himself with societal thoughts of the modern 'acceptable' man—he rises beyond them. He must remain very diligent as the animal and egoic energy is strongly encouraged in our society for the male. He wipes out thoughts of being weaker when it comes to sexual behavior, tendencies and aggression. Is the stamen of the flower more sexual or aggressive than the ova? Do the male and female trees bear any difference in this respect either? Do not delude yourself and excuse your weakness to male tendencies. There is no such thing. He wipes out his need for pride and competition. He no longer carries the cares of this world around with him, striving to live up to them. He rests in his own Self.

The male must be diligent to join with the female, with his own feminine energies and release the fear of female power in general. His rarity and uniqueness as a male are a precious gift. He must release his guilt for being male as our collective society sees him, and see himself as beyond gender.

The male healer has an interesting role to play with other males. Through gentleness, yet confidence and strength of love, he displays potentiality to other males beyond the cares of this world. No one can mock him when he is fully confident—fully at peace. He doesn't take heed to praise or blame from his peers any longer.

The balanced male healer sets the pattern for the God that he is.

Teaching the male

Although some males are more intuitive than others either in terms of background, culture, training or karma, they require slightly different methods to convey truths to than females. Males are easily devastated once certain mind or rational thresholds are reached and can react negatively, violently and irrationally to shame, disappointment and any other threat to their perceived manhood. This is why most males upon revealing sexual trauma or releasing suppressed trauma, are more apt to commit suicide. Most of this is due again to societal collective beliefs around what is masculine and acceptable for males. A teacher must be gentle with males and prepare him diligently and consistently for truths. A teacher must cultivate first, altered perception beyond societal beliefs and heightened intuition before truths can be relayed safely. Although this gentleness may seem a weakness, it is actually a great strength as it is devastating to fear. Ironically, the male is often more gentle in his true nature than the female and this can be used much to his advantage.

Female points of power

The moon cycle is extremely important for females, pulling on the tides of menses as most traditions teach us. (However, both genders are made mostly of water so the moon affects us all). Most ancient healing systems point to menses as a time of high intuition and sensitivity for females, allowing them full access to intuition, self-healing and unabashed honesty and emotion. Although not yet fully honored in our society, repressed, unexpressed and shunned feelings and behaviors often surface during these times. It's extremely important to watch a woman closely during menses for very clear cues as to her deepest subconscious issues and for answers as to her healing. A woman is best to seek solitude during these times so as to best allow for Self-communication without interruption, for Self-healing and expression. Creativity often heightens during menses and can be used to its highest potential at this time. The uterus (about four inches below the navel or at the acupuncture point of dan tian in traditional Chinese medicine) is a center of power for females and the pressure menses places on it at this time allows for nothing less than extreme sensitivity and clairvoyance. A woman can not only pick up every nuance of what's going on around her at that time but also the deep feelings, emotions and issues of others. A healer must apply her awareness without judgment of herself or others and allow for solitude so as not to be overwhelmed by it and by her surroundings. The response females have at this time is normal and must be used to its highest advantage. Menses can be a time of great peace for a woman if she fully surrenders to this communication and does not resist her knowing.

The womb or uterus literally holds great power. This chalice must be kept clean through the cleansing of the mind so that pure love can fill it.

As a woman reaches menopause, she becomes intuitive almost always. Full wisdom settles in now as she no longer cycles—she gets to keep her power all month long! Most women do not know what to do with this heightened intuition, awareness and sensitivity. They must be guided to use their powers in alignment with their destiny. Many women make drastic changes in their lives during this time—leaving partners, moving, new careers, traveling etc., all indicative of intuition taking its full grasp on woman. She now tells it like it is and knows it. Women who repress or suppress this start to experience symptoms of menopause, usually as hot flashes which is usually nothing more than repressed anger and emotion due to thwarted dreams, purpose and creative expression. Some women suffer from hot flashes for many years with no avail from any herb or drug due to the fact they simply have not changed their lives to suit what Self is trying to communicate.

Male points of power

The dan tian point is also a power point for the male and can be meditated or focused upon for increased power and accumulation of power. Although for males there is no particular time of month that he may become more intuitive, he must pay attention to the moon cycles as well. He must intuit his most receptive time in the moon cycle, as well as time of day and other power cues and seek solitude for full awareness. Cabins in the woods, retreats, caves and the like can lead to heightened intuition for a man in order to safely release all guards he's placed upon himself as social protection from daily life. For male healers heavily ingrained within societal rules and expectation, extensive stays of solitude may be necessary to provide sustained heightened intuition. Solitude becomes a gateway for the male into heightened states of awareness and possibility. Female healers can also be of great assistance in this way to male healers as they 'pick up' unabashed intuition from the female the more they are in their presence.

Finding your other power points

For both males and females, time of day, season, direction, land formations, power spots, totems etc. are all helpful to the student in focusing their power. It may be early morning where you thrive or late evening or afternoon—try to do healing work and/or meditate during these times if you can. Certain seasons will also attract you (or cause loathing) and you may choose to either retreat or work during these times. The direction one faces to heal and even how one sleeps is beneficial as power flows a certain way depending on your tendencies. Sit in different directions to provide you with cues. How you've already subconsciously situated yourself (at a desk, in your bedroom or especially at your favorite spot in the house) may provide you with helpful cues as to your most powerful direction. Certain land formations such as oceans, lakes and water, mountains, prairies or desert may also attract you. Listen and feel for these cues and use them to your advantage. Water may need to be flowing for you (river or creek) and not stagnant (pond, dugout or a lake) or vice versa to assist you.

Try not to apply your mind and concern yourself over details—simply use these power points as you can to enhance yourself and your practice. Knowing yourself and your body's preferences intimately helps you to know others in the same way.

The Setting for Healing

Make things easier for yourself and go where you can know Me best.
Here, I will train you to see Me everywhere.

Power places

There are many power places in the world and as we evolve consciousness, they also evolve and change. Physically, most are due to certain land formations, vortices, lay lines, water and underground springs or streams, electromagnetic influences, minerals, rocks, caves, crystal formations etc. The mind may not even like the power place from any aesthetic standpoint. A healer can tell a power place simply by how it feels and how it changes his/her perceptions of the world. A power place has a unique other-worldly feel to it as if one could be transported to another time, place or reality. Power places have given birth to the legends of fairies, nature, animal and plant spirits, and other entities— they engender a sense of peace and tranquility. A power place is necessary to provide a correct location for activity, healing, retreat and creativity. One must be astute to know a power place and utilize it to his/her advantage. A place you think of fondly or tend to return to often is usually a clear signal that it's a power place for you.

Some may be called to use these power places as retreats, new homes, as healing areas or simply for a one-time visit. Most healers however, will find a power place when their lives are ready for a change—for evolution or increased awareness. A power place is extremely helpful, if not necessary for this, as it allows through its heightened vibration, an energetic shift that may not be received elsewhere. We need a catalyst for change and power places are important in this and serve us well. It can literally reset one's energy, just as an enlightened or present individual can. To live in the presence of sustained heightened energy can help lead one into infinite possibility.

To the mind, a power place can appear in unlikely locations but one cannot ignore inner knowing. Pay attention to the feeling of a power place as it can be either positive or negative. A place with power but much fear around it is obviously conflictual and without advanced consciousness to overcome it, would be difficult to utilize. A place with power for you must feel right in all ways. What is a useful power place for one healer may be detrimental to another.

The Healing Space

The space that surrounds you is the Universe.
Within it You sit. All else is irrelevant.

Healing Atmosphere

Keep the office/work space simple and feng shui. The patient must feel very comfortable in your space as they may have to wait and may be very nervous at first. Coloring must be conducive to peace and health as well as furniture, literature and art. Your office literally reflects you so make it personal yet professional and clean. A cold and clinical space speaks of just that. Make your space warm, inviting and comfortable. In the actual healing space itself, you may want to use white on the walls so you can clearly see the patient—colors will reflect off the walls onto their skin and can change your perceptions of their health. One can also see auras and other energies more clearly using this background. Use colours, however, to enhance your own healing abilities and chakra strengths. Certain shades of green are excellent in their support for healing and love—choose colours close to nature such as earthy tones. Lighting is also important using as much natural light as possible to help both with healing and perception of the patient. Avoid fluorescent lighting and use more natural or full spectrum lighting if you can. Keep wall spaces clean and simple with meaningful, relevant or no decor. All things, including art, must be conducive to health and healing and vibrate within that accord. Natural fibre carpets, hemp, corks, wood floors and furniture lend a warm, natural energy and temperature to the office. To induce health and life, use nature inside such as plant life and water. Healing tools such as crystals, crystals lamps, bowls, waterfalls or misters can really enhance heightened awareness and prepare patients for a calm experience. Keep the temperature warm, not hot. Open windows for fresh moving air. Keep good water or herbal teas handy. Make sure all your reading materials, art and music reflect your own philosophies and energies and are light in nature. Keep a big box and play place for children full of toys (that make no noise), books and coloring materials. Keep computers off while working as both the screen and the electromagnetic energies can distract you both. It's also imperative patients shut off their cell phones and pagers and come undistracted (without busy children, relatives or friends that may interfere/distract from the visit.) Have tissues handy and chairs comfortable. All your tools must be easy to access and be at hand.

Keeping your space simple lends confidence to you as a healer. Clutter only clutters the mind and limits focus telling the patient energetically that you are trying to distract energy away from you because you are not clear and confident. Weed out anything that's not feng shui or that simply no longer feels right as you change and grow in your practice. Anything that induces a notion of presence within you is an important reminder to have in the healing space. Allow yourself to assess your workspace with new eyes on occasion to reassess it and make changes as necessary and as you evolve. It helps to do this after you have come back from vacation/retreat and can see the office space differently.

Choose a healing space that is a power spot for you and it will enhance your healing with patients. My patients don't mind waiting if they have to because my space is so inviting. Its music, art, colouring, lighting and general atmosphere are meditative and they become peaceful and relaxed before their actual visit. They will like coming, feel comfortable when with you and different upon leaving. Use your senses to detect just the right spot for you and do not settle for anything less no matter what the mind says. The office or space will choose you . . .

When choosing my new office, I chose a small, older yet quaint house in the middle of town. What sold me on it was the feeling I got when I went into it. It literally welcomed me and I felt 'home'. I saw green auras in the treatment rooms and knew right away this was the place for the practice without a doubt. It was not big, not fancy or in an office building. It was the vibration that I could work in without interference and in which my patients could also feel at home and comfortable. It does not have to be perfect and have all the latest and most expensive styles and shades, fancy desks and lighting. Most people do not live or work in fancy places and feel uncomfortable in them. You do not choose an office to impress or make yourself out to be better than. Make your office a reflection of you.

I find it so interesting how my office has changed over the years just as I have changed. Because I'm more comfortable with Who I Am now, I don't mind what people think or what they see in my office. I put up things and display things that I love and feel right for me. Previously, I had put up art and used objects that would be 'non-offensive' to everyone—bland and without the tint of my personal taste and style. I was afraid of offending. Now, with gentleness and simplicity, the objects I now choose are lovingly reflective of Me and where I'm at in my life. I set the intention that what they see in these objects no matter what their beliefs, is positive. Our perceptions may be different but the true source of all things is Divine. The office then becomes a subconscious reminder for others to do the same using their own style and taste—their own expression of the Divine.

The above are only suggestions (and can be made to your home as well). Work with what you have and mould your area to match Who You Are. Don't be afraid to let people see and experience that. Above all, you must be comfortable and enjoy the space in which you work and live.

Healing everywhere

Many of us are very good healers within our healing space atmosphere—at work. When we are out of our space, we seem to lose ground and become lost. Where do I fit in? How do I speak to others? How friendly should I be? What boundaries do I set? What social interactions do I engage in? What do I do with my free time? What is my purpose outside of work?

The answer to all questions is to continue being a healer in all settings which means to continue being present. Bring your healing to the rest of your life. Expand it and allow yourself to heal in every circumstance. You are a healer by your very nature and presence, not by anything you *do*. Not every situation calls for formal healing but every situation will call for you to be present. Even when you are not in the healing mode, practice remaining in reality—in focus and in the present.

The healing setting is usually a controlled one—a quiet space, one patient at a time—you know your place and so does the patient. It can seem like chaos to apply this to the rest of your life that's not so structured. Joy is not a structured thing. Well up joy wherever you go— in the grocery store lineup, at the gas station, with your family. You can become very fatigued outside of your space as chaotic energies encroach and you are not in your power. Practice seeing yourself as you see yourself in practice—your true present Self—which will stay with you, manifesting those feelings of joy and peace you have when healing, into the rest of your life. Every word you speak and gesture you make is healing. Every thought you think and action you take is healing. You cannot afford to be sloppy, ungrounded and lack presence. Fake it until you make it if you have to. Pretend you are that healer in these circumstances and as strange as it feels at first, you will soon get used to it and your entire concept of your old self in these settings will fall away.

Clearing your work space

Clearing can be done in any way you choose—it's all just intention.

Some use smudging (shamanic smoke like sage or incense), affirmations, prayer, hand-washing, meditation, water, crystals or other objects—the list is as limitless as your imagination. Simply bring awareness to the fact that the clearing of your space is necessary. Clear yourself first and then the space using whatever method you are comfortable with. Do this as often as you intuit. With the busy-ness of practice and everyday life, we sometimes forget but it is essential for your own well-being and that of the practice and patients. I often recommend healers wash their hands after every patient (as it is prudent to do for hygienic purposes anyway), only to do so with awareness that they are releasing the last patient and cleansing their energies. Another suggestion is to drink a large gulp of water after each patient to cleanse yourself of these energies and to increase your own energies with the power of water.

Staff

Staff is an integral and dynamic part of the healing space and must also be 'feng shui'—they too must be 'correct' for the healing place. They must have both a strong desire and love to be working with you. There must be a comfort and ease that is shared between you. Boundaries are key in any relationship and staff is no exception—open communication with them is paramount. Always gently speak the truth and encourage them to do the same. Listen and watch the body language and tone of staff. Be present and astute with them as well, even during practice. Pay energetic attention if they need healing or need to time off etc. Talk to them regularly and be childlike in your sharing as well—have fun! They are there more than just to perform a service for you and the patients. You are learning from them and vice versa. They are a vital part of the healing practice and many become healers themselves after watching you for a time. They are students and your love toward them must be aptly reflected with due time and attention toward them, the financial compensation you give them and your respect for them. A loved staff member can remain with you for a lifetime and is your ally. This spiritual partnership then serves both of you in limitless ways.

Communication with staff, as in any relationship, is a primary focus for the healer. Although there are certain job requirements, there may be things outside of this that need to be added, removed or discussed at times. Their suggestions are very valuable in terms of what's working in administration. Don't be afraid to try a new tactic for a while to see if it works out. You may be surprised! If not, nothing's lost.

As you change, so does your practice and so does your staff. Honor when a relationship is over and do not delay. If a staff member does not want to leave but clearly does not have passion for the work anymore, you must intervene with compassion promptly. You only do yourself, your patients and the staff person a great disservice by keeping them on.

I have found that all my staff promptly left happily and of their own accord when it was time for them to leave, without any intervention from me, with the next one waiting ready at hand to work! All shifts in your practice can come with peace and ease.

It stands to reason a happy worker makes happy goods and services. Give constant loving gratitude, pay employees well and yes, accept that mistakes do happen sometimes. When mistakes do occur, pay attention to what needs to be corrected—it may be your issue, the employee's issue or both. When mistakes occur repeatedly, you are simply ignoring something vital that you may be resistant to deal with. All my office managers at some point forgot to pay a certain bill. This went on three times before I realized I needed to change things. I switched to preauthorized payments and it was no longer an issue. I was unwilling to do this in the past and hadn't even seen it as an option because I'd had trust issues around money. I learned my lesson and the mistake was corrected. Most mistakes are usually minor and easily corrected. The benefit you and the business gain by allowing the trust of others however, far outweighs any risk.

Trust your heart, not resumes, when you're hiring and you will attract the right person for you, your business and the job. You will attract someone who fits right in. Trust your heart as well when their time is up and trust that you are literally making space for someone or something new that you need now, into your life. It's not always easy but ultimately, if you keep practicing this, it will prove itself to you time and time again.

The Patient

Be your own patient first.

Choosing the right patients

You are not here to treat everyone and anyone that walks in your door. You must carefully select those that are truly ready and willing to heal, and this is done quite intuitively. Everyone must always be treated the same; with love, compassion and politeness but boundaries must be clear or you run the risk of leaking yourself of precious life force energy.

The practice must always reflect the healer and if there are issues still present, the same patients and/or types of dis-eases will keep returning to 'teach' us. As I made the decision to help only those who are ready to heal, my practice literally 'cleaned up' and I found only those ready to heal came to me!

Sometimes these patients are difficult to pick out, other times it's clear. Here are a few signs of those not ready to heal:

- the patient never seems to get any better—sometimes this will show up as seemingly different symptoms or different life circumstances but it will always reek of the same story. (Be cautious with this as this may be due incorrect timing on your or their part or you are not seeing what the true issue is. You will have an underlying feeling that the patient is resisting you somehow).
- the patient is better/not better but always complaining and/or blaming
- the patient is constantly demanding of you to 'fix them' or heal them
- the patient comes to visits but refuses to follow instructions for their own health
- they have been dragged in by relatives or friends and clearly don't want to be in the visit
- they've 'tried everything already' and they doubt you can help them but are coming to say they've tried this too and add it to their list of things they've 'tried but didn't work' (victim mentality)
- they challenge and question everything you say or do
- they become obsessed with you with frequent requests to be with you and seem to listen but instead are worshipping you

(lost soul)

Usually we run into a combination of the above but for the most part, patients who don't want to heal are *consistently* this way. Every patient has moments of doubt and difficulty being diligent so invariably some of these issues will arise from time to time. Sometimes it will be you that's not seeing the solution to their issue. This is not a hard and fast guideline but gives you a clue as to those patients who are not interested in healing—at least at this time and space. Sometimes, a patient needs to warm to you before they can fully trust you or they may have other complications that need to be worked on first. Sometimes, it's just a matter of time for them. If I sense great resistance, I often ask a patient point blank, "are you ready to heal?" or I go into meditation and ask for a vision as to their intentions. Those who are not ready will always hesitate and usually they will avoid answering or looking me in the eye and talk about other things. In my visions, they will not sit down on my 'healing bench' (which is symbolic for healing for me) and they may also turn away or put their hand up to me. Rarely, some patients will be honest and tell you outright they don't want to be here. In those cases, I kindly show them the door and tell them I'm here when they are ready to heal. This is not harshness; this is necessary for your own and their survival. Some patients will return to you simply because you're the only person that's ever told them the truth and they've had to chew on that awhile and get ready for healing on their own.

Sometimes a long-term patient, who has been doing well, will need to leave the practice for a while to make some serious life decisions about their own healing and self-commitment. When they are ready to heal again, you both will know and progression can continue.

You are not in the business of proving yourself, defending yourself, fixing others, wasting your time or pleasing. The energy you expend in trying to heal someone who doesn't want to heal is neither worth the time nor the compensation you may receive. The time and space that's used up by those who don't want to heal is best used on someone who does or on yourself. Either way, let intuition be your guide in terms of who is ready and who is not. Someone who wants to heal has the will to do so and they will do it with or without you—that's your patient!

Types of Patients

All are the same yet unique.
See Me through others and apply Me to them in return.

The chronic patient

A chronic patient is in your practice for a reason. Look at them closely and look at yourself at the same time. What are they teaching you? Are you listening to the message? Be patient as you may not understand why for a time but set the intent that you will. Once you've got it, they either leave (if they don't want to heal at that time), or they continue healing.

Reset yourself every time an old patient comes in. Do not see them with the eyes of the past or you will skew the truth as they become 'familiar' to you. You cannot look at them or treat them the same way you did the last time—you must approach them from a new perspective every time. Pretend they are a new patient each and every time you see them. Stay present. Both you and the patient have changed since your last visit, even if it was yesterday. In this way, you allow new insight and intuitive healing to flow unimpeded.

The hiding patient

Sometimes, due to either physical, mental or spiritual reasons, a patient will literally 'hide' answers as to their health questions from you. Physically, they test 'normal' even though both you and they know there is an issue and obvious symptoms. Mentally, they usually seem open and ready to heal. During meditation, the patient is illusive or 'hard to catch' in visions. No healing can occur until they stop and face you as a healer. In most cases, you may have to palliate first on the physical level to correct electrical malfunctioning which 'hides' disease from you. If a person is very ill or has certain physical conditions such as severe toxicity or thyroid and diabetic issues, the body's electricity can be skewed and the kinesiologic[3] reflexes will be difficult to test. Simply treat a layer palliatively that intuitively feels right for both of you and the electricity will change.

If they are subconsciously eluding you, you make have to take a

---

[3] Kinesiology – or 'muscle testing'. A type of diagnostic procedure using the body's reflexes and biofeedback mechanisms to test physical, mental and emotional functioning.

break from each other for a time until they are ready to face you and heal.

The controlling patient

Sometimes a patient wants to heal but they also want to control how they do it and what tools are used. This can work as long as they don't become demanding. You have the right to say no if the tool simply doesn't feel right for you to use on them or if it puts you at risk. If you come to this impasse, refer them to someone else who will do it for them if you are guided to do so. Resist the temptation to 'pass a patient off' to another practitioner in these cases. Go within to ask for the best solution. A healer also has to watch her own issues around wanting to 'control' how the patient is treated. Ultimately, it's up to the patient and you both must work as a team toward their health. Flexibility and non-judgment are key here.

Sometimes patients come demanding a particular treatment or remedy. I then tell them what I do and how we treat the cause. If they still insist, I then suggest they find the remedy and treat themselves or they can bring it in for testing if they like. If we run across resistance, the patient is usually more interested in controlling than healing. People ready to heal could care less *how* they heal. A healer must stay in integrity and resist pleasing others as this will harm the patient and healer.

One patient I had, wanted only acupuncture as he couldn't trust taking remedies. I understood this and was compassionate providing him with acupuncture and making only dietary suggestions. Although he did improve (without other support that was necessary for him, full awareness and addressing his subconscious issues), he could not heal fully—not because of the lack of remedies but due to control. Control itself was making him ill. Healing must flow unimpeded for it to hold fast.

Lost souls

Many of us become lost from time to time. Life events, traumas or simply despair can lead us there. Those who truly choose to heal will be found.

Some lost souls do not seek to be found. They seek to remain lost. Often they have been lost for a long time and are used to it. You can only pray or meditate for a lost soul but you cannot heal one as they have not chosen to be healed on a subconscious level.

A practiced healer can tell a lost soul easily. They can be anyone—friends, family or strangers. You can always tell a lost soul by how you feel around them. They are needy in a very desperate kind of way, without wanting any true help or assistance but will 'bother' you somehow and may engender feelings of irritation, annoyance or guild and obligation. They appear to want to heal and seem to be quite attentive or even restless. They will ask questions like any other patient but upon you answering them, there is a distance in their eyes or in their attention. They tend to become very distracted and to go off into oblivion—they become vacant. They ask questions but do not hear the answer nor do they even *want* an answer. You will feel a definite disconnect with their soul. They sit before you going through the motions of this life and reality but are never present. You will feel that they're just not getting it or even wanting to get it. They keep 'telling you their story' seemingly without end, to elicit pity.

At times a patient that wants to heal may go into this, especially with regards to a deep truth, but it will not be a constant and you will notice them getting angry or irritated and usually honest with you that they don't get it. In these cases, anger or irritation becomes a catalyst or a motivator that can help them eventually wriggle into awareness out of pure will. With lost souls, this is not the case. They want one of two things:

to blame

to complain

These are the harbingers of self-pity.

Sometimes, they will even bring in children or other people to distract them from the visit. Often the children or people will be extremely distracting and demanding of attention during the visit, as the patient does not really want to hear what you have to say and the other person/child will reflect this. You must insist that they come alone or they cannot be treated. You will know their true intentions if they do not return at this suggestion.

The lost soul can easily cling to you for salvation. They look to you for it and they will not find it there. Salvation comes from within Oneself and with will. A lost soul is in the true sense of 'purgatory'. Some will look up to you, compliment you, perhaps bring you gifts or try to create a special relationship in some way with you. They may want to be 'special' and to have a needy relationship that goes both ways—as they're used to. They may even use you as a surrogate for someone or something that is missing in their life. Remain compassionate yet unattached to outcome, the patient or expectation. Since you've no time to waste, you must ask them pointedly before visits become leeching to you, what are their intentions—are they ready to heal? Often, the patient will not return at this point as they know you've 'figured them out' and will search elsewhere for salvation.

Boundaries are key here as well as clear guidelines for healing. They *must* want to heal or there is no relationship. Your only responsibility is to remain yourself and in your 'found-ness' or power until they remember theirs.

Lost souls must often be jolted into this reality and presence, usually by a trauma or shock of some kind. Trust their time will come and at that time, they will see the light and regain their presence. Pray for their awareness and send them away to finish their suffering in peace.

The dramatic patient

Some people are more dramatic than others. The ego likes drama because it's entertaining. The Spirit needs no entertainment as it's constantly content and joyful with anything and everything that occurs. Drama pulls out all the emotional stops in order to get a rush from adrenaline. Some patients will even try to pull you into their drama that can appear so real—we are all such good actors in life we can even convince ourselves of its reality. Don't be fooled. Do what you need to do to treat or palliate and if a patient goes into dramas, be compassionate and polite but like a child acting up, don't pay attention. They will soon see (subconsciously) that they are not being 'fed' and will usually stop. This can include angry outbursts, dramatic crying or forced and dramatic behaviors. All these will appear and feel fake to you, like learned behavior. True emotion wells up and serves a purpose to bring awareness, to clear and to heal and then it's over. Drama tends to lag on and have a forced or acted-out feel to it. With a more aware patient you can even bring this to their awareness—gently. The ego doesn't like to be embarrassed.

Some lost souls can go so far as to dramatize events and traumas to an extreme. Never go yourself into the drama of trauma. It never helps anyone let alone yourself. Ask yourself, 'without the drama and emotion, what do we have here?' This will keep you level-headed and you will be able to discern the wheat from the chaff. With a 'faker' there will be nothing underlying—nothing serious or even concerning. They are attempting to get a rise for some reason—to get you to 'care' in a sort of special relationship. Point this out politely and do not play the game. With a true crisis, people are usually quite level-headed—they have to be as trauma brings people quite into the present where they're able to function best.

The discouraged patient

To be discouraged is just that—to lack courage. Point out to the patient that they have simply forgotten the power of their will—the power of their innate courage. Sometimes, patients aren't aware of how much they've healed or how far they've come. Some of us have been entrained to be more negative than others in our outlook throughout life. Self-blame, inadequacy and self-pity can easily creep in for the healer at this point so keep a level head and understand these are not your fears. It can be so easy to fall into a patient's discouragement around their healing or lack thereof. Stay optimistic but truthful and point out all the things that have improved for them, with full confidence and faith. Keep your energies empowering and with a full energetic push back to the patient for ownership of their responsibility in healing. Journaling helps most people track their progress physically, mentally and spiritually. To observe oneself is a great tool and journaling can help immensely for Self connection.

If a patient is not healing, you must always ask them with compassion and pure observation, why they aren't. This places full power back to them. Now they must take responsibility and make a decision. If your energies are never offensive or defensive but purely observatory, they have no cause to attack you as you see only the truth (which they simply cannot hide from you or themselves anymore). Always remember the visit is not about you. You have no need to ever defend yourself. Truth has no defense. It stands alone and turns its head from proof and argument of any kind. It is neither arrogant nor opinionated or judgmental. It sits before you; face up, plain as day with only love and healing as its goal.

The distracted patient

Sometimes a patient or student will be doing very well on their own but they are not fully seeing it. They may come to you with a list of issues but doing very well overall. There is no need to 'treat' them. They need the simple reminder that the mind is leading them into distraction at the threat of enlightenment/presence. No matter how much they argue or 'want to know the whys', gently bring them back again and again into this awareness. Great fears can surface as the self's old foundations begin to crumble and it will frantically try to save itself. Do not fall into the trap of becoming distracted yourself with their issues but continue to remind them of Who they Are. You will have an underlying feeling that all is well with them—that the soul is happy and on track. Keep your eyes on this so they can turn their own eyes to it as well.

The understanding patient vs. the faithful patient

Patients, healers and spiritual students will fall into one of 2 general categories. They will either have a tendency to want to 'know' and therefore question to find answers and understanding or they will simply follow with faith. There is no issue with either tendency. Some of us require deeper understanding to bring us to awareness and to also share and teach others. Some of us do not. For those who need to know, spiritual reading/courses etc. are usually essential. For those that don't, (and they may or may not have a religious background) they simply need the action of it in order to heal. Cater teachings and recommend tools accordingly.

The wounded healer

Although martyrdom can seem attractive to the self, it is in no way helpful to the healer or patient. It brings with it the need to suffer, have pain, to seek and not find and to remain helpless. True strength lies in humility and asking for assistance when needed which takes great courage and insight. Weakness lies in succumbing to the need for pain, suffering and a false sense of strength through 'enduring' these on one's own. No one can truly help others in this state and it must be transcended for healing to occur. Be astute with the wounded healer/patient and point out to them this folly. They must be made aware of what they are creating and be empowered to change it. They must make the choice to release the title of martyr, bend down in humility and receive their healing.

The non-human patient

A healer will be called to heal animals, plants and even inanimate objects. You must learn to apply your skills to them as well.

Animals that one has in one's life must fit in to your life well. Always choose an animal for you and your family, from the wisdom and timing of Spirit. I chose 2 horses for my family. One was very sweet, one was mean. I worked with both and learned a lot from them. As I worked on myself at the same time, I realized that if the mean horse was unwilling to heal, she would have to go. I looked in her eye and spoke to her on a soul level. I told her that I loved her and that I could help her heal. I knew she had been abused from previous owners but if she did not choose to heal, I could not keep her. I felt a lot of sadness and pain from her but she would not 'cry' or let it out—she would not heal—at least not at this time or with me. I said I would give her time to make the decision.

If the animal 'stays in fear', then it will not heal, just like any human. It has a type of will in this sense. It may also simply be time to end the relationship.

One time, a patient brought me a hamster. I did Reiki (hands-on healing) on it but felt it was simply time for it to pass—its time was up. I informed the parent of the child that owned the hamster and told her to gently pass the impending news onto the child to prepare her. The Reiki eased the dying of the hamster.

The faith of the owner of the animal must be present for healing to occur. Like a child, the animal cannot respond unless faith is there. This can be very trying for some owners. We must always treat animal and owner together as issues are often reflected in the animal from the owner. You can use muscle testing and dowsing on animals to test them as well or you can use a surrogate tester. Simply ask someone to 'be the animal' for a moment and they will subconsciously reflect that animals' energies and can be easily tested for health issues.

Plants must be meditated upon for clarity and can also be muscle tested as in the above example. Often plants will speak to us subconsciously and once we 'own' a plant or imprint our energies on it, they will easily respond to us and give us messages as to their healing. They will tell us they need watering or a new pot or a different location.

Inanimate objects such as houses or cars can also be 'healed'. My partner is a 'machinery healer' and through intuition, knows exactly what the machine needs. He also has a deep knowledge of the anatomy of machinery and parts after many years of practice, making him a master in his field. He sees potential in machines that others don't and can fix anything that he's intuited to. The machines tell him what they need for prevention and what might become an issue if it's not attended to now.

Machines respond immediately to our energies. Once, I was so angry, I got into my vehicle and turned the ignition on. It would not start. I had never had this problem before. I kept trying to no avail and nothing was physically wrong with the vehicle. Then, it dawned on me that I was in a dangerous space and it was not safe for me to drive—I had 'shut down' the vehicle. I cleared my anger and it started no problem!

Like all other things with life force in them, animals, plants and inanimate objects reflect us. We also need to honour when they need healing, may be finished with us or when they are ready to pass.

The dying patient

Death does not have to be a subject we avoid or be afraid to deal with as healers. If a patient chooses to die (we all choose to die at some point on a subconscious or rarely, on a conscious level), we must assess what it is they need from us at this point and how we can best provide it. Death must not be seen as 'a failure' by the healer or she disrespects the choice the patient has made. Don't think that a life cannot be 'saved' (to be saved means to forgive oneself) before death either.

Some patients will not choose to save themselves or have peace at the time of death. They may choose to die with the same anger, fear or sadness they had in life. They may choose this either with or without any awareness. They may simply ask you to palliate them and make the end easier for them or they may be looking to you for spiritual guidance. Assess this as you would any other patient. Just because they are choosing to die however, does not mean you discontinue holding faith for them—this you must always uphold even beyond their death, that life is all there is, that it is eternal and that healing is always present upon our choice.

When the time is right, you will know how to prepare your patient. With some, you can be forthright. With others, you must be more subtle. With still others, you may have to let them know what they are choosing to bring it to their consciousness (some are not aware they are choosing death or that death is hovering around them) or you may be called to bring it to the consciousness of their close loved one instead so they too can prepare. There are many different scenarios that can arise.

With patients that are close to death, the thought of death will come to consciousness for you as a healer. Do not ignore it. There are tactful and subtle ways to share this information if you are intuited to. Sometimes, you will just need to keep it to yourself as they've already made a decision. With some patients that have awareness, it is prudent to inform them that they are attracting death at that point in their life. I usually see it as a kind of split or crack of darkness in their aura (or this knowing can also come from intuition or a vision etc.). This crack can be mended if we get to it in time and correct any physical, mental, emotional or spiritual dis-ease. Sometimes, this awareness of death for the patient is enough to make them alter their course and change what they are doing.

With patients choosing to pass, let them know their choice (if they don't already know) and then help them by preparing them for their passing. This may require answering any questions or concerns they may have regarding their Spirit, the 'afterlife', pain of death etc. You must go

Within for the answers as they are unique to them.

One such patient I had was gently preparing for death as she was simply tired. After a long relationship with her, one day she walked in the door and I knew she was ready and that this would be our last visit. I asked if she had any concern or questions and she said she was afraid of the pain of death and wanted instead to just die peacefully in her sleep. I told her she must command this for herself through prayer and faith. When she was ready (had the 'passion' for death), she would align herself with this manifestation and it would be fulfilled. There is no need for pain or 'to surrender to pain'. One must be firm around this subject. I also had the sense that although all her affairs were in order and there was nothing else she wanted to do, that she needed to do a ritual—to write a letter giving thanks to everyone and everything in her life. This is one method that can release one's past so the death is not stressful and full of anger and regret. The reading of the last rites is something akin to this and is an important part of passing so the soul can be at peace upon death. Gratitude to one's life and to others is extremely important at this point to allow forgiveness. She thanked me from the depths of her soul—I had never been thanked like that before. With My help, she had saved herself. I felt deeply honoured to have shared in her life and her passing. She died soon after the visit.

It must be made clear to the aware patient that the energy they pass with will follow them into the afterlife or next life—that energy has not been changed. Death is no respite from ourselves and fear continues if it has not been let go or 'forgiven'.

Despite this, some aware patients may not be able to do this. Give them compassion and healing work may have to be done after death instead by the healer.

When a relative of mine died, he had not forgiven himself and his soul was lingering. This is literally what is called 'purgatory' or a kind of nagging 'hell' for the soul. Other cultures say the soul still walks the earth, 'haunting' others. That energy cannot move on unless forgiveness occurs. I was called to help release him. I went into meditation and saw his soul looking back with guilt and fear at all he'd done in the past   he could not go to the light. I sensed a great urgency that I do this work to help him immediately. (If a healer such as me had not intervened, he would have missed his opportunity at that time to pass to the light and would still be haunting this earth and his relatives). I spoke to him in Spirit and soothed him. I cleared his energies with My intention and an angel came for him. The angel took him into the light and he was gone.

If you are sensing the 'haunting' of a spirit recent or even long passed, you must release all your personal fears and get down to business and help them. Ask what the spirit wants and follow Inner Guidance as to what to do next for them. It could be anything from a simple ritual such as smudging, clearing or helping them to settle a matter.

I have had other instances where I was called to do this work and sometimes, I haven't known the person at all. I had to help a celebrity once after his passing. Although I knew of this person, he was not someone I particularly paid attention to. I simply felt a very strong urge to help as he kept coming into my mind and I kept wanting to read and read about him. After I helped him to move on, I didn't think on him any longer—he was at peace.

Do not question your calling to help and do as you are commanded to release the souls that need your help.

'Seeing' the Patient

To look is not to see. To see is to be.

The likeness of everything

Your patients are a reflection in some way, of who *you* are presently. As you evolve and change, your patient base does too, revealing different people to you and your 'strengths and weaknesses'. Patients you have seen before will also reveal different aspects of themselves to you as *you* evolve. As you become more and more unaffected by everything, you become less and less affected by patients or by any other person or environment. Watch who you are attracting as this reveals many truths about yourself to you. Use this knowledge to help you heal and be open to the lessons. The visit essentially becomes a healing for both of you as you bring awareness to these reflections and clear yourself too.

I had a colleague who continually attracted a certain slovenly, repulsive, unhygienic, leering male into her practice. For many years they had a professional relationship and they both learned and healed from the connection. One day, it dawned on her that her own issues with these behaviors within herself (although not overt) were reflected in him. She secretly hated males of this description due to her own past trauma with one as a child. He literally could not leave the practice until she learned to completely let go of (for-give) her past and to become unaffected by it. He was learning that he was loved unconditionally regardless of his appearance and affect. She was learning to forgive.

Spirit and soul

When observing the patient, you must understand what you are seeing and connecting with.

When you are picking up on fear, you are seeing the ego or mind of the patient.

When you go deeper, you will see the soul which is like the 'inner child' of the patient. It is with the patient throughout all its lifetimes. It is affected by and remembers all the past traumas it has gone through. This soul is often what appears during visions you may have for the patient and shows you where it's at and what needs to be done. A person may hide many things on the surface but the soul knows. This aspect is what you'll be working with mostly as a healer. The goal is to connect the soul fully with the spirit.

The spirit of the patient is the Self. Unless one is on the spiritual path and can connect with their own Self, you may not see their spirit in visions per se as it is perfect and requires no work—it is always serene, content, wise and all-knowing.

Focus

A patient may not want to deal with underlying mind-body issues right away or ever and this is fine but you must always stay focused on the real issue, even if they are not, in your soul. If they are open and simply need reminding, nudge them once again with gentle suggestion so they can see the truth and deal with the underlying issues if they so choose. You are not here to 'let them get away with it'. You are here to shine the light of truth on the situation at all times.

I often see this with weight issues for women. Weight is extremely connected to the mind, although it's dealt with usually through diet and exercise only. It often reflects many things, the most common being a form a physical insular protection either due to past trauma or feeling generally unsafe as a female.

We all know patients who've literally 'tried everything' for years without any success. The truth is always before you. Speak it to them and share it with them. They must understand it's of their making in the first place and within their power to unmake. Often they come in once again begging for yet another weight loss remedy—show them the truth with unrelenting gentleness and focus.

Prayer

Although prayer is spoken of often in our world, it's rarely understood or performed properly. Differing religions have their own methods for prayer and each may have its own merit. Most people I speak to regarding prayer however, have little understanding of it, how it works or the power behind it. We tend to perform prayer based on what we were taught without question and most of the time, it's a formal form of asking, pleading or even begging. We can all act out a prayer but truly effective prayer is quite another story. Prayer is a two way street and requires both giving and receiving from Source/Higher Power/God. The method described here is based on the Hawaiian Huna system of healing and prayer[4] and draws from other methodologies as well. It has

---

[4] Long, Max Freedom. *The Secret Science At Work: New Light On Prayer.* Huna Research Publications: California. 1953:127-136.

70

served me well and I pray it serves you as well.

For prayer to be effective, it must always be done in a state of meditation or inner silence. One cannot be distracted because of the presence and focus that's required.

What is also required during either kind of prayer is the same as what's required for any manifestation:

Will
Passion/Inspiration
Faith
Self-Worth

It should be noted that the Will that's required must come from the Higher Self and not the ego's will or from wanting. Passion must be present (meaning the desire to create the effect) from the Higher Self. Faith is the knowing that the effect will be done. Self-Love/Self-Worth is often an aspect that's left behind and so the prayer cannot effectively be made manifest. One must know on a soul level that the request is worthy, 'deserved' and good. You love yourself enough to know you're worthy of it. Often people tend to feel unworthy of receiving and wonder why their prayer or manifestation is not coming about.

In general I have found there are two types of prayer:

asking
creating

In the asking prayer, one may simply ask for one's needs to be met. As long as there is gratitude in the prayer for what one has and is and there is a definite passion from Higher Self for change, the prayer will eventually be made manifest. As with all things, and especially depending on the faith of the participant, prayer may take time to manifest. Because I know the law of the Universe is attraction, I know that what I focus on will be attracted to me. I can't help but real-ise ('make real') my prayers eventually. This faith will make prayers and dreams manifest into reality.

The creating prayer is really the same as the asking prayer only the *time* between the prayer and its manifestation is much shorter and could be classified as a miracle. This requires even greater faith that God/Universe will provide not only the manifestation but the manifestation immediately. This type of prayer requires passion or inner desire to come about as well. Praying for a new car without Higher Self passion from the deepest part of you, will not manifest the vehicle because it's simply not important to the Higher Self. For example, when I bought my second vehicle, I had an inner passion and knowing that it was time to get a new (used) one. I knew exactly what type of vehicle, what price I would pay and what features it had. I was truly excited, like a child—I had passion. I went straight to the dealer and when he told me he didn't have one of those in stock right now, I told him to look for one for me and call me when it came in. He found the exact vehicle I desired not even a week later and upon seeing it, I knew it was what I'd manifested in prayer. Two years later, it came time to buy another vehicle (I thought I *should* buy another one even though there was nothing wrong with the one I had). Although I wanted one, my heart just wasn't in it. I couldn't decide on anything and the same dealer just didn't call me back! My Higher Self just couldn't have cared less so there was no Will, no passion and therefore, no car. Sure, I could have forced and struggled against this and found a car but it would not have worked out somehow and I would only have appeased my ego and wanting.

Prayer can be used to manifest anything. In meditation, send love, gratitude and energy up through the crown chakra to the Divine/God. No words need be spoken but a deep feeling of your passion from the depths of you must be present. Send that feeling up the same channel so the message gets there clearly. Then, know this prayer will be made manifest upon you, without fail because it's not only in your Highest Good to receive it but all of humanity's. Then, you let it be and put no more thinking or worry into it.

From a practical standpoint as a healer, prayer is extremely effective in healing as it literally 'showers' the patient with the desire. However, note this desire must also be the patients' desire. If you pray healing for them and they do not truly desire it, the prayer cannot be effective and will be a waste of time and energy.

Prayer is even more effective when performed by several people together for the same intent. This collective energy sent upward to the Divine creates more energy output.

Prayer can also be used to manifest changes in the weather, circumstance and even to change our physical abilities. When faith in Higher Power is paramount, anything is possible and limited beliefs are suspended. This is why 'miracles' often occur when people are in life threatening circumstances. The Will (passion) is certainly present during emergencies as it is dire.

One summer it rained for a whole month. Since we don't have long summers at the ranch, it's important to get as much work done as we can during that time. We did what we could for the month and I had tried several times to 'pray' the rain away but to no effect. I simply didn't care enough. One day however, when I wasn't even thinking about the weather at all, a feeling came over me that something had to be done. The sky was as usual, filled with dark clouds and it was raining heavily. A profound Will overcame me and a sort of confidence ran through me. I was in passion. I closed my eyes in meditation and focus. I raised my right hand to the sky (I was in my bedroom) and started to 'move the clouds' with it. I started to yawn as I do when energy is clearing and with ultimate faith, I moved the clouds along, asking the wind to blow. This was all done without words or thought, just feeling and hand gestures. The very moment I started this procedure, the wind started to blow and the clouds moved rapidly across the sky. If I were not in a state of meditation, I would have been surprised by the change in the weather. However, being as I was, I had nothing but faith that the sky would do as I asked and that this event was commonplace and already complete at My commandment. We had little rain the rest of the summer and the wind didn't die down until the winter came!

I didn't credit this event to little me or ego but to something inside me, My Higher Self, that required me to be the vessel for Its creation.

Ancient peoples were able to call animals by doing this, change weather, heal, grow crops, walk on water and fire and much more. We cannot forget our birthright to be a part in all creation and make ourselves useful as vessels for the Divine. Do what you can as a human and then, for the rest, employ the Divine.

The collective mind

Collective unconsciousness is not a new concept but it still hasn't reached mainstream thought. It is so real that many dis-eases will be based entirely upon it. It's simply a grouping or labeling that occurs due to race, gender, religion, culture, residence, marital status, financial status, educational status etc. Usually, one's collective labeling is not conscious and we can be almost completely oblivious as to its effect on our lives from day to day.

Labeling becomes a trigger that 'keeps us down' from fully succeeding as Spirits. Labels are not useful, save for the mundane implications they have such as a chair is for sitting, a tub is for washing, this is a man, that is a woman etc. They otherwise serve no other real purpose nor do they have any inherent meaning. However, our society has placed a vast array of illusory strengths and weaknesses associated with labels of all kinds. For women, it can be worthlessness, subservience and weakness. For men, it can be stoicism, duty, responsibility and aggression. For the elderly it can be feebleness, frailty and poverty. These characteristic labels can get quite complicated for people of mixed race, with the addition of gender, age, economic status etc. If one is a minority race, for example, no matter what other status one may also have, there can be an underlying sense of depression, shame and worthlessness. For majority races, there can be an underlying sense of guilt, elitism and an insatiable drive to 'succeed'. Different races can also have more intimate and defining characteristics depending on that race's status within society, its history within that society and the race's underlying issues about its *own* perception due to cultural background and past tradition. Although the above tendencies are merely generalizations, they do point us in the direction of the collective thoughts of our labels and therefore, subsequent dis-ease patterns.

As sensitive as these issues may be to our patients, they must be revealed and released for healing to occur fully. In some circumstances, they may be creating the entire dis-ease picture. For example, many people of certain races are so subconsciously tied to their cultural traditions and perceptions, it is simply seen as dangerous to release them and be truly free. If they release race or cultural labels, then they are no longer part of that group—a truly frightening prospect to the animal self that thinks it must be part of the pack to survive. Anything that attempts to differ from the label then becomes taboo and something not spoken about within (or without) that race or culture—something that just is and must never be questioned or ostracization results. The patient may go to the degree of defending their race or culture—and ultimately their own self-perception—in order to feel safe. Spirit requires no defense nor argument as it simply is—it is safe Within Itself. Other's perceptions (and labels) are no longer a concern.

Patients will also have difficulty letting go of what is perceived as the 'positive' aspects of being part of a group or collective. Some races and cultures take great pride in their backgrounds as well as some women, men, sports players, careers, clubs etc. Pride in a label then also creates something to be proud of and therefore, something to defend.

To be truly free, eventually all labels must cease to exist—both seemingly positive and negative. These labels are constantly changing as society changes its meaning around them. We must go beyond labeling of any kind to have full freedom and peace—to live fully in the present without the expectations and limitations our labels place upon us—to be children once again. Transcending one's labels takes patience, diligence, awareness, great courage and will.

Do not expect yourself or your patients to get this overnight or to have an easy time of this release. See them and yourself as limitless beings only, and you will uphold the highest vision and potential of them and of yourself beyond labels. Peace does not come from belonging to any club or group, race, family or gender. It comes from seeing yourself as you were before all labels arose—the One that cares not *what* It is—as long as it knows that It *is*.

The universal mind

People with similar energies or vibrations will tend to 'gather' unto themselves. This is why we have smaller groups of consciousness (races, cultures, clubs, societies etc.) within the larger, universal human consciousness. The universal consciousness affects the smaller group consciousness as do each of the smaller groups of consciousness affect each other. This is how we see vast changes in human behaviour when more and more smaller groups elevate their vibrations or consciousness. The internet (with all its positives and negatives) has been a great catalyst for universal consciousness shifts, (which affects smaller groups) creating even new governments in previously oppressed societies. Once the group has 'made up its mind' (i.e. applies it's collective will with all the necessary ingredients required for manifestation), it moves as a great force overcoming all and any obstacles to create its new collective reality that it has chosen. As each group elevates consciousness, they become closer and closer to the universal mind, the substrate for all consciousness and an enlightened society is made manifest. This is why it's paramount to remember that all thoughts, even individual thoughts, are powerful as a single person and their thoughts affect us all.

Boundaries

You will see beauty in the fox. You will see beauty in the chicken.
But the fox will eat the chicken when given the opportunity!

Boundaries

The healer must remain the same with all sexes, races, cultures and classes s/he is healing. Most healers will be used to different energies and it will not sway you as you are simply present and focused. Beware of some patients that are lost and looking to you for salvation. Do not allow the 'spiritual ego' to rise and succumb to this type of worshipping. Distrust and poor pattern setting from male and female authority figures and in the collective unconscious occurs due to this. Do not become distracted.

As You become more 'attractive' and you become healed yourself and a clear vessel for love, some patients may not know how to be with You or act around You. Some may become shy, timid and withdrawn. Others may become very smitten. Some may even cross physical boundaries and want to touch You in 'inappropriate' ways. Some may go so far as to even fall in love with You. The egoic self knows relatively few ways to express 'love' and it will usually do so physically. Men more often than women (although not always) will express love more physically through touching and sexual advance as they've been trained to know no other way to do so. The love they feel from You is real, strong and Divine and their animal self simply doesn't know what to do with it. If they are spiritually 'advanced' enough, discuss this with them, keeping it light. Show them it's simply a case of mistaken identity. They are really loving *Themselves*, as they see their own beauty reflected back to them from You—they just don't know it.

I often use examples from my own journey and what I did in the past to lightly point them in the right direction and to let them know I am the same as them.

I once met one of my ascended guides during meditation and was so drawn to Him, I told him I wanted to make love with Him! He simply laughed kindly and told me that was because he is God! Somewhere in my soul, I understood and the feeling dissipated from the base chakra as lust, to encompass all of me in a warm peace instead.

Inform people that it's natural to feel these things but explain to them the difference between animal self and Higher Self and its expressions of love. Animal self seeks to conquer, control and consume through sex, passion or dependency. Higher Self only sees love as beauty and ultimate intimacy as souls connect. In other words, the sexual act pales in comparison and is a poor substitute for soul connection and love. Explain that as with all things like eating or wearing clothes or going certain places, the sexual act also has its place and time and must come from the appropriate intentions of the Higher Self only.

Patient/healer boundaries must always be respected or the relationship and the healing itself are put at risk.

Do not succumb to the fear of boundaries being crossed. You are not your physical body—simply allow Wisdom to speak through you to the patient and to provide you with protection. Those who cross boundaries require compassion as they are often very needy and feel they are missing love in their life and its only expression is through touching and sex. Be compassionate but firm and ruthless. Look into their soul and tell them that love is deeper than this and needs no expression in this way as it is always present. By doing this, you can still be Yourself and not have to go into fearful animalistic protection of the body to defend yourself. Self will do it for you. When you are completely surrendered to Self (faith overrides all fear), you are safe. If you have the egoic need to protect something, it *becomes* unsafe by the very notion that it needs protection in the first place. Always keep in mind *you* create your reality and no one can affect this without your express permission on some level.

Sometimes emotional boundaries are crossed by a patient. This is when a patient gets emotional, attacks emotionally or blames. If your intent to heal has been loving, there is no issue at hand and their reaction is not your responsibility. Be firm yet calm and let it be known that you do not tolerate abuse of any kind. If intuitions come as to the true cause of their outburst, share this with them.

I once had a powerful student whose infant needed medical attention. The doctor was very rude to her. He was consistently terrorizing anyone around him. He was arrogant, attacked her outright for disagreeing with his recommendations and then threatened her. She calmly looked him in the eye and told him she would not tolerate his insolence or arrogance—that his disrespect was intolerable. She then asked him what had happened in his life to make him so miserable. He then stopped, bowed his head and did a routine procedure on the child, something he never did as it was 'beneath him'.

No one had ever stood up to him. She had no fear and no longer cared what others thought of her speaking the truth and standing up for herself. She said at the time she felt he should be honoured to be in her presence and to have the opportunity to help her baby girl. Not because of any pride or arrogance on her part but because she was simply a good person.

I felt this was probably one of the best examples I'd heard of someone staying in their power in this type of situation.

The conservation of a healer

A healer is always seeking to conserve energy. The whole goal is to prevent energy leaks, expenditures and thefts and to accumulate extra energy through energy saving techniques such as meditation, proper eating and exercising, proper speech and thought, proper activities, releasing all fears and pursuing one's life purpose. A healer literally cannot afford to waste energy and must do everything prudently and efficiently. She does not go to a party 'just for the sake of going' or because she feels she 'deserves to' in order to satisfy her ego. She goes because she is *called* to go for spiritual reasons—for herself and others. In this way, the party will not exhaust her but invigorate her. She will also leave the party when the time is right for her to do so and practice listening to this intuition so that she doesn't leak out any precious energy. She does everything on feel—on intuition around what is right for her. Nothing is frivolous. She can laugh and have fun still but there is always an underlying purpose, message and creation whether she understands it at the time or not. Nothing in her life is wasted.

Gift Giving

Gift giving has become a status symbol in our society, along with giving to charity just for the sake of saying you did. Gift giving is a beautiful thing when it comes from Within and you know it's right. You only give something that you are *told* (from Within) to give—that feels right to give. You also only receive something you're told to receive. I've had people give me gifts that didn't feel right for me to receive. They were given out of pride, as bribes, or simply out of guilt or obligation. An energy like that in your home or office is negative and will not serve you so it's best not to accept it or to recycle it as you are intuited.

If you accept the gift as you are told to intuitively, give gratitude for it but understand you have accepted it unconditionally, meaning without needing to return anything to the giver. This may be difficult for the giver to understand but if they come back to 'claim' their return on the gift, let them know you are not obligated in any way and that you only give out of love what you are told to give.

If you accept the gift and are told by Self it's not for you, give it in the spirit of love to the person it's meant for or destroy it. Go Within for directions.

When giving gifts yourself, no one wants more junk so gifts must be very appropriate. A gift is not always what you 'think' someone 'might' like—it's what you *know* they *will* need and sometimes, it will be right out of the ordinary. Gifts must be given without expectations or judgments of any kind. The receiver may even appear not to like the gift (although they will need it on a soul level), and they may choose to give it away or even throw it away. All this is irrelevant as the energy of giving the right gift is all that's necessary during the exchange. Gifts after all, are only symbols. Gifts given by a healer are very powerful because of the *intent* behind them and the healing energy they symbolize. Often intuition guides me to give something of my own to patients—a book, a rock, a painting—any relevant item—as a totem. As you become increasingly aware that the Universe is abundant, giving things away becomes easy, necessary and allows for more reception to the giver.

Gift giving has become a social norm in our society that you do for certain occasions and holidays whether you want to or not. A gift must never be given under obligatory circumstances as the energy with it will be negative. Gift giving must be done in meditation to determine what gift is appropriate and this can be very difficult to do in a store. First, you will be prompted to give a gift intuitively. Then, you will be shown what gift it is either through intuition, visions, dreams or other signs. It may not be when or what you expect. It may be recycled from your home, from nature, from a store, money, cooking for someone, calling them, or clothing from your very back!

Often we try to keep people at arm's length with gift giving or to appease the ravages of our societal expectations and consumerism. Gifts are loaded with meaning and energy so it's best to give something positive and correct to keep love in flow.

Relationships

Through your relationships with others and the world,
I teach you how to relate to Me.
You can only know Me through these relationships.

Soul mates

Contrary to popular belief, you can have many soul mates. A soul mate is simply someone (or even sometimes an animal, thing or place) that has a very similar or complimentary vibration. Someone can become a soul mate when you have made a soul connection or 'contract', usually to share some space in time together, supporting each other on your journeys. Sometimes people marry their soul mates, sometimes they do not. Sometimes soul mates are simply incompatible in this realm but there is still a strong connection and that feeling is mutual. These connections are what we call, 'marriages made in heaven'. No matter how far away or what happens to either of you, there is always that connection felt. It is not a pining or longing but a sense of correctness or 'home' within that relationship.

A soul mate can also be of the same sex. Some straight men can become quite confused upon the recognition of a male soul mate. A strong type of attraction exists that they cannot put their finger on. We also see this with two or sometimes more women. For women, these connections are more accepted by present society and their strength is even encouraged. 'Soul sisters' or 'sisters' for unrelated women is a common term often used.

We often say we are in search of a partner to 'complete' us—that we *need* this partnership. Usually, we mean this more or less physically. Our animal self is in need of connection through physical union. The Spirit needs no such thing as it is already complete. Upon finding one's soul mate, it can initially mean the end of long, even lifetimes, of searching. The attachments that are made at this point are deep and affect the navel chakra intensely. However, as one evolves spiritually, a soul mate relationship can become uncomfortable if attachments are not released. The soul longs for freedom and its own unique journey, but the egoic mind and body still want and desire soul mate attachment. As difficult as it may seem, unattached and unaffected is the way to peace. New vows must be made to Oneself as one must be fully committed to Self first and foremost. The soul mate relationship must never determine the individuals' path or life which is where most of us fall into the trap—it's expected of us to 'compromise' in love.

Marriage

After I married my soul mate, I was very happy but never the same again. Not having awakened spiritually at that point, I could only feel a loss of myself in some way as I gained the energies of another. One of my more enlightened friends at the time even told me my aura had changed to his colors—which I thought was a good thing. I was now in a way, subconsciously 'his property and he was mine'—as we are so taught in our society. After the honeymoon period, my perceptions and label of 'wife' started to creep in and I became more and more burdened, feeling more and more responsible for him. Emotions of bitterness, anger and blame can creep in at this point as we compromise and sacrifice for others, buying into the dependent relationship, fulfilling our set roles and losing ourselves in the process. If left unchecked, even those with strong loving foundations, can see their marriages start to crumble.

Over time, I started to see our union differently—to see it as an enhancement rather than a burden or loss of freedom. I learned to maintain my independence within a loving relationship. I learned to accept the support of his aura without having it control me. From then on in meditation I would see our souls entwined in a beautiful blue light.

Many patients may arrive with issues around their marriages or partnerships. However, the true issue always lies within themselves. If we are truly at peace and living in the present, we would not be concerned over what another person does or does not do. I have found that in general, there are three main ways a marriage can go if a person embarks on their healing or spiritual journey:

1) **the spiritual partnership**—the partners journey along together, pursuing their own individual healing and awakening while supporting and understanding one another and themselves from higher levels of awareness
2) **the supportive partnership** the partners do not journey along together but neither is interfering with one another, allowing each to live as they must
3) **the unsupportive partnership**—the partners do not journey together and one member actively resists and/or interferes with their partners' evolution and healing

In my experience, both a spiritual and supportive partnership can work and be healthy for both partners as long as dependency is released. Over time however, in the supportive partnership, the one being supportive but not journeying may find it uncomfortable being around the spiritual partner as their vibration increases. They then will have to make a choice whether to embark on the journey themselves or leave.

Oftentimes, all a patient needs is a reminder of where their partnerships are at. We can become so confused and blaming toward others, we may forget our partners are with us or are at least supporting us. Just because they may do things differently, irritate us or challenge us does not mean we are not meant to be together. Other times, we may be so used to their resistance and interference, we don't see it as creating a gross impediment in our own evolution. As awareness increases, the Self becomes more and more paramount, with relationships becoming less so as attachments are released. Relationships can still be healthy and abundant in one's life now—without the baggage.

It's wise to empower patients to only ever end partnerships when they are in a good space themselves—without anger or fear—and with the focus being on their own Self Love. Allow intuition to be your guide with this delicate counseling and send the patient love so they can make the correct decision for themselves. Resist the temptation to make the decision for them regardless of what you think you know. Remain loving, empowering and non-judgmental of any decision they make.

Vows

When vows of 'forever and ever' are uttered, they are not to be taken lightly. The contract made during marriage creates attachment and can damage one's energies if not done with awareness and a sense of independence. A healthy marriage or partnership must only ever declare the support, sharing and love for one another—nothing more. Independence must remain for relationships to last. Most marriages are based on dependency and rules. No one can remain truly happy within these bounds.

Recently, we are seeing a huge trend occurring where people are avoiding marriage vows, opting out of getting married at all, avoiding the traditional concept of marriage or the dependency it represents. This does not mean we go around hurting others, being irresponsible due to lack of integrity or even to adopt the concept that marriage is 'bad'. It means we essentially remain married to Ourselves first and by doing so, listen to and follow what's right for us (and by default, others at the same time). This is a huge commitment and for most, it's much easier to follow a set of rules that are set by marriage and its expectations. To remain unmarried to anything or anyone 'earthly' is merely symbolic for not allowing attachment.

Another interesting option that some are starting to choose is to get married but live in separate parts of the house or dwelling. In this way, a loving commitment is made but your own individual freedom, boundaries and space are paramount, recognized and important. Some find it extremely liberating to 'have their own room again' and this alone can save a relationship.

Yet another example is simply removing your wedding band (with love) or buying new bands, chosen by each individual to represent both your loving commitment to each other, but firstly, to Self. You can also create new, more up-to-date marriage vows that reflect your consciousness at this point rather than what it was years ago. Even changing to the terms 'partner' for your spouse or 'team' instead of family has huge subconscious implications and that gesture alone can change the dynamics dramatically.

Vows can also be made less formally or consciously in relationships as well and when releasing our past, these too must be released. Vows such as "I promise to look after you when you're old mum" or "I promise I'll never tell anyone what you did/said" or "I will be yours forever and ever" etc. can severely impede growth along your path, especially if you are unaware of any vows you have made in the past and to whom. Things, circumstances and people change. We can only ever make a true commitment to this moment.

All of these examples are simply symbolic gestures and must be correct for you—you may find your own way of releasing attachment while benefiting your marriage or relationship. Your new found freedom could save your marriage and even more importantly, save yourself.

Friendships

Usually early on in the journey, the healer releases any relationships that no longer serve them, including friendships. A learning contract may be over and this must be honoured or stagnation and pain occurs.

We are often led to believe in our society that a friendship is 'thicker than blood' and we sometimes even make vows to remain 'friends for life'. As with all relationships, the only 'special' relationship the healer must have is with Self. Traditional friendships require that certain 'rules' are followed such as getting together or calling when obligated, buying gifts for certain occasions and abiding by certain social norms such as avoiding conflict.

Friends often come and go in one's life as circumstances and locations change. However with the healer, it becomes even more paramount that those around you are conducive to your positive evolution. This can feel quite lonely at first when this change happens and as some friendships fall away. You will simply know when a relationship is over. Honour its release and give thanks for the friendship and what you've learned. All relationships are valuable on our journey, no matter what they entail.

When the time is right, I often suggest people give the friend a 'parting gift' that is meaningful in some way. Trust intuition to guide you. For most of my past friendships, I simply gave an appropriate gift with the intention to give gratitude and end the relationship as it stood. It worked every time. Most of those friends parted peacefully and occasionally, a friend would return later only they too were now on their spiritual path and our relationship had completely changed.

New relationships will eventually start to arrive that are supportive of your path after the old is released. You will find them stress-free, easy, non-demanding, without obligation or guilt and unconditional. This is a truly refreshing and empowering change from the dependencies and demands of traditional 'friendships' as we know them.

Family

Much of the above for friendships also applies to family although the ties are much stronger and more difficult to release. Be patient as releasing family usually takes more time and effort and is usually 'unsupported' by society in general. Again, it's not to say that attachments to family cannot be remade in more positive ways but changes in how one relates must occur as one evolves, therefore affecting relationships of all kinds. As you become more truthful with yourself, you become more truthful with others which creates new positive connections or distain from others. Some family members will be more open in their expressions and opinions of what they think of you now with your new ways of thinking and behaving. Others will be silent but cannot see you differently than they always have and will continue to treat you the same way. Others will see a change in you and celebrate that and sometimes, want to share in your joy. The key is to always hope but never expect.

As you become more self-loving, you become more loving toward others which may attract or repel others. As you do this, you also set boundaries to uphold that self-love and this too, affects others. Setting boundaries with family can be particularly challenging as you may have never done this before and neither you nor they are used to it. As mentioned, some will actively resist this, others will silently distain it and others will respect it. Tactics such as guilt, manipulation, bribery, control, withdrawal and generally conditional love can surface at this point from family. They are not to be blamed—it's all they have at their disposal and no one likes change. It's often at this point that the 'ante is upped' when they sense something different in you. To them, you must subconsciously 'remain with the pack', no matter how stressful and harmful it is to you.

You will know their subconscious intents by their reactions to you and the feelings you have around being Yourself around them. This includes being confident, assertive, loving, joyful and truthful. The light that shines becomes a catalyst for change and simply attracts or repels others, depending on where they are at this moment in time in their perceptions. No matter what, I always send love from the Divine to those I continue to love no matter how they perceive me.

Long-term close relationship release can be a painful and grieving experience. Over time, this release can mean a renewing of the relationship with new terms or simply a falling away with perhaps only cordial contact if any. Do not judge how it turns out—you may be surprised! Always hold faith for others that they too will join into Oneness. However, also remember that most family members are not compatible (in fact we're not *meant* to be compatible in order to stimulate growth)—we often wouldn't be friends if we weren't related.

Symbolic Relationships

All of life is a symbol of Me.
These things in the world are here to remind you of Me.

Everything in life is symbolic to the mind. Food, addictions and their symbolic meanings tell us much about the subconscious. Both food cravings and aversions can point to certain tendencies or habits of the mind and its fears. Listen with a spiritual mind when assessing the symbolic nature of foods. There are many volumes written on food's symbolic nature that can be helpful guides, however, always use intuition to determine the exact issue for your own or a patient's situation. Commonly, those foods or substances that are craved or addictive tend to be most significant in terms of mind-body symbolism. Below are just some common symbolic relationships we have with certain foods and substances.

Water

Water is symbolic for God/Self. Keeping yourself adequately hydrated allows for Higher transmission and communication with Self due to the fact that water acts as a conductor and allows for the free and easy movement of qi (life force energy). Water is also clear and lucid, flowing and dynamic; the very properties we seek in direct communication with Self. We are after all mostly water and are born from water (amniotic fluid). In Traditional Chinese Medicine, water is governed by the kidneys, the source of life and qi for the body. Water is a necessary substance (both inside and outside the body) for purification of the body and soul.

Amounts needed must be tested individually and can change over time.

Dairy

A common food intolerance for a reason, dairy is symbolic for nurturing oneself and the feminine—for self-love. It represents 'receiving' energy. Mother's milk is the ultimate in symbolic nurturance, mostly with female energies. Many of us do not properly nurture ourselves through self-love, attention or placing ourselves first. In this way, dairy can serve to irritate the system if the mind is not allowing for enough real nurturance. On a physical level, dairy is basically a mucous full of hormones and in many opinions, not a true food at all.

Traditional Chinese Medicine considers it too dampening for the body as it can cause dis-ease over time as mucous accumulates in the tissues. Soy is usually not a good alternative to dairy as it's still mucousy. There are lots of other great alternatives to choose from now.

Wheat/gluten

Another common intolerance, wheat is symbolic for male energy and issues with any authority. It represents the 'giving' energy. This includes issues with individual male figures in one's past or feeling collectively dominated by men (or women) or by the patriarchal attitudes in general from society.

On a physical level, wheat has changed (hybridized) a lot since its birth, and now contains more gluten (latin for 'glue') content than ever, creating difficulties in its digestion.

Sugar

Now reaching epidemic proportions, sugar consumption, sugar addiction and its ensuing health consequences are rampant in our society. In a world consumed with greed, consumption and success through accumulation of 'more', sugar has become the ultimate symbol of monetary wealth and abundance. Since neither eating sugar nor obtaining 'sugar' in our lives brings joy in and of itself, sugar serves to show us how detrimental this misplacement is. A massive shift in our sense of abundance and personal fulfillment must be created before our relationship with sugar can become balanced once again.

On a physical level, sugar is so refined and consumed in such large amounts, the body cannot recognize or digest it properly, creating a mass of health issues.

Corn

As corn is becoming increasingly genetically modified and used in most processed and refined foods today, intolerance to it has increased. Corn has been a staple for certain indigenous societies for eons. It represents the 'capability' energy (being 'capable').

Peanut

Peanut allergies are becoming alarmingly dangerous and wider spread. Aside from genetic modification of this food and the moulds it contains (as many foods such as strawberries and melons also do), it symbolically represents our general fear of the world—that the world is a dangerous place.

Food intolerances and allergies in general

Food intolerances are very common in our society and they always have been—we're just more aware of them and actually dealing with them now. Many foods are not really foods at all. Although there are others (such as preservatives, dyes, food additives and chemicals), the most common foods that afflict us are namely the 'white' foods; dairy, sugar (including alcohol), wheat and refined salt. By cleansing the diet of these, the body has a chance to truly heal physically and remain healthy (as long as there are no other underlying intolerances/allergies found). I have seen patients literally change their lives and health within a matter of weeks by simply avoiding completely what they are intolerant to. The body simply does not see these substances as foods as therefore, cannot digest and assimilate them. Not everyone has intolerances/allergies to these foods, however most people do not do very well consuming them long term. Testing for food intolerances/allergies is a key to addressing not only physical health but mental and spiritual health as well. Be sure the testing you use is accurate and effective. In my experience kinesiology (muscle testing), electrodermal testing and elimination testing are the most effective ways to determine food intolerances. Often the foods you crave are the ones you should avoid!

Avoidance of intolerant foods

Fasting from the above foods (or any other intolerant foods) from the diet creates not only physical relief but emotional, mental and spiritual cleansing as well. When a person becomes more consciously aware and literally 'changes' how they perceive and are with the world, these intolerances can fall away or improve. Your body processes anything, including air, light and moisture and the pranic energy from it is released into your body and the toxins expelled. Of course, this takes the release of all fears and purity of thoughts to enable such a pure process to occur. But, at this point, the awareness that 'takes over', the Self, chooses to eat well anyway!

Addictions

As mentioned, every food, in fact everything, represents a *symbolism* to the mind—it means something subconsciously. This in turn creates a craving or addiction for that substance to fulfill some emotional, mental or subconscious need that the food (or drug or behaviour) represents. The food can then serve to suppress certain feelings or emotions or to soothe the mind. However, true peace does not come from anything outside of oneself. We must learn to listen only to the Self to determine what foods are correct for us to consume at any point in time, discerning the difference between our wanting and craving egos.

Each person will have their own history attached to a food or addiction depending on their background, beliefs, culture, traumas, upbringing and exposure. Removal of intolerant foods allows not only physical ailments to heal very effectively but reveals the subconscious nature of the mind which can then also be healed if and when the patient is ready.

Although food intolerances may be similar for many people, their specific subconscious effects will be individual and must be treated as such. For example, two different patients may have a dairy intolerance, representing in general, issues with nurturance. The first patient, for example, is a young child and is too attached to her mother and has not learned how to nurture herself and instead relies completely on mother. The second patient is an adult that may have issues around over-nurturing her family and her children in particular, not allowing for any self-love and forgetting she is the most important person in her life. Both these are really just two sides of the same coin but must be addressed in different ways. These issues will also manifest differently, depending on what organs or systems are most susceptible. For the 'smothered' child, asthma is common as she is over-nurtured (which dairy will aggravate). For the female adult, breast issues and cancers are common as she over-nurtures and 'feeds' all those around her except herself (again, which dairy can aggravate). The breasts deserve special attention in this regard in our society today as cancers are so rampant. The breasts are the symbol of the origin of nurturance itself.

What should we eat?!

A good rule of thumb is if it's straight from the Earth (*healthy* Earth that is), it's good. We must go back to basics. Eating directly from the Source of life without alteration. Local and organic foods are more readily available now. Community gardens, container gardening and even small greenhouses indoors are wonderful options for those living in urban centres. If you have even a small amount of land at your home, you can grow a lot of food—you just have to get creative in how you do it. Get the whole family involved so they can nurture and nourish the very food that they're going to eat—it's truly an energetic exchange. What you love, loves you back—spiritually, nutritionally, energetically. Just like our pets, our gardens must be tended to and loved in just the same way so they can in return, nourish us. Food that's alive literally vibrates at a higher frequency than any processed or 'dead' food. The sooner we eat it after it's picked, the more 'aliveness' and vitality from the plant is transferred to us. You are what you eat…

Trauma And Suffering

You will suffer until you come home to Me.
You must suffer in order to do so . . .

Trauma

Before you can even broach the subject of trauma, you must be clear with respect to this subject yourself as a healer. Trauma is extremely common but rarely dealt with properly. There can be no fear from you as a healer when dealing with these subjects or it becomes confusing, uncomfortable and unclear for you in which case, you cannot help. Many times if a healer hasn't dealt with their own traumas, they will simply not be able to see it or recognize it in others at all. Go within when you are in doubt and allow all answers to come to you. Oftentimes, proper counseling and other assistance are necessary in addition to deal with these issues.

Never-well-since

Over time, you will develop almost a sixth sense for trauma as it arises for a patient and you will notice the signs and symptoms that go along with it. If the patient has never been well since a certain point in time, this is a very clear indication of potential trauma causing dis-ease. Ask the patient to search for themselves around this point in time while at the same time, trusting your own intuition on the matter. Gentle guidance is usually all that's necessary here. Many times, a patient will have 'dealt' with incidents from the past but they still don't seem to be healing. This usually indicates things are not yet finished for them. They are often still emotional when the subject is approached. They may be stuck in any one of the stages listed below and need assistance moving on from that. Or, they may not have dealt with some aspect of the trauma.

These types of traumas can by literally anything—physical, mental, emotional or sexual. A dental appointment, loss of a loved one, a move, change in job, change in income or status, marriage, divorce, childbirth, adoption, abandonment, alcoholism, new pets, loss of a hobby or past-time, surgery, increased stress of any kind, past trauma or accident of any kind, travel, war, strange encounter or incident, a fright etc. If the patient is willing, have them think on that specific timeframe before their next visit. Recurring dreams or nightmares since this time can also serve as pointers. 'Never-well-since' is extremely important and cannot be underestimated if clear timelines are present in the case.

Here are some examples of never-well-since. A patient may be born with conditions and they may reflect the mother or the father's consciousness or any trauma they had at the time. If the mother falls for example and almost miscarries the child or the child is birthed but it's soul had been previously miscarried by that same mother, it can be construed as trauma by the child. If the mother lost someone during this time or violence was present, this again can serve as trauma for the patient even though they were in the womb at the time. The soul is ever-present and remembers all. Sometimes, a child is born with dis-ease and is suffering from past life trauma or unfinished karmic business—at least on a mind-body level. Even though physical palliation and support is important throughout treatment, a healer must always be open to any incident(s) that may have played a key factor in the dis-ease inception. Many healers choose not to broach this subject as it can be painful and difficult for the patient. However, without some sort of understanding or faith, the patient cannot approach true healing and only palliative support can be offered.

One case I had involved a woman who was always sick and very angry at life. She blamed and complained constantly and could not seem to achieve wellness. I palliated her with remedies to help support her for a few years and she noticed improvements in her health but never a cure. One day, she was ready to delve into deeper issues and I asked her when she started feeling this way—could she pinpoint it. Being now ready to heal, she was no longer irritated at my questioning and started to cry. She told me how a relative had gotten sick and died from cancer many years before and she hadn't seen the connection until now—she'd been miserable ever since and thought she was 'over it'. I saw her in passing many months later and she was a different person. She said the power of that awareness alone left her stunned upon leaving my office and she doesn't even know how she made it home—all she could see and feel was beauty. She thanked me profusely saying she'd never felt better in her life and all her issues, physical and otherwise, were gone.

A very clear indicator that the patient has touched on the cause or trigger is when emotions arise—even if they deny the trigger for themselves. Point this out gently to the patient if you can, so they can see for themselves—through mindful non-judgmental awareness of oneself—that this trauma or incident has caused them dis-ease on some level. They are sometimes surprised to notice their reaction. At this point of realization, healing automatically begins and patients tend to carry on through the stages as long as no other blockages arise. This can be very liberating and relieving for the patient even though much healing work is still ahead for them.

Never-well-since vs. faith

Either one or the other or both is necessary for the patient to encounter in order for true healing to occur. The mind requires either an explanation (never-well-since a certain time or incident which *provides* faith) or simply pure faith (faith in miracles). These are the ingredients for success which is why they are so important in the questioning and discovering of causation. 'Never-well-since' provides an axis point in time and space from which dis-ease has begun. Once this is revealed, no matter what the incident, trauma or issue, healing can occur in the mind. Pure faith is a much more rare circumstance—most people don't have it. Sometimes, more religious patients will have been trained in the concept of pure faith and therefore, can heal dis-ease entirely using their faith. 'Faith healing' and the like are akin to this and there is no real need to go into the past to uncover a 'never-well-since' incident in these cases. However, until we all can come to this pure faith, addressing 'never-well-since' serves a valuable purpose.

Healing from traumas

Traumas of any kind or past incidents/triggers bring up a whole myriad of issues for a patient and the suppressed emotions that underlie the triggers create the stress that causes dis-ease. A patient may or may not be aware of how these emotions are affecting them. Oftentimes, they are so used to being that way, they figure it's just their 'personality'. It's extremely rare that a person doesn't have triggers of some kind. It's not important to focus so much on the trigger itself—there is no hierarchy of worse or better here. What's important is the understanding (and ensuing awareness) the patient gains from addressing the unhealed triggers from the past and observing them now as the witness to them. Eventually, the spiritual student will bring awareness to all triggers from the past in order to release who they think they are and remember Who They Really Are. We are not our triggers or our past traumatic events.

It's key to understand here that timing for the approach of triggers is very important. It simply cannot be rushed and must be guided by the patient as they near 'the end of their tether'.

Mental/emotional trauma

The list is simply too long to mention all the circumstances that may bring this type of trauma about but it's important to note that it can be anything—even seemingly minor things—that can create never-well-since. Abandonment, adoption, bullying, emotional abuse such as yelling or swearing or name-calling, the observation of someone else's trauma, chastisement, humiliation or embarrassment, loss of a loved one, changes of any kind, stress, war, violence, accidents, emergencies, job pressure, aging, near-death experience, financial pressure, relationship issues, divorce, marriage, children, family or even past life trauma if there is no other explanation in this one. All these and more can be triggers for this type of trauma.

If these triggers are suppressed, we see a range of emotions related to the trigger. For example, if someone has all of a sudden become ill after job pressure has increased and no other triggers are available, we can postulate the cause of illness is increased job pressure creating the stress.

For another example, if a man who has fear/trauma due to aging, he may exhibit subconscious feelings of weakness as a male because he's aging. This in turn, can create physical symptoms like prostate issues.

Many wonderful books are written on the subject of mind-body connection here (such as Louise L. Hay's book, *You Can Heal Your Life*[5] and Karol K. Truman's book, *Feelings Buried Alive Never Die*[6]) and should be studied for a general understanding of emotional suppression/repression and the physical or emotional symptoms that can result.

The following are possible generalized signs and symptoms that may appear in those suffering from past or present trauma of any kind (mental, emotional, sexual or a combination thereof) and is by no means a complete list. These are not in and of themselves determinants but 'pointers' to possible causation—a patient may have one or many of these pointers. As always, let intuition and the overall picture guide you.

- Fear of conflict or potential conflictual situations
- Chronic pain
- Sexual dysfunction

---

[5] Hay, Louise L. *You Can Heal Your Life*. Carlsbad, California: Hay House, Inc. 2002.

[6] Truman, Karol K. *Feelings Buried Alive Never Die*. Olympus Publishing Company; 4th revised edition. 1991.

- Poor memory, easily distracted, difficulties making decisions, poor concentration
- Yelling and anger issues or easily irritated
- Being very quiet/shy and unable to express oneself
- Low self-esteem and confidence
- Extreme weight gain or loss or eating disorders
- Loneliness and issues with relationships
- Manipulative and controlling or easily manipulated and controlled by others
- Guilt complexes or constant apologizing
- Constant need for approval
- Extremes in arrogance, cockiness and bragging
- Swearing
- Alcoholism or drug abuse to 'self-medicate'
- Certain mental disorders
- Irrational paranoia, suspicion and general lack of trust
- Frequent mood swings
- Post-traumatic stress disorder
- Nightmares or night terrors (recurring or memorable), insomnia
- Flashbacks to past traumatic events
- Panic attacks
- Mental and/or physical exhaustion
- Emotional detachment
- Depression, despair, suicidal tendencies
- Bullying or being bullied (even as an adult, for example at work)
- Physical self-abuse (consciously self-mutilating or unconsciously such as 'clumsiness' or always having accidents including car accidents)
- Poor self-esteem and confidence
- 'Hunching over' or trying to appear small, wearing only dark clothing
- Nervous habits such as nail biting, mouth biting or restlessness
- Jumpiness or nervousness
- Claustrophobia
- Fear of certain social situations (such as being alone with certain people or certain types of people)
- History of problems with authority or with the law
- History of fighting, abuse of others, verbal abuse

- Attraction to violent media (violent TV shows, video games etc.) or guns and weapons
- Risky behavior such as challenging or irritating others, physical risk-taking activities like driving too fast etc.
- Attraction to abusive relationships

Physical trauma

This can include not only physical abuse of any kind but surgery, dental work, accidents, drug or medication effects, heavy metals and chemicals, pathogens, birth defects, nutritional deficiencies or toxicities, injuries, prosthesis, labour and birth, structural and skeletal changes, the aging process etc.

Although these are much easier for a healer to approach because they are easier to discern, they may be still very difficult for the patient to deal with or even accept. They may be so used to having this pain or dis-ease in their lives that the simple explanation of a never-well-since at this point, throws them right off and can even launch them into denial of the actual cause.

Sexual trauma

Sexual trauma is usually the most difficult subject to approach with a patient. Helping a patient heal from socially taboo traumas can be challenging. The taboo itself tends to hide the trauma from the conscious mind of the patient as the shame is too great to bear. When a trauma remains hidden (suppressed) in the subconscious mind, it cannot be healed and 'enlightened', creating bodily dis-ease and mental turmoil. This can occur with patients who appear to be blocked in some way. However, the body will always attempt to reveal the trauma to the patient through various ailments and symptoms, sometimes to the point of extreme suffering. Until the patient is willing to heal the underlying trauma, (to for-give or 'give it up') the symptoms will remain and can only be palliated. Never listen to the patient's fears with sympathy or sharing in their pain—you will end up swallowed in the endless abyss of confusion around their ailments and of their minds—always look beyond the issues with compassion and help them into their souls for the answers.

Most commonly, patients will suppress painful childhood memories but in some cases, people can even suppress recent events. This mechanism is used by the mind to keep the patient 'safe' from certain information and at times you may come up against denial or repression when it is revealed. As a healer, the tricky task of gently revealing buried traumas must be done with the utmost care, timeliness, compassion and patience. Parables and stories bearing similarity to the situation/trauma can be very gentle and empowering toward the patient as they don't directly imply a truth but allow a patient to discover it themselves. Using your tools and intuitive skills, this is often not a difficult task to see the truth that they are hiding from themselves. Sometimes you may know a patient for years before they are ready to deal with past trauma. I find trauma does not reveal itself until it is ready to be approached. This approach must as gentle and cautious as possible as this can bring up shock, fear, denial and sometimes anger. Many healers choose not to approach these subjects as they themselves feel uncomfortable addressing them. However, with practice, a healer can learn to treat these situations like any other healing challenge. I have seen many cases in which no healing at all can occur until these traumas are addressed. Seek additional assistance from outside sources as you are intuited for further support for both of you if need be.

Most people with these traumas will not be seeking its revelation, only palliation from you. It is never safe to reveal sexual (or otherwise) trauma to the uninitiated mind that does not have the tools to deal with it. This is why some commit suicide (both 'victims' and 'perpetrators') after either sharing sexually traumatic events with others or due to it simply being revealed to them. The shame is too great to bear and they have no tools with which to alter their perception around the trauma and allow for forgiveness. Forgiveness is done through altering perception in alignment with Higher Self and the life purpose of the trauma. One must be ready for this to occur or it must remain in the darkness of one's mind until one is ready or has 'suffered enough'. At the same time, a healer must follow his intuition at all times or no healing can occur. Being overly cautious is also to the detriment of both parties.

On the part of the patient it takes great courage and humility to uncover repressions. For the healer, you must be unwavering in your confidence and love toward them and the subject at hand. Do not falter as denial and shock often surface. Observe these reactions as simply fears and continue seeing and focusing on the soul and on the cause.

On occasion (usually as someone's life purpose is pulling at them with some force or they are enduring great suffering), a patient will seek this deep healing from you. Many times you will be treating them for years without having any notion that any type of trauma even existed for them. As they approach their readiness for true healing and forgiveness however, the trauma suddenly becomes revealed to you and you will 'know' the patient's underlying angst as you finally reach deeper layers of the mind-body. If the patient is ready, you will have an almost nagging or recurring intuition for them around the subject. Intuition as always, guides you as to procedure.

Many patients at this point are actually relieved at this self-realization and memories and past issues come literally flooding back to them. They start piecing together their lives and many things now make sense to them as the dark parts of their suppressed subconscious is now seeing the light. They may spend the following month's journaling, remembering and detailing. Keep close contact with the patient at this time as they may need additional counseling from yourself and others trained in the field. Sometimes, a patient will simply want to remain in denial even though the subject has been broached. This is fine but let them know that no further healing can occur until their time is right. Palliate as necessary.

Interestingly, in some cultures, the attacker or perpetrator is not focused on as heavily as the victim is in terms of healing. In these traditions, 'demons' can possess the victim after trauma, as severe anger and fear wells up inside causing them to be very dangerous to not only the attacker but all others around them. These 'demons' must be removed so the 'victim' can 'be herself again' and return to society healed and 'forgiven' of the past. It is therapeutic to see this force of anger or victimization as something outside oneself, as a 'demon' of sorts, to dis-identify from not only one's actions, reactions and feelings as a so-called victim but also as an attacker. We truly do become possessed when we forget Who We Are and act out of animalistic egoic behaviors. Leaving the incident in the past where it belongs is paramount not only to individual sanity but to the survival of the society as a whole. Negative energy coming from the collective 'victim' is immense and must be neutralized in order to have an overall balancing effect in our world. Perhaps this is why we put people in jail—not so much to keep us safe but to prevent us from seeking revenge on the perpetrator . . .

One can go one step further and ask the victim to take her power back in terms of what she's attracting into her life and encouraging her to set proper boundaries. She will forever remain a victim if she does not realize the power she has to create her world and her reality.

Once a patient is ready to heal, you can gently point out to them certain behavioral characteristics you have noticed in them. Listed below are just a few 'pointers' and by themselves, they do not necessarily mean sexual trauma in one's past. Some who've been traumatized may have one of these cues—some may have many of them. There must be many factors that come into play for accurate assessment and a burning intuition around the subject. In addition to the above cues for traumas in general, here are just a few common cues that are specific to sexual trauma:

- very poor memory of one's past or for large/specific portions of one's life
- dressing either very provocatively or very conservatively
- issues wearing clothing that reveal their gender ex. Women that only dress in masculine clothing or men that wear more feminine clothing—may or may not be homosexual (homosexuality is not a determinant in and of itself for trauma)
- exhibiting the extremes of either frigidity or promiscuity including prostitution
- very unique sexual desires, addictions or fetishes
- speech and behavior will often point to their trauma (collecting pornographic materials, obsession with breast size or reduction, obsession with physical fitness or with weight loss, attraction to certain types of media or hobbies, obsession with appearance etc.)
- how they treat their own children or speak about them (mothers may be very overly attentive to male children and fathers to female children as an example)
- worse since the birth of certain children (usually of the same sex as they become 'reminders' of their own childhood self)
- chronic genital and reproductive organ dis-eases/issues
- chronic swearing, especially of a sexual or lewd nature
- rude sense of humor often with shocking sexual content
- chronic seductive-destructive behaviors
- obsession with violence, sexual or shocking media
- extremely needy behavior and love-seeking

Sex is very prominent is our society and many things are now socially acceptable. The subconscious mind of the sexually traumatized patient will always and consistently point to the trauma, often through the physical body, usually through dis-ease, whether the patient is aware of it or not. As a healer, we must simply observe with an always open mind, allowing intuition and cues to lead both us and the patient gently toward healing.

Sexual trauma is like any other dis-ease, it must not be judged—it simply is. And, it is common. If it is approached with neither fascination nor repulsion or fear, one can simply help to heal it as one would any other dis-ease.

Releasing the victim

As with anything is one's life, there is no need to blame a person, place, thing or incident as this takes away our power and places it directly on that object. Traumas and triggers must be realized, then released. It is never beneficial to encourage 'confrontation' with one's 'attacker', regardless of the type trauma. Fear only begets fear and no good ever comes from this as only denial and attacking back occurs, sometimes toward the healer as well. If a perpetrator is truly ready to heal, then gentle healing can occur for both parties but this is not common. The information revealed to the patient is private and must be dealt with as such. Only they can change their own consciousness and heal themselves. Our past is not who we are now.

Identification in some way with one's attacker is very prominent in most cases of trauma. As one feels sorry for oneself as the victim, one also feels sorry for one's attacker, impeding any true healing or forgiveness (or 'giving it/them up'). This is different from compassion where we can lovingly understand another's pain and suffering without being affected or 'caring'. Those who have been traumatized tend to try to help the perpetrator or others like them, usually subconsciously. This creates a vicious cycle of dependency as the perpetrator, usually subconsciously, 'lures' the victim to feel sorry for him or her. They often believe their own story and often they themselves have been a victim of trauma in their own past, creating this vicious cycle. This is a very subtle form of manipulation that can seem quite innocent to those involved in the trauma but clear to the observant onlooker of the case. The only way the perpetrator has survived thus far within society is by eliciting pity and denying responsibility and they will do anything to keep that alive. At this realization, the 'victim' must become ruthless. She can no longer afford to play this game and pity another, let alone herself. She is so used to being pitied and pitying that this can take immense discipline and awareness on her part to overcome. She must practice being unaffected yet compassionate, something we have no practice doing in our society. We are taught to be either angry, vengeful and vicious or nice, pleasing and accommodating.

Fight or flight

With any type of trauma, fight or flight are the only options we have. Once we are trained to use them, they become habitual. Some of us attack, become fearful and/or defensive at the slightest sign of potential conflict. If we are used to reacting in this manner, we tend to exhibit more outward symptoms of stress, anxiety and anger. Some of us shut-down, numb out, hide or run away. If we are used to reacting in this manner, we tend to exhibit more inward symptoms such as high blood pressure, stomach ailments and addictions. Discovering which way you react to fear is very helpful in overcoming it. Understanding your personal tendencies and why you are this way is very important for retraining from unhealthy reaction into healthy response.

Stages of healing trauma:
When the patient is ready for this deep healing, it's important to tell them it can be very difficult and challenging to deal with emotionally. Even though they may not be conscious of the nature of the trauma, they will tell you the truth about their readiness.

There are four general stages in the healing of a repression of any type of trauma (physical, mental, emotional or sexual):

1) Shock and Disbelief
As difficult as this first stage is, it often accompanies a feeling of knowing that this is a truth they cannot deny. If the patient cannot go beyond this point, they will suppress this revealed information back into the recesses of the mind in denial and continue to suffer or wait until the time comes when they can better deal with it. Sometimes they will go into blame and seek another practitioner that will 'agree' with their ailments and their supposed cause.

2) Anger, Grief and Emotional Healing
Perhaps the most difficult stage and can take some time to overcome. Journaling, emotional releasing, counseling, physical, mental and spiritual support are paramount here. A sense of great relief even amongst this turmoil is felt as the missing parts of their lives are being restructured and put into proper place now. This stage can include flashbacks, vivid dreams and the return of old memories. Patients will sometimes have flashbacks many months or years after their initial flashbacks, depending on what they are ready to heal at that time.

If this stage is left to fester, the patient becomes, 'the angry victim'. Sometimes patients will come to you already at this stage as they are consciously aware of their past traumas but do not know how to 'place them' (forgive them). It's paramount for the practitioner at this stage not to circulate or place heavy importance on the actual content of memories or the trauma itself but simply encourage the allowing of their surfacing to the conscious mind where they can be healed and released without judgment.

3) Frustration and Confusion

The 'whys' come up during this stage. Deep spiritual, soul healing must occur at this time to help the patient put their trauma into proper perspective in terms of its purpose for life path, learning through suffering, past life karmic tendencies or unlearned lessons etc. With proper guidance the healer can help release them from the victim mode into acceptance. Healing methods like Emotional Freedom Techniques™, neuroplastic therapy, Belief Repatterning™ or Conscious Awareness Technique can help immensely to change the mind through 'deprogramming'.

The patient can take responsibility now for their own involvement (spiritually) in the events and in the trauma itself (like attracts like). They will also be able to focus on how they've created other issues in their present life as well. We continue to be 'raped' when we say yes when we mean no, for example. They are learning at this stage to set proper boundaries and practice true self-love in all areas of their life. Most importantly, regardless of their findings, they must become blameless— to remember that it's not their fault. Many people think that to be responsible means to take fault and that's not the case. Fault implies guilt, responsibility implies taking proper action and understanding.

This stage also involves helping them understand that their consciousness has now shifted from what it was in the past—they have a new outlook. The patient must be led to see that nothing in and of itself actually 'means' anything—we have only placed symbolic or temporary meaning on events or things, as we have been trained to. Those healing often get stuck at this stage because they keep placing meaning on events or situations and therefore, continue to judge the event, situation, others and themselves. There can be no escape from judgment without the release of it. Falling out of a tree could be just as traumatic as any other traumatic event to a person but it is not *seen* or *perceived* as such by society and therefore, is deemed insignificant to the mind and placed in the unaffected memory banks of the brain. Non-judgment and unaffectedness on the part of the healer must be paramount at this point so it can be shared with the patient to prepare them for forgiveness.

The patient can also become stuck here and be forever trying to 'figure out' why these things occurred to them leading to self-blame, depression and continued frustration. It's important to remember; the mind can never forgive or understand—only the Spirit can.

4) Forgiveness and Relief
Forgiveness is Self-guided and can be prepared for but not given until the time is right. This is guided by the patient's Higher Self and their karma. They must truly surrender past notions of right and wrong for self and others to become unaffected. Great relief and spiritual evolution can occur at this point. The past traumatic events become merely like any other memory with no special significance or trigger left to the mind. The healer is only to hold the patient up with faith in terms of their highest potential—a simple knowing that they can   and will succeed.

Forgiveness literally means to give away or give up. We often ask, what it is we are giving, with forgiveness? We cannot condone nor can we forget so how can we give up something that was once real and once traumatic?

Forgiveness is assisted by compassion. First to oneself, and then, to the other. Forgiveness can only occur when one forgives oneself first – there is no reality outside the Self. We must then, aim to see ourselves and others with the compassionate eye. We are all ultimately looking for God, no matter what our outward actions or intentions may be. The drug addict seeks love through the high that brings him falsely closer to God. The pedophile seeks the purity and innocence of God through control and tries to take it. The hungry dictator seeks God through the ecstasy of power. Through all things good or evil, comes the lust for Oneness warped by the ego's desires. Understand this and compassion—and ultimately forgiveness is yours. Then, forgiveness is given where all things go – into the stillness of the present moment.

Although forgiveness is not understood by the mind, it can be understood by the soul as a change one undergoes, bringing one fully into the present. We often think forgiveness means forgiving another person and/or ourselves *in time* but it's not a one-time thing. Forgiveness is what you do every moment—it is ongoing because it requires us to be present. It means we no longer define ourselves by our past—our history, traumas, suffering, our so-called personality or tendencies. It's often difficult for us to see that we are different—that we have changed and to even believe that it's possible for us to do so. However, as you slowly watch your interactions and perceptions of the world around you change, you must know deep Within Yourself that *you really have changed* and you must honour this. Forgiveness comes from knowing we have changed into Who We Really Are and none of what has happened to us is relevant any longer. We can simply *be*.

The length of time it takes to heal through the entire process and even to heal each stage is determined by the patient and can take minutes or years. As with any healing, do not judge the time it takes for it to be revealed or the time it takes to heal. All that's necessary in cases of trauma is the awareness of it and the will to change perception around it.

The patient may naturally have questions that you can help them with from a spiritual or mind-body perspective. There is never any need to circulate over and over an issue or event from the past. We must look at all things equally, recognize our learning from the situation and move forward. We must as with all things, become unaffected and stay present.

Childhood trauma

A special note needs to be made here with respect to this subject. As adults, it's difficult to remember how the child was. How he saw the world, reacted to it and his fears. We have changed as adults. We tend to blame the child for its 'wrongdoings' of the past and even for its involvement in traumatic events. This can be sticky, even after most healing work has been done because essentially, one hasn't forgiven oneself. We still think we should have known better, stood up for ourselves, said something, fought back, ran away, told someone, whatever. A child is a child and does childlike things and has a childlike perception of the world. We cannot compare the child's mind to the adult's mind. We cannot expect the child to know better.

This concept alone helps to bring peace and self-forgiveness. One heals the child as one forgives oneself. And to forgive oneself, one must forgive all others—to see their infinite beauty—to see Who They Really Are right at this moment. And forgiveness—is truly—being present.

Awakening

There is no real hierarchy for trauma—one cannot say one type is worse than another. The key is to realize it's all just a process of revelation—of awakening to truth. Even as all so-called traumas and repressions are revealed from one's past, there are more fears that we have on a daily basis that must be revealed and realized. These can sometimes be even more challenging as they have become habitual to the point we don't even recognize them and perceive them as simply part of our 'personality'.

The realization (even more so for the advanced student) that some other fear has been uncovered often elicits frustration and depression. An example of my own journey was a deep fear of authority or patriarchal domination. My ego was always chastising me for some thing or another so this created a fear of chastisement from sources outside of me as well, which ultimately through feeding this fear, I attracted. I continually blamed outside sources for this and although I knew this couldn't be true, I could not 'see' how I could forgive it. Then, a healing occurred after I listened to my own phone message I'd left to my partner. I couldn't believe how authoritarian, demanding and dominating I sounded! I was astounded. Another layer of egoic self was being revealed to me. At first, I was angry with myself for not 'seeing' this sooner, and then I became irritated, with all over body itching and extreme frustration. Only journaling (a tool of awareness) relieved my angst. My ego did not like this truth to be revealed—it feared giving up its pseudo-authority. We don't like to be told what to do, even if it is God speaking. I had literally been blind as to my own behaviors and attitudes—they had kept me safe. I was relieved in my soul as I knew I was healing on yet another level but my ego was plain mad. I finally broke down emotionally with deep, heavy, angry sobbing that was not within my control (this is healing emotion). I ran outside and put my hands on the wet evening grass to dissipate the release back to the Earth which relieved me. After this, my irritation lessened greatly and over the months that ensued I was gradually 'shown' each and every way in which I'd been authoritarian/dominating myself and how I'd allowed others to be so toward me, so I could be free of one of my greatest and deepest fears.

Karma will continue to cycle us through our fears again and again until we release them fully.

Elation then depression after revelation

The journey is fraught with these episodes where spiritual revelations are shown to us and great peace and wisdom ensues—for a time. Then, as this new vibration must release the old, depression and anger sets in. I would often find this type of cycling after resolving an issue or gaining spiritual insight that the very next day, I would be irritated, sour and sometimes plunge into anger or grief after a simple trigger like spilling water. It's never about the water we spilled—follow the release, understand what it is, do not suppress it further and allow the emotion to take its course. Again, grounding oneself by going outside, walking, touching the earth, through music, journaling or talking to 'God', prayer etc. can assist greatly.

Not everyone has emotional tendencies such as this but a release will ensue all the same. Be aware of your personal tendencies and the way your ego releases and you will not take these episodes too seriously. They are simply part of your evolution toward Oneness.

Traumas and suffering as the keys to evolution

Suffering is a great catalyst for change. When we are suffering enough, we only have two choices; pain and death or salvation and surrender. To stop suffering must be a personal choice—to choose differently. When a person suffers hard enough, they now have an opportunity to change. They can choose to suffer and eventually die or to evolve their consciousness. As 'cold' as it may sound, it gives a great opportunity to us and we must employ gratitude to any opportunity that arises to allow for this change.

Many times have I seen people change vastly and permanently after trauma of any kind—they are usually the wisest people I know. Part of your job as a healer is to show them the beauty of the trauma and suffering and where it can take them—the gift must be extracted out of it as all things, even seemingly 'bad' things, are essentially good. Sometimes people are not ready for the change and must endure suffering longer—sometimes for a lifetime. Let it be so. Send them life force and love and it will be there waiting for them when their time to change comes. For those willing to evolve from trauma, seize the opportunity to show them its gift and change their minds from victimization to triumph. Go within to find the right suggestions and guides for them as individuals. The main focus must always be on your faith that they *can and will* fulfill their highest potential. This focus you provide as a healer is your hallmark. You must provide the setting of motivation, of knowingness, and if they so choose, they will pick it up and express it themselves. This is the setting for the manifestation of healing you provide.

During the Visit

Do only what you can through Me.
The rest is taken care of by the nature of its existence, with or without you.

The feeling of fear

Many people will come to you in fear (especially on the first visit) and at first, you will feel and pick up that fear. You will literally start to shake and feel 'nervous'. Do not mistake it for 'your own'—you don't own any fear. Send it back to them (release responsibility back to them, clear, reset yourself and be the observer) and you will find stillness—the truth lies within that focused stillness. Many patients will come to you with physical ailments that may at first appear serious—and to you and to them, they appear very real. Be assured they are neither. They are trivial, powerless and temporary. To give them space in reality is to give them power. This is not to say we are flippant, unrealistic or disrespectful but we must not buy into fear or we cannot heal it. Many times people heal simply because someone has told them for the first time that there's actually a possibility that they *can* heal and that it's simply not as bad as they think. Intuition will guide you as to exactly 'what to say' and how best to treat these patients. For some, you may need to start by slowly helping them heal layer by layer, gaining their trust. For others, they have 'tried everything' and are ready to hear the truth right away.

For those that have come to you, the truth lies deep and is something they are not always consciously aware of yet so you cannot ask them for it per se. You must go within and ask Yourself what it is they are really here to see you for and what they are presenting with. It's usually an ailment/fear of the mind at the root. Once this is surfaced and made conscious, the patient has the option to heal from it permanently. You must question them until you intuitively put the pieces together.

One case I had was a man with a pain that would come and go but never leave. Upon deep questioning, I found he had kept his father's ashes and not disposed of them—20 years after his death—and had been ill ever since. After this emotional release, the answer of what to do was now in his hands. The pain got better and less frequent after the conscious mind realized this connection. Still frustrated with the pain, he asked me what more he could do. With full knowledge that he needed to release the ashes, I only told him to be patient with his healing as he needed to be ready for this. He finally released his father after considerable time, and the pain disappeared.

Another case I had points to how unconscious these triggers can be. One patient I had had gout in his feet. He had tried many different things and seen many people for it for many years. Nothing really helped him. As I touched his feet, I told him that he did not like his present career and was not satisfied on a soul level—his soul had another purpose he had not honoured. He looked at me puzzled and said he loved being a stay-at-home dad. His wife then jumped in and said that he really wants to be a farmer and always has. He was in complete denial and wasn't even aware of his own unrequited dreams.

Do not back down in these cases. Be sure of what Inner Self has told you about the case. Your words are true—the receiver may simply not be ready or aware enough to recognize them. This takes great courage, discipline and faith as a healer—to know and stand ground with Self.

When fear walks in the office, simply be aware that it's there and know it too will pass. Ask Higher Self to deal with it and lay the fear out on the table for you both.

One patient I saw was vibrating in fear even before she walked in to see me. My intuitive office manager had picked up her angst right away and thought she was going to run out at any moment. I was allowing of the fear but could not figure out why it was there. I asked internally for Higher Self to reveal it and she then almost immediately told me she had had a bad experience with a previous healer (which had traumatized her on a soul level). As I reassured her and gave her loving compassion, her energy *completely changed*. We ended up laughing together during the visit. She patted me on the back and was clearly relieved. Unknowingly, she had already healed from this fear just from that awareness! I didn't see her again—this was the real healing that she needed.

A patient like this will rarely know they're nervous, they will be in denial about it or they're simply used to it. They will also rarely know what has triggered their fear—all this is up to You to know in the process of healing.

Listening

Many patients will tell you what's wrong right away (if you are truly listening). They may tell you through clues in their speech or body language or even by the nature of their symptoms. Other times, patients will talk and clear their own issues right in front of you without seemingly any assistance from you. In these cases, avoid the temptation to 'step in' and provide your 'expert advice'—they are already speaking to their own expert in your presence—Self. Be content to observe, listen and support silently. Celebrate in their Self-communication and empowerment and offer advice only when intuitively prompted. Point out to them that they are in fact healing themselves at that moment and that they have found all the answers themselves. This alone is extremely powerful and awakens further conscious communication and connection with Self when they realize what they are doing. They can then do this outside the practice setting from then on.

While listening intently to the patient, always turn an ear to yourself. You do not need to strain to hear messages for yourself as well—they will come to you with ease. Every patient has something to show/teach you about yourself. Have humility and remember that souls seek souls and speak to one another at this level regardless of outward appearances, formalities and contracts.

Asking for guidance

Whether a patient has awareness or not, you must always go Within and ask for guidance. This is usually most necessary when we are stuck on a case or an aspect of a case. Don't ignore recurring feelings or messages even if they seem odd to the mind. Answers always lie Within You and your duty will be clear. Visions often come swiftly so this doesn't have to take long. Self communicates with us with ease—there is no need for long meditations and contemplation over a case, which can lead to doubt.

At times, you may have to leave the room or go outside to gain clarity. Simply remove yourself for a moment if there is too much confusion or fear. Do what it takes to discover what the patient needs as those willing to heal don't really care how you do it—they just want to heal.

The dire need to be present

As a healer, you must stay present at all times. The only way to do this is to 'convince' your mind that the matters at hand are very serious ones—life or death. Most of us become very present in moments of trauma or near-death as we have no other option. At this point, the mind gets out of the way or at least is not heeded. Every moment and situation with a patient must be 'dire'. Some may use the guise of professionalism or reputation to convince the mind that what they're doing is a serious matter and the 'life or death' of their career is on the line if they lack presence. A hairdresser may be present if he desires above all to be the very best. An athlete will do the same. There are no other options for them to the contrary. A healer does this action consciously and is aware that she is 'tricking' the mind so to speak into succumbing to the Spirit. The mind backs down because survival is at stake and it will cease its chatter in the face of it.

Eventually, the peace and power that comes from being present will be desired during all aspects of your life, not just during your working hours. Using this presence provides for the very essence of healing and without it, no true healing can occur. Presence provides the background for ultimate Will, Faith and Love. Within presence, all things are possible and healing is at your very whim, without effort or thought.

After mastery of presence in one's profession, one must also master presence in the rest of your life. Convincing the mind that being present is 'dire' in the presence of relatives, friends or at the gas station takes intense dedication, discipline and practice. (This is why after a near-death experience, some can stay present permanently—they see all life as dire and precious now which commands their presence). One must cease to see the gas station and the interactions one has at it, as unimportant. All actions are extremely important to the healer and he never knows when he will be required to heal.

Fear will become more obvious in the other areas of your life outside the practice and you will wish too for its demise. This may be more challenging unless you find a dire reason for presence in the rest of your life. Some use the love for their families and spouses or animals and friends. Find your reason.

A good practice is to assure the mind that you are the most important person (dire) in that patient's life at the moment they are with you and that you are the only one that can help to heal them at that moment as well. This is not done out of any arrogance but simply because they are with *you* and have come to you specifically for healing at that moment in time. This perception creates the dire situation required to elicit presence and focused intent for accurate healing. This method can be used to 'trick' the ego into being present because the situation is seen as 'dire'.

This practice is also useful to recognize the person or situation in front of you is also dire for *you* and your learning! We must be present or we may miss something—some awareness, lesson, message or sharing.

If all of life is seen in this manner, nothing is wasted and it becomes dire to be in this moment—to exist only in what's real—in the reality of now.

Miracles

When a patient picks this truth up and knows it to be true in their hearts, they can no longer fool themselves into believing it's all physical or it's due to this dis-ease or that label or this symptom. This is when miracles occur. They have literally woken up from a bad dream and taken back their life and their power—they have chosen, consciously or not, to change the dream. They have simply chosen to remember the original perfection of Who They Really Are.

Hawaiian Huna medicine explains the mechanics of instant healing to us beautifully. Our True Selves contain an etheric blueprint or mold of Who We Are, perfected, unbreakable and eternal. Since we are made in this image, our bodies are a reflection of this perfection. When a body is injured, it heals itself through copying from this etheric blueprint once again and making new cells. We have limited thoughts in our minds around how long it takes to heal and what can heal fully and therefore only fulfill our limited beliefs. In reality, there are no limits. In the Huna tradition, a prayer (energy) is made to the Higher Self to heal the broken part. This energy then returns to the body and 'dissolves' the broken part into the etheric blueprint once again. Here, this dissolved energy molds to the original etheric blueprint and this new 'copy' becomes solidified in the physical as an instantly healed part of the body[7].

Perhaps the 'phantom limb' sensation occurs not so much because of nerve endings but because the arm (in its original mold or form) is still there in the etheric (or blueprint) form but has simply not materialized into physical form. Another interesting note is that perhaps stem cells are actually the same as this 'etheric mould' from which other cells miraculously arise to create whole new organs and physical structures.

The power of love

There is no need to answer questions in a manner people 'want' them answered. The ego/self loves to distract itself from the truth. A healing patient will often answer their own questions in front of you. Your presence is simply a carrier frequency on which they reside for a time to remember themselves and their own connection and answers. Never take away anyone's power by answering their own questions for them. They must find out for themselves. You will answer simply

[7] Long, Max Freedom. *The Secret Science Behind Miracles*. Wildside Press. 2009:118-121, 236-237.

according to what Self tells you or, what comes to you. If you have a vision, you tell it. If something comes out your mouth, you say it but never *expect* any particular outcome or result from the patient. Allow it all to be said by the Self and you will always, see, say and do everything in accordance with that. You will only ever be shown what you need to know and see for yourself and the patient. You can only share with the other person what you have healed in yourself. You cannot see or know more or less.

Essentially and eventually, as many teachers say, there is nothing *to* say. Anything will do in terms of conversation. But this is something your ego does not guide. What's said is not from the ego or animal self, it's from Higher Self and your patient will be left in a state of peace and calm. This calmness comes if they are open and receptive, grateful and loving. This is soul conversation—speaking soul to soul. And there will be connection—deeper understanding. The words will mean deeper things to the person as they do to you—they will speak to you on many levels in many ways, not just superficially. Everything will have multiple meanings and become a parable if we allow ourselves to really hear the deeper meanings. This is a determined by karma.

Regardless of age, education, language or so-called intelligence, the person will hear you and understand, usually without words. Then give thanks for the glory of God shining in them back at you because they are shining forth their true light and love to you—the greatest payment and reward of your service to them. They will teach you. Listen. What they say, do and come in with will show you where you are at in your own life and what you also need to work on. They will test your faith and challenge you to love them at all costs. They will come at you with harshness and anger and blame at times and you will just love them because you will see their souls only and their fear as something on the outside only, easily cracked like an thin-shelled egg, with your love for their being-ness. How can we but give thanks for those who are harshest to us? Most terrifying? They show us, yes—I see myself and my fears and my own frailties in you at times when I feel lost. As you give only love out to them, love is all you can receive. Their outward expressions will no longer terrify or affect you. You will soothe their pain with your words and your love—you will cool their brows with your compassion because you see them as your own child and self that is lost and afraid. You will comfort and remind and never back down. You will love them unconditionally in whatever state they choose to be in because their fear is no longer a threat to you. They will break down in front of you—all their fears they will see are no match for your unending love and compassion and it will simply not hold. They are naked before you and you see their souls. You think this is God. It is not outside you—it *is* you! This *You* will see! How else can God know itself but through us?! I ask you! We are sons and daughters of God sent here to express ourselves as Gods—to serve and love each other and the world. To help one another to awaken and be powerful like God. These words inspire you because they are the truth. They excite you because they speak to your soul. Accept yourself, your true Self, and sit in this faith—this ultimate confidence of Who You Are. Sit with the assurance of yourself as a child of God and *all* is yours—I mean *all*—you *have* heaven on earth! Feel your power and share it always—withhold nothing. Share your frailties as well until they are all gone. Share your fears until they are all gone. Your brothers and sisters help you heal as well—sometimes in the most unexpected ways. Never underestimate a person or anything for that matter. God will speak to you in many different ways and forms if you are listening. God will show you His hand through the miracle of healing, through words of wisdom, through the glory of a sunset or the march of an insect, through a boss's kind words, through a friend's desperate call on the phone, through your mother's advice and her love of nature, your father's diligence with his work and love of art. God will show up in the eyes of children and infants, in cashiers and store clerks and look straight at you and say "I see you. I see your beauty, your soul" and they will serve you—bend forward to you like lovely flowers. You will marvel at how life bends to Your Will and serves you fully without effort. Others will come to your palm and rest and be comforted. Your simple words and kind thoughts toward anyone in your life will always create service toward you. The joy you express and exude will attract the same back toward you and through this you are limitless and God-like. Others will do things for you they may have never done for anyone ever. They will say things they have never said and think things they never have before. All because you see them—their real Selves—their true Selves—their Godliness and beauty and they will shine in your presence. This is your only task, your only assignment. To just look—look and really see. Every day will bring you God. Everywhere you look, if you only take the time to look and listen. God is always speaking. There is nothing *but* God speaking! We just often don't take the time to listen. This is how everything in your life will run smoothly and bring you peace, love and power beyond measure.

As you see others, so you will be seen and so you will see Yourself.

Changing the mood

We've all experienced times where we may have been just feeling ok or even down and all of a sudden, good news, a breakthrough or some other positive outcome occurs and we are instantly in an excellent, cheerful if not excited mood. This shift seems involuntary but can actually be trained. All that's needed is the awareness of one's triggers to happiness and joy. It could be as simple as a thought, a place, a thing, a person or a situation. Regardless, it lifts and launches you into that joy and can be utilized as a tool to do so whenever you desire. You must practice this with your patients in order to bring them into their most positive state for healing to occur and also, within your own personal life. If you love your work, it seems almost nothing can get you down—you thrive on it and it gives you ultimate joy. You literally manifest that feeling and even change those around you no matter what mood or state they may be in. You can even write down your joy triggers to acknowledge them and recognize as well when you are not in joy. This can also be applied to others who are open to it, during any opportunity, at any time. A patient may come to see you in a foul mood, despairing or negative in some way. Gently, firmly and consistently apply unbending faith and love to them. Do not waver and succumb to their superficial negativity that seems to taint the air. Do not bend down to it to appease them or think that by agreeing with their negativity that you are bettering the situation. Nor do you need to prove yourself or defend your ego. Insert gentle and compassionate remarks to the positive and continue to relay the deep truths that come to you about their situation.

A man I knew well came into the practice and was in a foul mood. He was scared of the future and had forgotten himself and his path upon his retirement. He had pains in his joints which plagued him on and off for years. He had once been healed but could not hold the faith and the pain returned. He now had abundance, time and nothing to do. I kept reminding him his pain was due to not paying attention to his intuition and gentle Self. He waved my comments off and continued to look at the physical and complain. Although I supported his decision to seek surgery, I pointed out that the surgery itself would not heal him—only his peace could do that. The timing was ripe for this surgery but he had to understand that to sustain any healing from the surgery, he was to change his mind and embark on a new path—the path of his true Self through love, gentleness and helping others. He had been the true 'man' in every sense in his life as provider and successful businessman and now was left 'adrift' as to who he really was now. I pointed out that this was good as now he had to look deeper into himself and see himself for

Who He Really Was not who he thought he was or should be. As love continued to assert itself throughout the visit, his energy noticeably softened and he silenced his complaints and truly listened to the words that I was speaking. His soul had released its restlessness and quieted itself enough to listen to the healing. He now understood and was in the correct state to commence his true healing.

Another such time the mood was changed was when I unknowingly parked a little too close to a handicap parking zone and to the vehicle in it, stopping the person from getting into the vehicle. I rushed out of the store immediately to move my car when I saw the angry look from the woman trying to wheel her daughter into her van. I felt great fear coming from my ego, as I was in the 'wrong' and potential 'conflict' was in the air between us but Higher Self came through. I looked in her eyes with full focus and said sincerely that I was sorry and that I did not mean to park that close. Her mood immediately changed and she softened as she sensed my love and sincerity. She said she was just frustrated as this happened all the time.

I had learned to love not only others but myself in the face of fear and potential conflict, even while being in the 'wrong'—that I am always safe. She had learned that people are ultimately loving and most do not mean any harm. Just perhaps, due to our interaction, her outlook will change as to how she sees herself as a victim in this world, to one of freedom and limitlessness.

Once, my husband and I were parked outside a store and bitterly fighting over something. We grumped into the store and then heard on the intercom to go outside to our vehicle. I knew right away I had attracted something negative! Sure enough, someone had backed into our truck leaving a large dent in the bumper. Matt and I started to laugh because we realized what we'd attracted. The man who hit the vehicle was in tears because his house had just burned down and he did not know how he was going to pay for this damage. We were simply not upset at all and at first he took this as quite a shock. We exchanged information and told him not to worry—besides I needed some work done on the bumper anyway. I hugged him and blessed him—his gratitude and the experience itself that certainly 'changed our mood' were worth more to us than any bumper.

We are here to be joyful—how we get there and what tools we use make no difference. When you practice joy even in only one area of your life, it can spread to all others easily.

Life purpose

Often, a soul becomes 'sick' or 'lost' because they have forgotten their destiny—their life purpose. The patient must be reminded as to their destiny here on earth. I often ask people, what are you doing 'here on earth'? I sometimes get a shocked look as they have to go deep for this one. They have forgotten why they're here and what they're here to do. In fact, this is a very important and pertinent question to ask yourself once in a while – am I still on track? I have seen people pine away and die due to lack of purpose. The real focus necessary for healing must be on the present moment and what one is doing here and what one's purpose is on a spiritual level—what are you here to create?!

The soul is here to create and to be the light of the world[8] unto itself and others. It has no other purpose. The technicalities of *how* and *what* a person does (through being a healing practitioner, a missionary, a florist, a technician, a salesperson etc.) is irrelevant in terms of delivery but vital for individual soul expression, learning and satisfaction. What a person does must stir passion within them (the desire to create) and that is what moves them forward and provides the soul with a reason to be here. Lack of purpose leads to depression, dis-ease and ultimately, to death. We must remind people that they have work to do here and cannot afford the luxury of being ill or stalling their destiny.

If a patient cannot fathom what it is they are doing here, I ask them what they loved as a child. No matter how 'silly' what you loved seems to be now, these things are important keys to life purpose. Dreams of being a fireman may have been a call to help others. Playing with mud may be the gift of working with one's hands or using creativity. A love for playing dress-up may be indications of a flare for drama, entertainment or comedy. These passions never go away and must return into adult life and be fulfilled and embraced into present day life.

One patient had dreams of being a healer and had even taken courses toward that. She said she just couldn't do it because she had no energy—she was waiting to get better so she could do it. My approach to her was that she must do the opposite and start now! A vision came to me during meditation of a child in South America and I asked who this was. She told me she sponsored a child there. I told her it was prudent for her to visit her and to do some outreach work there. She looked at me in shock but realized I would not support excuses for her or focus on 'licking her physical wounds'. After all, she'd been everywhere and tried everything. I only saw her as temporarily stalled and well in Spirit.

---

[8] Matthew 5:14

Her soul was dying due to lack of purpose.

Purpose must come first before any healing can occur—which takes insight and great courage. We must never support the 'victim' mentality, or the patient forever remains a victim. I had to see her potential and hold it as the truth in my mind, with the full faith that she can and will do it. If she so chooses and when she chooses, she will live up to it. She has to tune into something better, something higher and if there's nothing around to show her that, how can she heal? Her lack of energy is precisely *due* to lack of purpose. It takes immense energy to push against the Will of the Spirit and deny our true purpose—this causes great fatigue. A person has to want their true purpose more than any other goal.

'Do the do'

My partner often says "stop talking and do the do. Fear always feels the same anyway—where you're at now isn't working so you have nothing to lose".

It helps to 'get busy' in one's life doing service work in the area of one's passion, even if at first it's not quite what you would like—it's a step in the right direction and that energy will catapult you into getting to your true passion. During this, no one has time to focus on fear of the past and future. You are forced to be in the present where peace lies, no matter how noisy or busy your life is. Remind yourself you do not have the luxury of remaining idle, waiting for someone and something else or something better to come along and save you—you must save yourself and show others how to do the same through your example and through compassion. One almost 'forgets' their so-called ailments when they are 'caught up in the moment'. Forget them until they are no longer in your reality! They are again, trivial, temporary and not real! Forgetting does not mean denial. Look closely at your fears and address them but do not *dwell* on them. This only empowers them and makes them into huge monsters that eventually take over you and your life, becoming your only focus, labeling you completely. Things that are not focused upon do not exist. When you are busy doing your soul's work, you do not have time for frivolities and random thoughts of the mind. Thoughts and fears do not exist until we make them manifest—until we pull them in and believe them. Remember, as thoughts and fears come, they also go just as easily.

Many great people I have learned from have one thing in common. They do simply what they love and don't worry about the future.

117

Compassion

Compassion always plays a huge role and is integral to any true healing work. Compassion means understanding in a non-judgmental manner. It does not mean to feel sorry for, to pity, to join in or to allow abuse of the relationship. I often see healers who 'feel badly' for their patients and exhaust themselves trying to 'heal them'. As mentioned above, you must not treat those who have not chosen to heal. You must be fully charged and present for those who do choose to. Trying to give a gift to someone who doesn't want it, will only exhaust and frustrate you and it's disrespectful to the person who does not want to receive it. We can still be compassionate toward them and understand the difficulty they must be having in changing their mind. All we can do is palliate if possible and let them go while sending love to them through focused prayer/meditation. The patient will know on a soul level that you love them and unconditionally to boot. They will return when they are ready.

Humility

Humility comes from the root word, 'humus' or 'ground'. It means to be real, grounded in Oneness and sanity. With humility, there is no room for the illusion of pride and ego. Humility means simply being present (grounded) without judgment. This can take practice as one must constantly bring awareness to oneself and one's behaviors. You will be triggered by certain situations, people, patients and circumstances. Pay attention to what 'humiliates you' and you will know what areas you need to let go of. You are not here to be right and to argue with others. You are not here to prove yourself or allow others to 'get to you'. You are not here to take responsibility for others which is none other than self-importance. All these are just the ego's attempt to stay liked by the pack. You can be in the pack but not *of* it. To be a healer, you cannot afford to play with pride as it will cloud your vision, love and healing ability for the patient. You must remain clear at all times to allow the flow of life force through unimpeded. Even if you feel you've made a so-called mistake, remember you are learning—you are here to evolve through learning into Who You Really Are. Humbly admit to and correct your mistakes and humanness while being kind to yourself.

Pride is not always something conscious. It is a well taught and ingrained behavior that comes ultimately from the fear of being attacked or being 'wrong'. With pride, we can hide the truth from ourselves and others in order to save our skin, usually without awareness or malicious intent. Always keep pride in check through constant awareness and humility—it's OK to be wrong or to not know. Admitting this to yourself and the patient sets the ground for further trust and compassion. Once we admit we don't know, we can finally find out what there is to know.

I once had a patient I'd been treating with some success. I had gotten to know her too well and could not see her clearly with fresh eyes every time she arrived. I was too full of pride to admit this to myself or to her. Although she had some minor physical complaints, nothing appeared on her muscle testing (which can happen if the body is hiding something—at this point it is paramount to use intuition and employ other assessment skills and tools)—I simply found that she was stressed. She fortunately, did not listen and kept searching for answers elsewhere. I was too full of pride (unknowingly) to refer her or to clear myself to gain a new perspective on this case—I simply couldn't see. She kept getting no answers elsewhere either from other healers for quite some time until she finally found out she was allergic to a certain food. She called me to kindly inform me. I was humiliated. How could I miss such a thing? I was embarrassed, apologized and told her I was happy that she had found what she was looking for. Although at this point on my path, I knew it was pointless to beat myself up over this and she was not upset at all with me as she understood that I had tried many things and my best with her at the time, I needed to understand what had occurred here. She had become a needy patient in my egoic judgment, and my subconscious mind had literally 'passed her off' to allow her to nurture herself. I also realized that I had previously diagnosed myself with the same allergy but had since ignored my own diagnosis as I could neither commit nor believe that this was the case for me—that I should somehow just 'get over it' due to my spiritual awareness. She had opened my eyes to my own condition and the need to fast off the allergen as well. As synchronicity would have it, I had several patients come in that same week with the same allergy—just as an added reminder! Lastly, due to my fears of what others would think if I made a mistake, especially my patients, my 'nightmare' came true. To my surprise however, she was anything but rejecting and blaming toward me which I had experienced my whole life in the past when I was 'wrong'.

No harm was done to her in the long run and she eventually returned to see me later for deeper work as her soul trusted me. However, I realized acutely at the time that I could not help or even *see* someone else's condition if I could not help or see my own or at least admit to myself the truth of the situation and my issues around it. I could not gain this perspective because I hadn't allowed for it myself yet.

119

She was the one who had healed me (and also herself in the process). She taught me humility and through my 'mistake', she learned self-empowerment, self-connection and faith.

A fresh perspective

Sometimes, it's as simple as discussing the case with another colleague you trust if you are stumped on a case. You can also pretend the patient is a new patient and you can even tell them you are doing this. Choosing a different room or setting to assess the patient can also help. Sitting in different chairs or facing a different direction in the same room can also do it. Sometimes it helps to type out a case freeform and see what thoughts come to you. Try not to go back over and over a case and what's been done in the past as this will simply lead you down the same path again. If all else fails, refer to someone you are told from Within is right for this person. You're never losing a patient, you are gaining trust and you are doing your job—healing—whether it's 'through' you or not.

A healer's responsibilities

Just as all other labels in our society hold their list of responsibilities, so does a healer. Do not fall prey to them or you will lose yourself in protocol and rules. You are not responsible for outcome, healing, cure, experience and perceptions the patient has. You are responsible only for doing your best in love and diligence for them.

Recognize when a patient chooses not to heal and point this out to them with the option to return when they are ready. Do not become distracted by the lost souls and patients that seem to want to heal but are not. Know when your job with them is finished and move on. Sometimes palliation is all they're asking for. Plant a seed and speak to the soul, if you are guided to, even during palliation. Only the soul responds to healing and this will make the difference as to whether they 'take to' the palliation or not. Everything you do and say will be perfect for them and used when they are ready to use it. You don't have to 'think' about it.

Have faith that all visits are:

- meant to be
- perfect in every way
- healing
- loving

You are only responsible to say and do what Self tells you to—to be present. You are here to tell the truth even if you 'think' it's unspeakable. Patients often get uncomfortable or irritated with the truth and their body language will tell you so. They may even not like you for it or may find you strange. You are not here to make friends, seek for people to 'like' you or to appease others. You are here to speak the truth while the world may not be and this takes great courage. You are here to be the light of the world.

Making 'mistakes'

A great healer once told me, 'there are no mistakes, only learning'.

Healers often suffer from 'too nice-itis' and we can unknowingly go out of our power to please others. In most cases, this is at the root of any mistakes we may make—ones made out of good intention. To be truly non-judgmental, we must release our need to please which ties right into our fears of 'hurting others'. The irony is that as you go along this journey, you will make 'mistakes'—it's inevitable because you are not yet infallible in your ability to stay present. Until then, all you can do is your best out of love; admit your mistakes, correct them and move on with forgiveness. As we all know (but despise) is that these 'mistakes' lead us to great wisdom and insight that could have been gained in no other way. Life is perfect just the way it is, no matter what good, bad or ugly is seemingly present. The suffering lies in your *perception* of what you think is perfect in the first place.

Losing the patient

Many of us are afraid to speak what we know is true for fear of losing our credibility with the patient or losing the patient altogether.

You always risk 'losing the patient' anyway. They are not yours to own and come and go as they please. Why not tell them the truth if they're going to go anyway? They will never forget what You've told them, even if they don't believe you or 'like' what You've said. Remember, these are not 'opinions' that come from you—these are intuitions from the still, calm place inside you that 'knows all'. They will know You are telling them the truth—they just may not like it.

I once had a patient who had a large blood clot in her leg. I told her it was prudent she speak to her medical doctor about it and get some tests including an ultrasound and I would treat her with the proper remedies on my end of things. She was outraged (or rather, just scared). I never saw her again but I knew that information had perhaps saved her life.

Most of the time, people are actually OK with and ready for the truth otherwise they wouldn't be in your practice in the first place! If you speak with love, integrity and confidence, you have done your job and done it well. You must not so much share the physical message with them, as the *faith behind the message*. You *know* this to be true not from some learned fact, statistic or opinion but from your heart. You may not even know why you know it. It matters not. It's more a *feeling* than a thought. Speak to the patient's soul. They will come out with many fears and disbelief's but know you are not to engage in battle with their fears and lack of faith—those are not concerning to you. Let them speak but hold your faith in a sure and confident manner. Do so without judgment of the need to prove anything to anyone. You have said the truth and that is enough no matter how hard they may resist. Only they can choose to pick up this faith when they are ready to do so. It may be next week, years from now or at the end of their life or even in the next one. It matters not. You have set the truth into motion—the catalyst is now in place for healing.

The Departure

Whoever said 'parting is such sweet sorrow⁹' never knew what peace comes from a timely and honourable ending.

When to say goodbye

Sometimes someone has chosen you as their healer or teacher for a time. At other times, for only a few moments. Either way, it's irrelevant. Simply go with the flow and allow them to determine it as they, and you feel fit. Within a visit itself, there will be a finality to it and you must cue the patient at this point as lingering can create other issues for both of you. Both you and they must follow inner imperatives. Sometimes a patient will give you body cues and these must be heeded as well. They may shift position, look at the clock or watch, lose their focus or simply start to leave. Do not push. Sometimes a patient will want to linger, which is more often the case with spiritual students, and will keep asking you questions. Remain compassionate yet firm. Getting up is an excellent cue and most people won't carry on after that. If they do, simply touch them on the shoulder and look in their eyes if you can. Connect with the soul and let them know it's all right to go now—that You are always with them even after the visit. For the more aware student, you can point out their tendencies of lingering during visits and discuss this directly. Often people simply feel good in your presence and they naturally, do not want to leave. Going out into the 'real' world can be daunting after such a pleasant respite! Remind them that they take that feeling with them and that it's not 'from you (self)'. You are simply reminding them of how they can be and feel all the time as they love themselves. Have them use books, music, life purpose, disciplines, meditation, nature and other tools to help them between visits and to find that comfort from within Themselves.

Usually saying a 'permanent' goodbye to a patient is agreed upon for both of you. These patients are not usually spiritually aware. You have provided a service and service has been rendered. Other patients with more spiritual awareness may leave for a while and return perhaps even years later as they are ready to take the next step. Do not attempt to force contact or make contact out of obligation. You must stay true to

---

⁹ Shakespeare, William. *Romeo and Juliet.* Act 2, scene 2, line 184-185.

123

your inner imperative and if it doesn't feel right, don't do it! Sometimes, your contracts with one another are simply over. Once souls have connected in a spiritual manner however, it is forever whether there is a physical or otherwise connection in the future.

Letting go of the student
As mentioned, you will know when the teaching is finished. Have no expectations from the student as to their 'loyalty' to you or even of their return. They may also exceed you in terms of material wealth and worldly 'success' or so-called spiritual success. Keep egoic jealousy in check with humility and understand that your own path is unique and tailored just for You, by You. Celebrate fully in your students' success and their joy and success will be yours also. Remember, they *are* You, just in different form and expression. Be joyous to see your brothers and sisters excel and spread light and love throughout—the greatest gift to You!

Practice Management

Look after Yourself and the rest is looked after.

When the practice is too slow:

- *you are burnt out and need a break*

Clear and take a break. Work on a balance in your practice that works better for you. Try different tools and hours of work until you find the perfect balance that feels right for you. It could be one day a week, it could be five. It could be part-time or full-time. Weed out any negative patients, staff, spaces, equipment, energies or issues that need to be addressed.

- *you need to focus on another task at this time or go within (meditation, retreat)*

You simply need to be recharged within, without the need for any outward changes. This is called pressing the reset button. Often travel helps us to gain a new perspective as well. Try not to see this as 'selfish'—you are recharging. You will return refreshed and ready. Do not push yourself or you and the practice will suffer. Healers would be wise to retreat or travel at least once a year and take regular breaks to refresh.

- *you are pushing away patients out of some fear*

Clear and address any fears around treating others or particular patients. This issue may require you to take a retreat away from practice to gain clarity or assistance from other healers.

- *you are not allowing abundance into your life*

Know that this is your destiny (if it's not, everything will have an ulterior motive and agenda for you such as money, fame, prestige etc.) and that you are worthy of abundance. Clear any sabotages and feelings of unworthiness. Allow love, confidence and faith to enter and abundance will come. You cannot help the 'poor' by being impoverished yourself in any respect.

- *you are not working enough*

Reassess your work schedule to see if you are working enough. You may be trying to avoid your career out of some fea

- *you are just getting started*

Be patient! It takes time for a practice to evolve and for word to get around. No matter how much you advertise, word-of-mouth is always the key to your success. Advertise a bit at the beginning of your practice but once you get rolling, it will have its own momentum through word-of-mouth. Many practitioners waste funds on advertising. Make sure you get to know all the other healers in the area so they know who you are and go to functions as intuited. Frequenting health food stores and getting to know staff also helps immensely. I found it took 2 years before my practice took off—this seems to be pretty standard for most if you are starting off alone.

- *your destiny as a healer in this particular manner is coming to a close*

Recognize the intuitive signs when your career may be coming to an end. Self may command you to do different things now as your passion guides you. This is not in any way a giving up but a shifting. You may find you need to write a book, do research, change fields, go on a lecture circuit, change tactics, location or countries, work for someone else, go on sabbatical, do outreach work, teach others, or pursue another passion. Go within and find your answers. Change always frightens the ego and you will be guided as to what will be best for you. Resisting only brings about pain and suffering as the practice will eventually fall away anyway whether you listen and follow or whether you resist.

When the practice is too busy:

- *you are on the right track but are anxious about pleasing those that are waiting*

It's not abundance if you're stressed all the time trying to fit everyone in and make the practice work for everyone. Waiting lists can serve to weed out those who are not ready to be healed yet as they will fall off your list if they're not serious. Only those that are truly meant to see you will ever come into your practice. Stick to the hours you feel comfortable working. Do not compromise. Others will find other ways to heal as Self always makes a path. This is not your concern. Be very careful not to become enslaved to the practice or your patients. You are here to be of service but not to be a slave.

- *you need to work less*

You may be resisting working less out of fear of lack of abundance, trying to serve too many patients or your overhead is too high and you are constantly trying to catch up. Don't forget, just because the rest of the Universe is working full-time, it doesn't mean you have to. Abundance is more than money—make sure you have time to enjoy it. I only ever worked part-time because of my commitments to family and to Myself. For many years I worked only mornings, 4 or 5 days a week out of a basement office in my home. Then, I worked 6-7 straight days at the beginning of every month in a small house/office that we purchased. So many practitioners leave their passion in an untimely manner due to burn out. When you are chasing large overhead, paying for too many staff and renting, the practice soon becomes a worrisome burden. So many practitioners and healers want it all now and start buying and spending it all now too. Abundance takes time to manifest. Walk slowly but surely and you will reach all your goals. Talk to a good financial advisor to work out what you can do to change things.

- *you need to hire help*

You simply need better/more office assistance or someone else to work along with you that shares the same philosophies.

- *you have created a monster and believe the only successful practice is a too busy one*

I have seen many businesses of all types fail when they reach a certain 'busy-ness' threshold. The business becomes a monster that's out of control ending in its own demise, consuming you and itself into oblivion. All businesses are a reflection of their owners. There is a perfect threshold that you must find and then honor. Start out the way you want to finish. Abundance doesn't mean building, building, building and accumulating as we're taught so well to do. It means joy and peace. More stuff, busier and bigger doesn't make you joyful. Besides, you won't have any time to enjoy material life anyway as you'll always be so busy in your pursuit in searching for more.

- *you need to clear out any fears*

Clear out any fears around lack of abundance, competition with others in your field or with society in general—about pride and power. Balance is key to a sustained, naturally flowing and peaceful practice. This in no way means you can't make money and be comfortable; you need to simply ask what your real agenda is and what abundance really means to you.

Practice Guidelines

Answer to no one except to Me.

Referrals

There are two types of referrals. Those who refer to you and those whom you refer to others. Those that are referred to you are usually one of two kinds:

- difficult patients to treat physically and/or mentally/emotionally
- referred to you for your expertise in a certain area or for your abilities as a healer

For the first type, assess them as you would any other patient and if they are not ready to heal, do not do another practitioner a disservice by then referring them on. Speak truthfully about their situation and leave them to chew on it until they are ready for healing either from you or from another. It eschews integrity to refer simply to 'get a patient off your back' or to escape telling them the truth. You must be very courageous as a healer and willing to let go all of society's expectations of you. (This, as a side effect, helps build your reputation as a healer with great integrity).

If you are referred to for your expertise, then use this to your advantage. Many patients will have seen many other people before you and precision, clarity and truth are paramount to their healing at this point. Many practitioners from all fields will refer to you as word gets around quickly when you are a true healer. Teach other practitioners by example and send them love and gratitude in return. Even if they come from very conservative or conventional backgrounds, work at staying in Your own truth and power and speaking of Your truth in their presence. Listen, be respectful yet true to Yourself, point out their own power and gifts when applicable and always see them at their highest potential, even if they are not ready to for themselves. It can be very difficult to change ourselves from conventional thinking to the Divine—be compassionate but relentless in your inspiring example to them. Seeds of wisdom and words of thanks from Within can change someone's life. You are not to bend and sacrifice yourself to make others 'comfortable' but you are to love them. Do not be afraid to show love, to say it, to express it and to be completely vulnerable. Their reactions to love are not your concern.

Do not fear you will not be taken seriously. When love from Self speaks, you will be taken more seriously than you can imagine.

House and hospital calls

With all decisions you make, they must be done from Within, including whether to go someplace or to see someone. There are always rare cases in which house and hospital calls are prudent and intuited, however, a patient that is well enough must make the commitment to come see you. It is symbolic in gesture (to themselves) of their commitment to self-healing.

Visits and scheduling

Both the length of a visit and duration between visits must be individually determined. With set times to practice, this can be difficult to manage but the Universe always works in everyone's favor. Set your intent to heal efficiently and you will stay on time and schedule without rushing or having patients wait. However, there are times when this is not possible and you must forgive yourself and heal without regard to time constraint. A committed patient will wait and they know you would spend the same amount of time with them if need be. Sometimes patients are simply late to start your day and you end up stressing to 'catch up'. Give it up and inform incoming patients of your time lag or call them so that they are informed ahead of time. Most are understanding. If you never over-schedule yourself, you will not end up in chronic difficulties with respect to this. You are not in the business of 'getting in as many patients in a day as possible'—this is not truly healing as you need full attention and focus on each patient which can take time. Be realistic with your scheduling and you will look forward to your healing work. A stressed healer cannot heal.

Sometimes a patient is finished after one visit. Sometimes they need several or just a few. It always depends on them. You will just know this intuitively and always leave it up to them to return to you as they choose. With more physically focused cases, it's often prudent to schedule regular visits. With spiritual students, encourage them to assess themselves when is the best time to return.

Be aware of your schedule and what it looks like. Are there gaps in your day? Do they occur with certain types of patients only? Do they occur when you are feeling a certain way? It could mean you need a break if it happens consistently or that you need to clear your issues around certain patients.

Be precise about visits and do not waste time on procedures

because they are simply what you've been taught and are ingrained in you. Practice intuitively. A focused practitioner can tell right away the areas needing address. You do not need to look in the ears if the eyes are wanting attention. Trust Higher Self not to miss details—they will be told to you if you are truly listening. Silence inner chatter and allow pure listening. Do not be afraid of what you hear for it is the truth. It may even seem illogical to the mind and against what you are used to. The mind will want to go back to its old standby's and protocols as they are 'safe'. Take a risk and allow yourself to be Yourself—a true healer. Be precise about what remedies and therapies are needed, without adding more or less. Be precise about when treating a patient is over—whether they're healed or not (as this is up to them). Be precise about length of visit and know when you and they are done. Be precise about what to treat, when and how. All these things take practice but are easy if one listens to inner imperatives—you can only do as you are guided.

You do not get to choose—Life Force chooses for you and the patient.

Fear of lack

As a healer, we are often subtly taught to 'keep patients coming' under the guise of 'managing a successful practice'. Many well-intentioned practitioners get caught up in 'selling' their practice to the patient, developing a needy, dependent relationship, where the patient can't live without you, your advice, products or services. A true practice runs of its own momentum, carried by the power of healing and the empowerment given to the patient.

We may never know if a patient will return as healing is up to them. They may return days or years later or never again. Even if they choose not to heal at that time, they often will refer you to others—their soul knows your integrity.

The paradox is that as you let go the fear of lack or not seeing patients, the busier you become. A true healer is known by all and they will be sought out. A true healer never 'runs out of patients'!

A healer cares (worries) not if he sees his patient again or not. He loves the patient unconditionally and sends him Life Force energy to guide and assist him in life. He cares not if the patient 'likes' him or not or whether the patient speaks good or ill of him—not out of pride or arrogance but because it's irrelevant. As a healer, you must be prepared for the wind to blow through your office at times and at other times for droves of people to be there. Healing must always be done with conscience. You heal because it is your life's mission and purpose.

Money and payment

In days of old, healers and spiritual teachers were well respected and invited into homes for food, shelter and to share what little others had. We cannot apply the trades of old to the trades of today and there is no room for guilt in exchange of services, even in healing. By this you only teach unworthiness, guilt and lack. By your example, others learn to get what they ask for in their own lives, including material wealth as one aspect. I find it curious that healers and especially spiritual teachers are somehow morally expected to offer services for free. There can be no moral hierarchy here as all occupations and services are the same. Until we can exist on pure air, it is our right to be paid fairly, as it is also our obligation to work for free for those who cannot pay and who still need healing. Only Self can determine the individual details of exchange and it must be listened to for proper guidance. Every patient will demand something different of you. Most people will gladly pay for services rendered. Others may need assistance and you will feel it. Do what's fair and 'ripe', not what's 'nice' out of guilt or obligation.

One must always be cautious with the lure of money but at the same time, keep our guilt in check. Just as charging very little leads to worthlessness and failure, so does charging exorbitant amounts of money lead to the attraction of extortion and excess to yourself. There is nothing 'bad' about money or payment—release this judgment and be at peace. Go within and clear any fears you have around this as abundance in all respects is yours to have. There is a difference between greed and sustaining yourself, between over-consumption and contentment. You must do this in all aspects of your work and life. As you must not work too much or too little, so you must not charge too much or too little. All things must be in balance.

Those who can pay you, always pay you gladly. They are not only paying you in thanks but paying themselves by caring enough about themselves to commit to healing. They are investing in their own well-being. Spending money is an energetic form of commitment that says 'yes' to something. They must come at least this far to meet you. It does not take 'long' to heal and it is always up to them when and if they need to return—all this is their choice. Often patients must make a serious choice and commitment to themselves in order to heal and spending money is one way to do this. Some patients even feel they need to spend in excess (especially if they are very ill) in order to get 'good results'— this is all just a matter of belief as we also know healing can occur instantly and it does not have to 'cost' anything. The mind however, seems to subscribe to the old adage, 'you get what you pay for'!

You will be called to heal all the time—not just in practice. You will do many works without payment at all as you are a living, breathing healer at all times. Always remember, the service you extend outward, returns to you over time.

As one starts in practice, the fees are usually lower. As your confidence increases, so do your fees. There was a time in my practice where I was seeing a lot of patients who 'just wanted to see what it was like' or 'to try it out'. I eventually had to take a good look at my fees as they did not reflect my inner imperatives and where I was as a healer anymore—my fees were reflecting me as worthless. I was feeling guilty asking for more—of having my own needs met. A fair increase in fees then weeded out those that were coming 'just to try it out' and my practice became much more efficient and attracted committed patients that were ready to heal.

Qualifications

Many lay healers that come to see me tell me they don't feel as worthy as those who've been formally trained at college or university. Even though many of them have been trained through other respectable programs or had years of intense experience in their field, they still feel they are lacking. It's important to remember that the healer is one who is present. Period. It doesn't matter if you wave a stick over someone—if you are truly present and have will, faith, compassion, knowing and self-love, healing must occur. Qualifications should never be a measure of a healer. They are only background and although useful to a degree, can never replace the power of a true healer.

Phone consults

Use this method of communication as you are intuited. Most everyday questions must be answered by your staff so you can stay focused on the healing aspect. Anyone who needs 'healing' however will require a consult. I personally only do consults after an initial visit. I have connected with the patient and 'know' them and their history and can better serve them over the phone if need be. Some patients will be physically unable to see you or are far away. You can still be extremely effective with this form of distance healing and have wonderful results. Always make it clear you are booking a phone consult with them so they know the terms. Some people have the idea that a phone consult is not a 'visit' and take advantage of this. Intuit what is fair and correct for both of you. My consults are the same price as a visit of the same length. Some patients will want a phone consult when they really need a physical visit and others may only need a quick follow-up over the phone and don't need to come in. Use intuition to decide what is best for the patient.

The only time consults of this nature become an issue is if someone feels they can call to 'complain' to you anytime about their ailments or their life. You are not in the business of being a sounding board, even if you are being paid for it. It does neither you nor the patient any good and will leach you of vital life force energy and exhaust you. The patient at all times must be ready to heal. Otherwise, we can only send them love and wait until they are ready.

Resistance

Occasionally, you may run into others that find you threatening in some way. These patients will usually just not return. Other professionals or institutions may challenge you at times due to your seemingly radical ways. When things are done with integrity and love, never fear. Hold the faith and know that you are safe. Always counter hostility with love. People expect conflict when they are hostile—but not love in return. Be true, factual and assertive in your response but ultimately loving. When others feel that you are unshakable in your faith and you have unconditional love for them, they will fall away from you. They will only harass you if you are in some way fearful. Clear yourself of any fears of authority or conflict. The pack animal/ego always fears this as it feels it risks a huge rejection from the societal pack if so-called authority starts challenging it. Your only authority is Self. You answer to no one. This does not mean you are stubborn, inflexible and hard-minded. It does not mean you need to prove yourself in any way or that you are 'righteous'. You simply continue on doing what you are told to do from Within. Watch your agendas—are you doing things to be righteous? To prove a point? To challenge authority? To be a martyr and allow for your own persecution? To sabotage yourself? If intuition tells you to change course of action, you do so. If it tells you to continue doing the same, you do so. If you feel any fear, do it anyway. This can be a great challenge so don't expect to get it overnight. You cannot be guided by the rules of this world.

The best way to deal with a forceful authority is not at all. Force always attracts more force (arguing, proving, anger and righteousness). If you run up against resistance, simply go around—ask Within how this can be solved another way. Do not see it as any obstacle. The 'me' authority tries to do these things to is merely ego or animal self. There is always a way and Self makes it for us if we listen. Nothing is impossible or impassable. Do not fight. Do not resist. Be flexible and go around. Move out of the way. When pushed, move yourself in the direction of the push, not against it. In this way, your opponent falls over due to their own momentum.

Only you can create in your reality. No one can do that for you (or *to* you). Your fears attract your fears. Recognize, clear and deal with them. They are passing illusions that there can possibly be someone or something greater than Higher Self/God. We don't have the luxury of worrying about what others think and what's accepted at this time. You do not have time for martyrdom or victimization. You are here to be the light of the world. You are safe. You are free.

Teaching and Learning

You are the fish and You are also the school of fish.

There really is no teaching or learning as we already 'know'. There is only awakening—remembering.

Learning

To learn means to raise one's vibration (or energetic 'understanding') to the teaching. The teaching is revealed to you on a deep and spiritual level. It is a revelation. Sometimes you may feel you have already learned something before. However, you can never learn something or be revealed something twice. It has just been revealed to you on an even deeper level this time and the lesson may be very different although the method may seem the same. Do not kick yourself—you are still learning—life is still being revealed to you. When all is revealed to you, there is no more learning. Only presence, creativity and love are left. When all is revealed you become that All—The Oneness of All.

Learning will happen in many different ways and come in many different disguises. All of life and its challenges are for your learning. Listen to and use your lessons well. Then they don't need to be repeated.

Learning from a teacher

When a teacher of a 'higher' vibration (or rather, 'different' vibration) comes to you, through whatever medium, it will literally change you if you are accepting and willing to receive. The 'teaching' that ensues is more than the words spoken, written or the new skills learned. Especially when a teacher is in your physical presence, their vibration will become part of your own. As they 'give you this gift', your own consciousness will elevate accordingly in sometimes surprising ways.

After a visit with one of my teachers, she told me she had given me a 'gift'. The most profound and permanent change overcame me. I had experienced a change in my consciousness—to pure presence without thought. This is called a satori. This 'satori' lasted 3 days where I was completely present, calm, all-knowing and powerful—I felt I could have parted the road with a mere thought. Nothing disturbed me. The satori left and I then spent years 'getting used to' that satori and the new vibration she had 'gifted' to me. Satoris or states of higher consciousness

135

do not *leave* us—we simply must incorporate these higher vibrations into our lives which can take time—sometimes a lifetime.

Another teacher I had was much younger than me and a very gifted clairvoyant. During a session where I was teaching her, I asked her to go into meditation for me. She revealed to me many important aspects of my life and future that confirmed and eased my mind. I was grateful after the session but not prepared for the 'gift' she left me during this interaction. I found myself able to clearly 'see' and obtain any information about anyone or thing, effortlessly, just as she could. I had this ability before but not to this extent—I found I could only do it in certain settings and the information that came to me was limited to my practice. Her vibration revealed a whole new world for me. She had given me a gift without even realizing it or formally offering it to me. I had picked up her 'Way'.

Another teacher I had was a trip to Sedona one fall and a visit to the Chapel of the Holy Cross there. Stunned by the sheer beauty of the area and its unique vibration, I knew immediately I would never return the same person as before. I experienced satori on the very first day there and was in awe by the ultimate beauty of all the things and people around me. It had shaken my perceptions so much by being there that I couldn't help but feel at One. The satori dissipated after that day and I was left with a type of depression as often happens after satori. Down but not out, I felt attracted to the Chapel and decided to take a look out of curiosity. Being of no particular religious affiliation, I simply approached my visit as an observer but I was stunned by what happened next. Upon entering the church, I looked around the entrance as any other tourist would and then placed my hand on the gate. I immediately, without control, fell to my knees and wept. The emotions I'd held within me for so long could no longer be contained and I wept long and hard. I was shocked at how such a simple gesture and physical structure could bring up such deep release for me. The vibration and love of the place and what it represented moved me to the core. At that point, I forgave myself for carrying such a load and burden (trying to save the world, my family, others), for past persecutions and my grievance with religion and church. I actually bought a small rosary as a token of this release and honor of what the church had at least tried, in its own way, to 'save the world'.

Teachers can come in any way, shape or form—be prepared for teaching at any time.

The irritating teacher

You know you are doing a good job when you are irritating to your students and patients! Of course, we do not *strive* to be irritating but speaking the truth is always irritating to fear and the egoic self. 'Irritating' vibrations shake things up and allow fears to clear and surface. Speak the truth even though it may be perceived as 'rude' or irritating. It is neither and you and your patient will know it on the deepest levels. The truth can never be denied and is always necessary for growth and healing.

After giving birth to my 3rd child, my belly was still sticking out a little and I felt a little overweight. I shoved this notion aside but it still bothered me—I still hadn't dealt with the societal notion of 'having to look super-slender'. One day, a little boy came up to me, looked at my belly and said, "you're fat". I laughed and thanked him for his wisdom. He walked away without care or malice—he had irritated me by speaking the truth—he had seen right through me and told me what I was thinking—and so shall You as the healer.

One of my greatest teachers would irritate me constantly. She would never answer my questions with a straight answer and would often go off on tangents relaying some seemingly unrelated story or parable which drove me to distraction. When I would ask a question, she would always have me ask it to myself and go Within which also drove me nutty. She was teaching me self-empowerment and was unwavering in her persistence. Like water off a duck's back, she would keep diverting attention back to me and my own inner connection rather than to her for all the answers. At times, I knew she could clearly know my irritation and anger but she stayed perfectly serene and unmoved (which irritated me even more). Strangely, I always felt love from her and compassion but she would never sacrifice the truth to please me. She cared not if I spoke to her or not, if I listened to her or not. She had no expectations. She had her own inner guidance and the rest of the world and its rules of social acceptance were not her concern. Sometimes she would silently listen to me talk, which would make me very uncomfortable at first as I was so used to comment and vocal interaction. She would allow me to determine entirely the length of the visit and I had to pull away when I found myself rambling. Other times she would tell me she had to go sometimes mid-conversation and promptly leave, always polite but efficient as if she were simply being pulled in another direction—to other affairs at hand—truly living in the present.

As a teacher yourself, students will often have many questions. Observe the temptation to be flattered by this attention to 'show off' your knowledge. Provide with simplicity and efficiency, only what is needed. Often, a question a student may ask becomes a teaching tool in and of itself and may never be answered directly by you. Their question may be just specific for their own journey and their attention must be brought to the true nature or meaning of their question.

One such student I had kept asking me for clarification of terms, to define them. I pointed out that this need for clarification was just their habit; to know in the mind how things work and what they mean. Instead of giving the student the definition of the term, I pointed to where their awareness must go so that they can find it not in the mind but from Within themselves. They already know the meaning Inside.

As pleasing as we want to be, we are not here to please nor purposely irritate. Use every opportunity to awaken and to shift perception. Go Within for guidance as to your response and you can never fail.

The attractive teacher

It's not uncommon to have people be very attracted to you or completely avoid you when you are a true healer. Consciousness or love has a powerful way of augmenting both attractive and repulsive forces. You will not be surprised to already see certain people fall away from your life as you evolve, as your focus and interests change and as love and presence within you increases. This is normal and resistance only creates pain and persecution. Allow relationships to fall when and where they must and to stay true to your path. Many will not understand what you are doing and why but most will not offer resistance as something within them knows you are following your purpose. There are less repulsive forces now than ever in human consciousness—we have evolved. You are safe this lifetime to pursue your destiny without interference. Some people will simply try to ignore you or scurry away back into fear. Self will always inform you what to do and what to say without judgment, keeping you free and out of harm's way. If others are very fearful, they will not be able to stand your presence. Do not descend and go out of your power. Clear through the release and walk forward. People may return when and if they are ready to face the Truth.

Most will be curious of you and come to you for assistance but once assisted, will leave your presence to learn and evolve and suffer as they must. Pray for them as they come to you in mind and to you physically. Most will not choose to learn until big changes come to mass consciousness on this earth.

Those who truly choose to learn from you will make themselves known to you intuitively. They will choose you. Those of strong will simply learn from you as they would from any other teacher and take what they need to carry on with their own life's work—their paths will unfold before you and their empowerment will be clear and sure. They will not 'need' you. Some beginning on the spiritual journey may look highly upon you almost to the point of worship and they must be constantly and gently reminded of their own inner power, constantly turned from what seems like only yours, back unto Themselves. This may at times mean leaving them to their own devices until they are sober enough to go within and listen to Self. Pray earnestly for your students as they enter into consciousness, as they are the light bearers of this world and must be supported. All students and paths are different and you must listen to Self for specific directions as to their teaching. Sometimes the teaching may seem to lack compassion both to you and to the student but be assured when listening to Self, love is always foremost. You must show students by example that there are no special relationships, hierarchies or preferences. This can seem harsh as the ego wants to be special. Show them the freedom they will obtain through 'non-specialness' or sameness.

No matter how patients or students perceive Your decision, always extend love to them. Some of my students have been very irritated with me but if I happen to see them, I always tell them I love them somehow. They are often stunned that someone who shows such hostility toward Me can love them still, unconditionally. With patience, I find they often return to finish their healing when they are ready. This can involve a chance encounter or something more planned by them. Assess the situation and ask Your Spirit what their intentions are and act upon that intention to continue learning. Remember that all is perfect and that your Spirit may not be ready to teach them until a later time as well.

The false guru

Those that see you as a guru and treat you as such deserve special mention. Apart from being simply attraction, this enters into the realms of worship. If a student feels unworthy, he will worship her teacher and follow him/her around or attach to the teacher in some way. The student will have difficulty seeing the teacher's weaknesses and have trouble seeing the truth about the teacher—that she is no better or worse than him. The teacher at times may provide great insight and clarity during higher states of consciousness and at others times, seem to know very little or act as we all would in everyday life. This can become confusing to the student and the student must always be reminded that the teacher and student are both the same. You are no one's guru and you must empower others to find their own guru Within. Sometimes this means leaving them to their own devices until they've done so. A true teacher is ruthless in their intent for humanity—small self and its agendas are not part of that. This requires humility and awareness on the part of the teacher to point out to the student what they are doing—to make them aware of how they are judging themselves as less than and you as greater than. This dilemma is very similar to the lost soul scenario with the only difference being these students/patients are more consciously aware.

A student/patient must use you as a guide only and although may go through times of self-degradation and doubt, they must continue on their path with or without you. They have their own inherent will and karma driving them forward. These are the only students of the spiritual path you are to 'take on' and 'assist'. For others, you will only succeed in misguiding them as they will hang on your every word and action—as something to be worshipped outside of themselves. Students must only use you as an example or pattern—to set a vibration. The aware student shows great interest in their own destiny and purpose and pursues it with vigor and great will. Those that remain idle and clinging only leach others of life force energy. Be aware that students can also go in and out of stages of neediness and independence as the journey can be variable and many fears must be released along the way. Respond to each as needed and as guided at any given time.

As you become more 'attractive', others bend toward you in this manner, and sometimes pursue you with obsession. You are simply a vessel for Self and you must recognize this as you guide others. I have seen students try to gain 'exclusive access' to their teachers and this becomes their only pursuit. As if you are a rock star, they will try to elbow their way in to see you and get your attention in any way they can. They may use bribes, fear, stories of serious pain and dis-ease, guilt and manipulation. Some have even read and tried everything in terms of 'spiritualism' and seem to be very wise and well-read but are unwilling or unable to *use* their wisdom in action as the light-bearers they are meant to be. The pursuit for them becomes the constant *seeking* outside themselves, disguised as something 'greater' than what everyone else seeks—disguised as spirituality. This is seeking just for seeking's sake. Nothing, therefore, can be found.

Others will replace you for their lost 'parent' and worship you like they are a child and you the all-knowing parent. Remain compassionate yet unaffected and resist the temptation to be drawn into this. Keep boundaries and remain neutral.

140

Many enlightened teachers in the past have been caught in the traps of others' obsessions toward them, only to their own demise. Recognize obsession as merely the whim of the ego, not wanting to look Within, misplacing and mistaking you for their own Self. The light bulb is not the source of light. Redirect their attentions toward Their Own light always. A true teacher knows they need nothing outside themselves—a teacher is carefree of both praise and blame—a true teacher is fully free.

Asking for help

Setting pride aside can be one of the most challenging aspects of being a teacher/healer. Ego fears it cannot afford to look 'weak' or 'needy' or even to risk others knowing this especially if we have been 'burned' before by asking for help. Being ultimately vulnerable i.e. *Knowing* we are safe, is the key to mastery and full wisdom. Admitting to yourself that you need help is the first step. How, when and with whom or with what you get this help is not relevant but will come to you as intuition. The only thing you ever need to do is ask. The person you ask is Yourself. Go Within and ask for Higher Self/God to help you and then listen for the response. Your help will arrive to you in a timely and awesome fashion. Although you must listen to what steps you need to take, you may never know quite how this help will come to you—just trust that it will. The added benefit of receiving help is that new revelations come to you that you can then pass on to others.

Sometimes the help does not seem to be forthcoming and frustration can set in after meditation/prayer. It takes utmost faith, courage and patience to listen for your next course of action—which may require nothing less than you ironically doing it yourself! As one advances along the spiritual path, less and less assistance is necessary from outside of Oneself as you will have developed all the tools and know-how to do it Yourself. The ego does not like this as it feels unworthy, that others have all the answers, that it's ultimately lazy and doesn't want to help itself. It takes even more courage to do things yourself.

I bought two horses as I was intuited to. I thought I could just jump up on the horses like I did when I was 16. I was scared to death of them. I got bucked off and was humiliated, hurt and angry. I cursed those horses and yet I couldn't bring myself to get rid of them. I asked diligently for help from Self and from others to seemingly no avail—no one would come and help me. I resigned myself to the fact that only I could help me. I very slowly and patiently worked with those horses every day starting with the smallest things until I was able to ride again.

No one else *could* help me with this at that time. Our relationship was just between us and I had to learn, through trial, error and humiliation, to release my doubts and fears, stay in my power and not to give up. Ironically, as I gave up the need for someone else to help me, help from others started arriving as well.

Even though I'd asked for help, somewhere inside I felt unworthy of it so I didn't get what I'd asked for. We only literally get what we ask for and if our hearts aren't in it, we can't fool Ourselves. The horses had taught me that it's ok to ask for help—and it came when and how I needed it.

The joy of work

One of the saddest parts of living in today's society is our lack of joy surrounding work and labour of any kind. Physically, the body likes to work. Balance sedentary behaviour with physical work and your system will work optimally. The concept of work as being 'bad' is only a perception and must be altered for life to take on full joy. Work is a blessing, a treasure and a great reward for a job well done. We are here to create, to work and be active in this world. The healthiest of us and those that live the longest are those who embrace and enjoy work.

I used to hate work and would do anything to avoid it. I would complain and grumble if I had to do it and do whatever I could to avoid it, especially domestic work. I eventually found myself feeling more and more tired and weaker and weaker until I 'knew' I was literally dying of boredom. I moved to a busy ranch and now work constantly—the best and more joyous cure to my 'near death'.

The craving to 'know'

You will have many teachers on your journey. Some are aware, some are not. All are equal in potential and all can and will speak to you if you are listening. Some of the most 'unaware' people have given me the most insight and the best teachings. As one of my teachers cryptically once told me, "you never know when God will come down".

True teachers that can help you raise your vibration and evolution will come to you (or you will go to them) when you are ready. Be patient and alert because they can be disguised. Also recognize when the teaching is over and when to move on. Eventually, you go within to the ultimate Source, Self—the greatest teacher of all—and no more teachers or guides are necessary.

As you embark on the journey, you will have many questions and will be bursting with 'the need to know'. Do your best to keep it at a

142

healthy curiosity instead of information overload and obsession with reading, courses, cards (tarot), divining, studying spiritual material or constantly asking teachers. This is literally a whole new world but we must approach it more in faith than with the mind. Getting out into nature and being creative (doing what you love to do best) helps to curb this and you will then naturally evolve with peace and ease.

I used to buy many books on spirituality—I had to know it all. I read and read. My mind thought that if it had all the 'training', the know-how, I could manifest 'it'. But no one else's story was like mine. Mine was unique to me alone. This craving eventually fell away as I realized that although they had given me great wisdom and helped with understanding, I had to put what I had learned into practice in my own daily life—only by living in this world can we become truly enlightened.

The call to teach and heal

You have been given a gift. You will be called to share it. As you learn, so you will teach others—in sometimes the most 'unlikely' and expected situations. Remember that *what you have not learned yourself, you cannot teach.*

If you do not listen to this inner imperative to teach, the soul becomes unhappy, restless and ultimately lacking in purpose. This high energy needs an outlet and must be shared—it is never for just you alone.

The potential student

Many times, students will come to you and the relationship will be clear. They are ready and the opportunity is right. Other times, you will only 'sense' someone is a student or has potential. Follow intuition as to the assistance you can provide toward their awakening by being ultimately patient. You may have to use other premises before you can 'speak' to them and this may take you a while.

One such example I had was the need to see a practitioner. I knew he was a potential healer but he was as of yet unaware of his power and his destiny. I went to see him in the guise of receiving help from him (which I did) but with the understanding of why I was *really* there, was on a spiritual level. At first, he did not know what to make of me and was nervous, thinking I was testing him somehow. I continued to ask him many questions about his work on me and his life and I remained consistent with him in this manner, although humorous, gentle and non-judgmental. There came an opportunity to address and share how I practiced at which time, Higher Self came through and spoke to him. He

143

received well and understood which I took as a good sign that I could continue teaching him. Although still confused by me, he became more relaxed with me over time as each time I saw him, my Spirit/Self showed him something else, although he was still not consciously aware of what I was doing. Once I showed him to be more relaxed and to laugh at my silly jokes. One time, I showed him the joy my children gave to me as the feeling welled up within me and its 'intent' directed at him. On another occasion, I indirectly showed him where his other passions in life lay. I continued seeing him until I knew from Higher Self to stop going—he was no longer responding and I could not afford to waste life force. It would be a long time before I saw him again—when I was guided. I had set the potential for him to pick up if and when he was ever ready.

Sometimes, doors open for us to make major life changes either through another person, event or thing that comes our way. Sometimes we take these opportunities, sometimes we don't. Timing is everything and our readiness to see them, predominant. The healer has the unique ability to be aware of these moments and acts as a catalyst if he is commanded to do so. Outcome however, is never his concern.

An important note to know is that the teacher always learns from the student as well and must be constantly aware of the teachings the student is providing them—it is *always* a two-way street. The wisest healers understand what they have attracted into their reality and observe it.

A potential student must have their own internal desire for awakening and no one can *create* that desire for them—it can only be coaxed and encouraged. Do not see it as a 'failure' if potential students fall away—whether you have taught them anything or not, you did what you were intuited to do and in this way, you are honouring Yourself— the greatest service of all. Through setting this intention into motion, you create an energy that goes out into the world and is picked up by others whether you or they realize it or not, such is our connectedness.

Most people that are ready will be female simply due to the fact that females have the tendency of being more intuitive. Not because they are that way by nature but because it's more *socially acceptable* to be intuitive as a female in our world. Most females are not as 'surprised' as males to find themselves pursuing a spiritual path. Many potential female students I have seen have started out completely unaware, sick and depressed only to find themselves eventually aware, content, healthy and pursuing their own destiny in what seems like a very short time.

Males are more apt to pursue a spiritual path after a certain shock or traumatic experience in their lives such as bankruptcy, divorce, illness, loss of job etc. This trigger point in time can cause a male to question his existence and mortality and he will go deeper. It's important, in fact paramount, for the healer to seize this opportunity before he goes into despair. This portal in time is like a gateway and the healer can help lead him through it to his awakening.

Your daily learning

Practice during daily life, to remain at ease during any situation. Many situations will be presented to you as a healer and many outside the 'comfort zone' of the practice. Those situations that are most uncomfortable to you provide the most teaching. Embarrassing situations, various social interactions or activities, new changes or pursuits can all provide the background for intense and deep release of attachment to certain behaviors. If you cannot at first be at ease, practice being at least observant of your behavior in different situations. You can also practice *faking* feeling at ease or relaxing into certain roles. This works wonders to change the mind and to create the knowledge that you can do it and *are* doing it. We're only just *used* to our responses and we are already 'faking it' when we are in fear as our True Self is perfectly at ease at all times anyway. Align yourself with this through practice.

One of my patients told me whenever she felt nervous, she pretended she was her confident friend and all nervousness left her and she *became* confident! The only thing left for her was to now identify this new found behavior as hers—to convince her mind that it had been her all along.

As you master ease within all social situations, fear leaves you and you can be truly present and at peace as both observer and actor—you can truly be Yourself.

The student as teacher/healer

When the student is ready, an extremely powerful teaching tool is to engage the student in helping you and others to heal. As you are intuited, have a student use their healing abilities, clairvoyance etc. on you. Not only is it helpful for you to have another's perspective, it's extremely empowering for the student to help a respected healer or teacher. This levels the playing field and shows your humility, vulnerability and 'humanness' in a very real sense as a teacher and clearly shows the student the awesome power they also possess to do just the same as you.

Use that student's particular aptitudes and gifts to help them see their own power. Some students are adept at visions so have them read

145

your aura and tell you what they see/feel around your body. Others are adept at hands-on healing and their abilities can be displayed by doing a healing session on you. If it is in your Highest Good to have them help you, then make sure a proper energetic exchange is made. In these cases, I may offer as intuited, my services in exchange for theirs. Even if they are just beginning, not quite adept yet or clear, the intent is very powerful to have them see they are just as valuable, respected and capable as you through the honour of this exchange.

One such student of mine after doing a healing session on me (which helped me immensely), said that she knew she had the abilities as a healer and had worked on others before but after she worked on her teacher, all her doubts as to her abilities and purpose fell away—it had released her from feeling unworthy and incapable and into true confidence and faith that also was a true healer.

This not only sharpens their intuition and empowers them but it also shows them that they too can teach the teacher! Show them you are not above healing yourself and that the power of the Self comes through all of us and must be heeded, no matter what vessel the message comes through. Teach them to be great teachers.

The teacher is teachable

The key to being the ultimate teacher and healer is to know that it is not little you that teaches and heals—it is big You that does it. With this constant understanding and humility, one takes no ownership, praise nor blame for one's actions and becomes simply the vessel for the Divine. With this, all things are possible and the teaching and healing from this Source flows unimpeded. The humility that comes from being teachable provides the greatest power and wisdom of all. Little you will never know it all but you do have access to the Divine and Its knowing at this moment—which is all you'll ever need.

Communication

Speak softly so others can hear you.

Communicating

The most subtle and powerful of healing forms, communication is always from Within. You must 'know' the person without taking on their fears. Practice feeling the fear or at least knowing it's there. Allow yourself to know that all fear feels the same—it's simply a low vibration. This method keeps fear *outside* of you and allows you to remain the observer. This allows you to communicate not with their fears (as we normally do) but with their spirits—their Selves. Find the 'problem', focus on it and pluck it out. Then, wipe it out with confidence that it's nothing to be afraid of. With your (and their) faith, they are healed. In reality, only this can you share with them, whether their minds believe it or not. None of this you need to necessarily share verbally with the patient—it will only serve to confuse and scare them further if they are not aware. Share as intuited, the seeds that you must, but retain the inner knowing of the power you are placing with them.

People are no different than objects, animals and places. All have a resonance, a 'feeling'. That person that comes to see you has already chosen his healing and how to heal on a subconscious level. He has chosen his remedies, his new settings and environments and ways of perceiving. You are to share those with him and remind him. Ideas will speak to you and jump out at you. These are not just fantasies of the imagination or fleeting 'thoughts'. Sometimes they appear to come out of nowhere—the best place to come out of! Trust is essential and faith, paramount. You are only seeking resonance with object and soul, food and soul, remedy and soul, place and soul. Nothing else is relevant. Most people need something tangible, like a remedy, a solution or taking something out of their life to make it 'real' for them. Use whatever tools they need at the time. As your own faith builds, you will use less and less tooling in your practice. Eventually and simply, by faith, it is healed. Remember, the patient must also share this faith or healing cannot occur so use what you must to assist. You cannot take someone into limitlessness who refuses to go—we have free will.

Speaking the truth

You are not here to please. You are not here to just make money. You are not here to perform. You are not here to appease others with

147

social pleasantries. You are a healer and you have the job of presenting light, truth and limitlessness to the world.

Pleasing others is actually a very selfish endeavor. We are attempting to please others out of a selfish, animalistic need to be 'accepted' as part of the pack, so we go out of our way for that person, putting our own survival at risk. Accept the fact that you will never 'fit in' in a conventional sense and you will stop trying and accept your uniqueness while at the same time, knowing we are all cut from the same cloth. 'Fitting in' requires great sacrifice, suffering and drama. Once you release this, great relief overcomes you and you can finally be Yourself. Ironically, as you do this, others are even more attracted and accepting of you because you serve Yourself first and have no need for approval from outside Yourself. In your presence, they also feel free to be Themselves and for Themselves.

All your material needs will be met because of this integrity but money must not be a primary focus for you. Your passion must be your focus and abundance is always the side effect of passion, integrity and presence. If money is a big concern, simply bring awareness to it and consciously work through it as go you along. The irony is as you focus too intensely on anything, it falls away from you anyway! Ask for it for sure, know it's yours, and then let it go. It will eventually lose importance to you as Self takes over in a stronger and stronger manner over time. You can't help but be ultimately successful in all respects if you listen solely to Self—It is perfect, knows all and Its guidance is flawless—only It can lead you to ultimate abundance.

Some healers almost perform for their patients in an attempt to win approval. You do not have to make someone smile or work to elicit any response from them. You do not have to abide by the rules of society and smile when others are smiling or agree when something doesn't sit well with you. Our survival is seen as literally being part of the pack. This can be subtle and tricky to master as we are brought up with these behaviors and they are well-ingrained. Just observe them when you are able and be diligent with self-honesty. Once you 'don't care anymore' and tell the truth, you become even more 'popular'. For the first time, people know someone is speaking to them with integrity and honesty. They know in their own Self that only the truth can heal.

Speaking in parables

We are all unique and have our own way of communicating that comes through us. Communication occurs in a many and varied fashion and cannot be limited. Sometimes, a 'story' may come to the healer which he must share with the patient. The story is multilayered and speaks to the patient's Spirit, as seemingly irrelevant it may seem to the mind. I have sometimes used stories from my own life to avoid placing direct attention on the sensitive ego of the patient while still 'getting the point across'. One can also use parables to 'awaken' the patient as to what they must now become aware of in terms of egoic fears and tendencies.

One of my healers was an excellent 'story-teller'. She would keep saying certain things or stories over and over, even though I knew she wasn't senile in any way. One such story was her constant mention of 'coming over to visit my house'. For some reason, I found the notion terribly uncomfortable although I loved her and have invited people over to stay in my home in the past. It only dawned on me after I'd surrendered to Higher Self/God, that she was speaking a parable—that I must allow 'God' into my home—my being and my body. She never mentioned it again after I'd come to this realization.

Another story she told me was that someone had offered for her to live in a log cabin by a lake in the mountains. It was so beautiful but it was too far away. However, she could always visit. I recognized immediately (a little wiser to her ways now!) that this was my very own mind's 'dream' of perfection—what I'd always wanted but somehow, was not coming to fruition for me. She was teaching me that perfection does not live in only this type of physical place. Perfection lives where I am and where I am meant to be, which is not ego or mind's choice. Later on, another revelation came to me from this same story. I had actually purchased a ranch in the mountains after this—that is beautiful and far away from my home that I could only visit at the time. The symbolic reference of the ranch to my own life was clear. It symbolized how sustained enlightenment (beauty) I could only visit (during states of heightened awareness), so far away (seemingly unattainable).

Parables can have many layers and each may be revealed when the listener is ready. When using a parable yourself, the mind steps aside and Higher Self will present it or bring it up for you—there's no thinking involved. You will just feel the need to tell it. You may not even understand fully the parable yourself at the time. The patient may not either. They may 'hear' it sometime later as it percolates into them.

Let the story flow from you unimpeded and you'll be amazed at Its wisdom for both yourself and the intended recipient.

Speaking the patient's language

The main message is always the truth and from this you must never waver. However, the way in which you deliver the message can be varied according to the patient's comfort zone. The last thing we want to do is make patients more uncomfortable than they already are with their condition and state of mind. If they are religious, you can easily incorporate religious terminology into your discussion. Not to please them but to better communicate with them the ideas you are conveying. Do so without reservation, as if you have spoken this way all your life and you know (which you do). For example, I often replace intuition with The Holy Spirit or speak of prayer instead of meditation to help with comprehension. You do not need to go out of your way, simply ease your conversation and make a few simple and thoughtful adjustments. Many religious people are wary of religious speech outside of the church and outside of their own preachers. You are not in the business of preaching but in the business of sharing truth. Focus on love first and the right words will come. Do not be afraid to use the word 'God'—use it with confidence and that's all that will be picked up by the patient. This can take practice so be patient and kind to yourself.

You can do the same for children, teenagers, people of different races and backgrounds, even if you don't know a lot about them. Simply be sensitive to the collective consciousness around them. All this is easily accomplished when one is focused and present. You do not need to think before you speak. Allow speech to simply come through you with peace and ease. When you speak with truth during meditation, there are no thoughts. You are channeling in a sense. *It's not you or ego speaking— Self/God is speaking for and through you.*

Speaking to the child

Children must be treated like any other patient. We are so ingrained to think of children as 'less than' that we often talk down to them, fail to listen or take them seriously. I call this kind of treatment toward children the last 'ism'.

Although speech can be altered slightly, just to simplify, maintain your energies' focus on the child, even when speaking and looking at the parent. Even beyond speech, you are speaking to the child's soul and this is healing. I trust all the children that come to see me have 'heard' me in this way. I have actively prayed/meditated on them and seen them in their highest potential—thus their healing comes about. No matter what I 'use' to facilitate this, whether it is dietary changes or remedies etc., I know deep in my soul that only faith heals. The child picks up that faith and, the child is healed.

Even if the parent does not have faith but is as least supportive enough to bring the child into your presence, the child can heal. You must maintain the faith for the child and encourage the parent's faith but it is not necessary. The child *themselves* must maintain this faith as well for healing to occur. If they do, they will remain well despite any outside influences. In these cases, I sometimes find the parent gets 'scared' after the visit because the child is healed—the child has *aligned* themselves with healing. The parent's lack of faith has been shaken in these cases, creating fear, with the child's healing as proof of miracles. Maintain both parent and child at utmost potential in your mind as to their abilities to heal whether they return to you or not.

Often, the child is not the one who needs healing—it's the parent(s) or family. Children often act as reflectors or mirrors of their current environment. In these cases, the focus must be on the parent(s) to recognize the reflection and on the child to release the need to reflect. Allow intuition to guide you as to the true cause and solution. Your eyes or attention will automatically focus and turn to the one needing healing at that moment—do not ignore this as it could come from anyone in the family. Be aware of your body and where it's focusing its attention.

I once had parents that brought in their 10 year old child. The child whined, was uncooperative and was coddled by his father throughout the visit. The father pretended to be very interested but my Spirit knew better. The mother however, was attentive and listening, truly wanting the child to heal. My 'attention' kept looking at the mother and 'ignoring' the child and father who clearly did not want to be there. Although the parents had brought the child in, the only person I could help was the mother so Self focused on her.

If the child is quite young, they tend to reflect more, have less independence from their parents and rely more on their parent's faith for healing. In these cases, although healing can still occur, it's very important to address faith on the part of the parent(s) to *maintain* the healing.

Parents and children

Sometimes, a child will come in doing fine and the parent is worried that they are sick. If you know the child to be well, ask the *child* how they feel (if they are old enough). This helps them to stay in their own power and to get a sense of their own diagnosis. If they say they are well, and you also know they are well, all is well and share that with them. Oftentimes, the parent will want confirmation, so do what you must within reason—kinesiology is one safe and easy way to confirm. However, let the parent know very clearly that you are only doing this to confirm what you and the child already know. Your faith must never waver. If the parent is open, you can then work on the parent to help them eliminate fear and doubt and increase their awareness.

Keep a keen eye and ear on the parent the whole time a child is present as a patient. Children and animals almost always reflect the nature of the household and authority figures within it, as mentioned previously. I often find the underlying issue is not with the child at all—it's with the parent(s). If a parent is willing to deal with underlying issues, you simply change focus to the parent. If not, plant a seed regarding the truth and let them know the child is healthy—on a soul level. Stay in your truth. A parent who is unwilling to deal with their own issues will invariably try to 'offload' (subconsciously) onto the child. Do not allow them to get away with it. Be gentle but the truth must irritate them into self-healing. Also muster personal power within the child so that they no longer reflect the parent. At this point, the relationship has the possibility to change with the focus off the child and onto the parent or family. Sometimes the parent will still be unwilling to heal and will simply choose someone or something else to offload onto. All you can do is hold them high in their potential and keep faith for the child and for those around him.

If the child is old enough, you may want to speak with them on their own. If this is not possible, there are ways to give messages in very gentle and loving ways that clearly get your point across. For example, if there's turmoil in the household regarding parents getting along, speak to the child about staying in his/her own power and remembering Him/Herself amongst any family stress. Remind the child that they are simply picking up on the negative energy in the house and you need to be aware of this, clear it and learn not to take it personally. These are very general statements but with careful and focused meditation, you can speak to the child's soul, no matter how old they are. Sometimes, you will not be able to speak to the child or the parent due to their intense fears around the subject. Simply go into meditation on their departure and connect with the child and/or the parents' souls and send them love from Self. See what it is they are suffering from and what you can do about it, if anything, in terms of distance healing. Listen and follow.

I once had a patient whose son was continually going into severe and uncontrollable diabetic episodes. He was very sickly when he came to see me and I did all the usual of changing his diet and remedy support as they were not open to deeper subjects. Not much changed. At our next visit, a deeper root was revealed and I found out he had injured himself when he was younger. I adjusted him gently and he was testing well afterward. I didn't see him for quite a time as he was doing so well, without any episodes. Then, suddenly, he came in very ill. The mother was angry and accusatory toward me and said she just wanted another adjustment to 'get him better again'. This layer had already been healed and no more work could be done there. I could sense a lot of drama and stress coming from the mother and despair from the child. I asked what was going on right now in the mother's life and she said she had just left her husband and broke down in tears. Suddenly the picture became entirely clear to me that this child was simply subconsciously trying to get his parents attention away from stress and drama and he had to resort to extreme illness to do so—they were not allowing the abundance (sugar) of love that was already right before them, into their lives. I saw in my visions that the husband was a good man and this woman was simply never satisfied, always wanting more. She had had a neglectful childhood and had never dealt with her issues, placing them firmly on her husband. I told her what I had seen and she went into hysteria but no denial and stormed out of the room. She didn't like that I'd discovered her 'secret'. I knew I could do nothing for the mother at that time—her fear was too intense and the drama, too addictive. I looked at the child and told him he must not take on the family's pain and drama. That he must see this for what it is only and become an observer. He must love himself first and cease taking on their issues of lack of abundance—they were caught in their own suffering for which he had a choice whether to participate or not in. He had to know on a deep level that it was his choice whether he chose to be sick or not. He must now take back his power. The child didn't understand me on a mind level—most people won't—but I knew he got it on a soul level— he was listening. Of course, I never saw the family again. The grandmother of the patient however, told me that the parents got back together and the child was now doing fine.

Sometimes, parents have been told by other health care practitioners that the child has this or that diagnosis and there's nothing more to be done about it. They've been given a dire label with no hope of recovery. This tends to be the most challenging aspect of recovery—eliminating this 'curse' from the parent(s) minds. We can use these systems in place to inform us and help us within their limitations to do so but we must never buy into prognosis, statistics, labels and limitations for ourselves or our loved ones. To do so is to take away our very right to heal—no one can determine that for us except Ourselves. You may have to spend quite a bit of time reinforcing this concept to weed away this negativity from the parent(s) and to help them see a new way or other possibilities.

Work within their scope. Some patients have more faith than others but this can be cultivated over time and with patience. You as a healer must always keep your own faith very high so they have at least have it available to them.

Sometimes a child will be sick and deny illness. Sometimes teenagers will be involved with illicit behaviors and drugs which you will know of intuitively right away. They may even believe *themselves* that they are not doing anything incorrectly, such is where they are in their fearful vibrations. If the child chooses to heal, treat as necessary. If not, approach the parent and child together. In a gentle way, inform the parent and the child of the path they are heading toward so they are least aware. This is not to scare the child; it's simply to place responsibility in the correct areas again. There is no judgment of the child as his path may require suffering but the parent must understand their role and release their responsibility for the child as well—to allow them the 'space' to heal or suffer as they choose. This is the most difficult part for parents so be patient and compassionate. You will know what can be done to help heal or improve the situation and this you must share with both of them. Uphold faith for the child always, regardless of their decision, and share this with the parent but be clear about expectations as it is after all, the child's life and choice.

Channeling and mediumship

It is only ever beneficial for you to 'channel' positive energy. This means channeling your Higher Self or God/Universe essentially. Angels, guides, masters etc. are all extensions of you in a higher realm and channeling them can be very helpful to you and others however, focus must eventually 'come back home' to You. These are never separate entities that simply invade our bodies once in a while. We must realize these Gods and Goddesses are truly Ourselves and we must manifest them permanently into our lives and into this reality.

It is never beneficial to channel lower or negative energies, entities, fear or spirits. Channeling fear simply attracts more fear and low vibratory energy, causing you eventually to become quite ill and scaring patients, without any healing effect. Ask again to just *know* instead of feel fear or have fear take over your body. There is no place in your high vibrating vessel for fear, nor can you heal with it. I know my patients' fears and they are displayed to me if they serve a purpose in their healing—if there's some information they need to know that will help them *out* of fear. I simply 'read' them. I cannot help them if I go *into* their fears. I must maintain an unaffected yet high vibratory frequency in their presence in order to help them heal.

When you are tuned in, present, focused and relaying only love, you are always 'channeling' God/Higher Self.

Automatic writing

Although this is more of a personal tool rather than something done during a visit, it can help you and your patients uncover deep truths about themselves and train you both to become connected to Self and to listen only to the One Voice. I like using my computer to just journal out any thoughts, fears, questions and then have Me answer, without thought interfering. Anyone can do this and you'd be amazed at what comes out and what guidance, love and assurance is provided. It is an active form of prayer and it's important for anyone to access when on the spiritual path. Self is after all, all-knowing and your best friend. Why not open the lines of communication?

Speak no evil

You are not seeking to be 'pure' or to 'behave yourself' in a worldly sense—you must speak with childlike honesty and innocence even if it's not 'accepted'. However, work at refraining from speaking ill of anyone or thing, not out of some fear of karmic return or punishment but out of damage and injury to your own Self. If the fish is in the school, each fish affects the others, (including itself) in the collective consciousness. Clear and release any ill will toward others you may have as it only affects you as it is ultimately directed toward you in the first place. Remember, only *you* can create in your reality. If others speak ill of you, disrespect you or confront you, see beyond their illness and into their soul. Release their negativity back to them to deal with for themselves as it's not really your business. It cannot affect you unless you allow it to. To be clear healers, we must become unaffected. Many people assume this means indifference or lack of caring. One can still care, be kind and compassionate without being affected in any way to what's happening around you. This takes practice and diligence as the present observer. A healer never feels sorry for him/herself or takes anything personally. This will only serve to weaken you and those around you.

The power of silence

Those of us in authority are taught to say much and listen little. A good healer does the opposite. It's not that you can't use your voice as a tool—as a communicator it comes in handy! Silence does not always mean quieting your speaking, it means silencing the relentless chatter from the mind and the egoic fears running through you so that you can channel love and higher forces and speak the truth. Sometimes I would speak ceaselessly throughout a visit and at other times, say very little.

Silence means pure listening without thought. It's the deep thought below everyday mind and its ramblings—it's the thought you simply know as the truth within you. Do not censor it. Practice knowing, recognizing and speaking the truth from this place—the deep, private, quiet, still place within You. Practice this with patients as you lay ego and mind aside and enter meditation for every one of them during every moment. Only healing can occur when you are purely present. Words will simply come to you without thought, mind or ego. You will simply be the speaker without agenda, without expectation. You become the channel for Self.

You don't have to listen to a litany of complaints or distractions the whole visit—your words must be aptly and carefully placed so as to allow the patient to stay on track. You are not here to appease the ramblings of their ego and fears. Knowing when to speak and the allowance of speech from Within is vital to healing. Speak what is deep Within and your words will work like miracles as they stir up fears and dis-ease out into open view. Many times your messages will have many meanings for the soul and you are only ever speaking to the soul when you heal. You do not have time, nor effort to pay attention to the ego or the stiff logic of the mind. Go in gently with a light heart and without expectations—keep your words loving and gentle. This will come naturally as you listen inwardly to the truth of the situation. When a patient is connecting with you, there is no need for words, only silence and listening on your part. Don't listen so much to their words per se but to their soul, their body language, their eyes, their energies—use your senses to know them. After you hear what they are communicating to you for their healing, go then even deeper into their soul and see their beauty, potential and what they have ultimately come to you for. Then go in and deliver it.

Dreams and Visions

The dreamer of the dream is dreaming . . . always dreaming.
What you see is not real.
What you know from Within is real and is also what you really see . . .

Dreams

Michael Talbot sums dreams up beautifully in his book, The Holographic Universe when he writes about psychiatrist Montague Ullman:

> *"During the course of his practice Ullman noticed that when one of his patients failed to recognize or accept some truth about himself, that truth would surface again and again in his dreams, in different metaphorical guises and linked with different related experiences from his past, but always in an apparent attempt to offer him new opportunities to come to terms with the truth."* [10]

Visions and dreams are very similar and function in a similar manner. One occurs when one is awake (vision) and one occurs when one is asleep (dreams). They are forms of deep communication with the soul and Self and they communicate to us our true issues. Continual practice in dreams and visions leads to deep understanding and healing connection. In this sense, dreams are more real than our waking life.

Visions

Visions are not special in any way and anyone can have one. An accurate vision requires presence (focus) and zero distraction. One can have vivid visions or symbolic visions, waking or dreaming. Having a vision is as simple as:

• Asking permission (from your Higher Self) to have visions for healing reasons and assistance.
• Quieting the mind completely into stillness. Closing the eyes in a quiet setting or during meditation is helpful.
• Having no fear around the subject. Being fully present and calm.
• Watching your vision with unaffectedness or as an observer.

---

[10] Talbot, Michael, *The Holographic Universe*. New York: HarperCollins Publishing, 1992: 62.

- Speaking, writing or otherwise communicating your vision in some way to the patient or to yourself until the vision changes or displays a scene of 'finality'.

All these steps take practice but can be done. A person becomes more clairvoyant as they clear their own issues and subconscious fears and literally practices being clairvoyant. A safe and easy way to practice is by doing so with a friend that you trust. Set aside practice time to sit with the friend and go into meditation with them. Then speak whatever thoughts come to you. The friend can then give you feedback on your intuitive session. You can even practice being more precise by envisioning or intuiting certain objects in another room or in a box on in the other person's mind. Aura reading, reading tea leaves and positive oracle cards, palm reading, muscle testing, dowsing etc. are just a few of the many ways you can practice with others or on your own.

I once sat before a teacher. Although respectful, my childlike self bounded toward the teacher to relay a story. I had just remembered her from a vision I had and felt bound to tell her about it. I was also very nervous because I knew that if I was guided to share something, it was coming from a place of power—from my true Self and goodness knows what would come out of my mouth! 'I remember you from a dream many years ago! Now I know why I had to come here to see you! I need to thank you for saving my life! You told me I was sick and dying and I was so distraught that I begged for mercy and said I'd do anything for my life. You said I needed to study every day and from that day forward I committed to my spiritual journey.' My innocent words were met with complete shock and silence. I was excited before to tell her but it seemed she didn't understand me so I sheepishly sat down. I felt so embarrassed, I asked the person beside me what I had said to cause such a reaction. 'You just told her about herself. That vision was also about her. She's sick.' I had shocked even myself as I had no idea the effect my story would have or what this teacher's story was. I just knew I had to tell it as I was commanded to from Within. Through the parable of my story, something was shaken in myself and in her—we were both the receivers of the message from the Divine. Self told me that both she and I had not forgiven ourselves which was why we were 'sick'. We had accepted 'punishment' for our 'sins' and I was telling us both through that story to be cheerful and that we're worthy—that we must fight for life or it will be taken.

Visions are very powerful because they speak to us on a soul level even if we don't understand them on any other level. Both parties in this case had received from this vision, even though on the surface it seemed shocking or socially inappropriate. Out of innocence, truth will be spoken.

I still don't understand this vision fully and I may never because I cannot grasp the depths of it—it is not understandable to the mind. Who can understand forgiveness? It is not from the mind. But, through the sharing of innocent love and the *energy* of forgiveness, peace enters for both of us from somewhere beyond the mind. The need to understand is then forgotten as all that's necessary is peace. And peace can only come to us through this very moment—no past, no future, just now.

Life is entirely symbolic and beautiful because of its symbolism. Speak your truth, even though it may take great courage to do so. You may have a chance to help save someone's life—or even your own. In this manner, we are all connected and no interaction between us is unimportant or meaningless.

Visions of these types can be symbolic or actual depending on the situation/person. Symbolic visions are very important in relaying to the conscious mind the true nature of the issue. They can at first appear nonsensical or like a fantasy to the logical mind. Be open and allow intuition to guide you as to their true meaning. Usually, they are quite literal in their meaning. This is usually easier to do for someone else than for yourself but with practice o

n yourself, this too can become simple. Ask for assistance when needed from Higher Self/God. You may also use your tools such as muscle testing, dowsing or cards to assist you. Symbolic visions speak in parables and one must be in meditation, have confidence and no fear to interpret correctly.

Asking permission for visions is foremost and can be done silently as part of your routine and of course, must include the patient. You will know if a patient is not ready for this type of soul communication and there is no point in pushing the matter. Treat palliatively as guided if this is the case.

You will know when you are finished as no more visions will come to you and you will have a sense of finality to the session. Often, once the soul has 'gotten the message', the vision will immediately change to a bright, joyful and loving scene where all is well. In my visions, my patients would look toward the 'Sun' (God/Higher Self) while sitting on my 'healing bench' (seeing the truth and healing), petting a little white dog (unconditional love) when the healing for the day was finished. These symbols in the vision were not premeditated on my part but simply arose naturally from the Self and became markers or guideposts as to where we were at energetically at any given moment. Your own guideposts will be unique to you but you will understand them.

I would also see a blue light whenever angels were making their presence known to me. It came to be a symbol for me to allow God/Universe/angels to take over now when I saw it.

In some cases, it may take a while and several visions before full effect takes place. Be patient and wait for your cue. If the soul is left unsettled even with your best efforts to communicate, it could be because:

- You have the issue yourself and need to clear it.
- The patient is not ready for the communication but for some reason needs to hear it now for future healing.

In these cases, ask yourself during the session if this is your issue as well and it can be easily cleared in the patient's presence openly or discretely depending on your relationship. If the patient is not ready for the communication, ask for Higher Self to show you in the vision what you can do to palliate for now. Send them loving and protective energy so that their healing occurs with peace, ease and Godspeed. It is helpful to also use this in conjunction with other diagnostic and treatment tools you have acquired.

It is paramount that the mind is quiet or vision will be muddled, confused and difficult. This is perhaps the most challenging part of the procedure—ignoring the ramblings of the mind and its tendencies to stray. Too often, we don't believe what we see because we don't understand it. It's still the truth albeit symbolic. Ask as well what can be verbally communicated and what can be simply healed through soul communication. Do not doubt what you are seeing in the vision—the vision is always correct—and the vision will stabilize. Sometimes you may even have patients that challenge your visions which can be distracting and create doubt. Do not be swayed. With compassion yet firmness of confidence, stick to what you see. You and the patient may never fully understand it on a mind level but your souls will. There have been times in my practice while relaying a symbolic vision which neither myself nor the patient understood, the patient would clear the issue anyway as confirmed through kinesiology. You don't always have to interpret the visions—they are simply there for you to relay. If a meaning comes to you *from Within*, share it, otherwise, let it be.

If a student is aware, have them go into receiving their own visions.

This can take practice and patience on both your parts but if a student is ready, visions will come. It's extremely empowering for a student to have their own visions and see the truth *for* themselves, from *within* themselves.

If you are nervous or have fear, visions will either simply not appear or be difficult and confusing. Do not attempt visualizing when you are in this state as you will create further fear and confusion for yourself and/or the patient. Practice first with patients/friends you are comfortable with and regularly with yourself to develop your skill and confidence. I even ask my own children to go into their visions and tell me what they see.

Sometimes visions can be shocking and even grotesque or disturbing. Some visions are extremely pleasant. Do your best not to indulge and keep watching as an observer only. Do not get caught up in any drama. Watch your tendency to crave drama or indulge in it. This only distracts from the truth and healing. Sometimes the vision is not necessarily actual but symbolic and through fearlessness, this will easily be extracted.

Most clairvoyants vocalize what they see. This is usually fine as long as they have loving and healing intent and the patient is ready for the message. However, some clairvoyants are caught in the dramas of fear and the occult and subconsciously enjoy fear, leading much of the vision toward fear and the negative. These are not true visions but only reflections of the patient's fears or egoic tendencies. This is in no way helpful or healing and can even be detrimental. Remember no one can determine your future as all things are your choice and you have an infinite number of choices before you. A vision simply communicates to the soul what is needed for healing at *this moment in time*. It is a form of deep, loving, unconditional understanding.

A patient may feel fear in your presence as you bring up certain subjects or relay certain messages. Treat all subjects with the same unaffected nature and compassion. None need to be dwelled upon and all is healed as the truth is revealed to the conscious mind. Allow the patient to do their own healing through your positive and loving support. It is not your job to please them or 'take away fears'. They must learn through your guidance to also become unaffected and fearless.

Visions can interchange between 'knowing' and actual visions—they are really one and the same. As you practice clairvoyance, eventually no formalities will be needed and you will just 'know' in your mind's eye without having an actual vision per se.

Auric visions

Another type of vision is auric visions. These are visions (usually of colour) that appear around a person, animal or object. In meditation, you may see your own aura or colours in front of your eyes, that seem to 'pulsate' or appear like a heatwave. Take note of the colours as they represent your chakra strengths. Usually one sees the physical aura which is closest to the body but one can also tune into the mental, emotional and spiritual auras. Sometimes other entities (angels) can be seen in this manner and may appear during certain situations. I would see a blue light often when treating patients and sometimes before sleep or randomly during the day. I knew this to be an angelic presence. The light was there to remind me of the support, assistance and protection I have.

If I tuned into a patient's aura, you can see or intuit the colours. You can tell if the colours are bright and pulsating well that they are healthy in that area. If the aura is muddy or darker and has poor pulsation, they are unhealthy. A crack or darkness in the aura indicates severe illness or potential death if not corrected. Over the course of the spiritual journey the aura colours can change or new colours are added.

Visions of all kinds are a handy tool that can be used anytime and anywhere—practice with them regularly so the dreamer can master the dream!

Recurring dreams

Dreams that occur over and over or at least have a repeating theme remind us of what we haven't dealt with. Usually the meaning is symbolic and you must meditate on its meaning for you or for others. They are very important indicators of where you are at at this stage. I used to always dream that I was always late for my flight and couldn't decide on the clothes to put in my suitcase. This was symbolic for perfectionism, impatience and fear of loss of control.

Sometimes, a patient will come to you in a dream or they will enter your thoughts quite a bit. If it is a recent patient, you may need to address an issue that is arising for you around them (that's affecting you personally). For example, they may be triggering some fear or unresolved issue within you when they visited. Otherwise, it may be something you've simply forgotten to do or inform them of. Meditate on it and the answer will come in the silence. This 'knowing' comes from deep Within You and is undeniable. We may try to rationalize but the truth lay before us in our deeper sense of knowing. Many times, we do not want to look there as it brings up issues for us—pride, 'mistakes', teachings and learnings, our past etc. that disturb us or reflect us on a subconscious level. Be brave and look for both yourself and your patient. Only good can come out of this humility.

Other times, patients, friends, family etc. will come to you from the past, unannounced. This usually signals to you that they are 'calling you' and may need your help. This is almost always spiritual and the nature of the dream or vision will usually give you a clue. Oftentimes, the patient or person will physically reappear as well into your practice or life somehow. Regardless, you must still address the issue that's arising on a spiritual plane. Go into meditation and speak to their soul. Just this reassurance, support and acknowledgment are often all that's needed. Be gentle and know that power extends far beyond the physical. Send love to them which heals all and sets them back on their path.

If the patient is lingering (in mind or in dreams) they are usually 'lost and needy', you have developed a dependent relationship with them or you have some fear around the subject matter the patient brings up for you. They are literally being allowed to invade your personal space. With unconditional love, this nagging connection must be severed to allow for their own inner work (and yours) to be done alone. You cannot enable them which is what they are asking of you. This attachment sucks you dry of life force energy and will fatigue you. A healer must always save his/her energy in order to be powerful.

Symbolic dreams

Often a dream or vision will appear to make 'no sense' to the logical mind and is usually symbolic in nature. It's very helpful to write or talk about the dream to someone supportive or even just to yourself! By speaking about it, you will often come to an awareness of its meaning all on your own. Otherwise, meditation can help you. It's important to practice interpreting your own dreams as it strengthens intuition and confidence. The true meaning of a dream may not come to you immediately, perhaps not for many years. By asking Self for help, the help swiftly comes and some trigger (often something someone says or does, how they listen to you, some event or your own correct timing), will bring on its meaning. Release the 'need to know' and it will come to you more easily.

Actual dreams

Sometimes a dream or vision is actually what's going on in your life, in the future or in the past. It may signal something you still need to address or acknowledge. Write, speak or meditate about it for clarity. Sometimes you will have actual visitations from beings from other realms (ex. Angels and guides) or see those you love as present. In these dreams they 'come to you' so to speak in a form of vivid dreaming.

Often I would have guides or angels visit me this way to show me support or bring me messages of guidance. Sometimes someone from my past would appear and an old or forgotten memory would be shown. In this case I would know that that memory needed to be cleared.

Vivid dreams

Vivid dreams are what are described as astral travelling, having out-of-body experiences (OBE's) or as remote viewing. Your Spirit is translocating and you are literally viewing another reality. It is as real as what you are doing right now and can come during sleep or meditation or near death/trauma. You can also learn to command it at will to come and go as you please. By mastering vivid dreams, one can master all realities and this life merely becomes a 'game', mastered by Self-will. However, resist the temptation to get caught up in the act itself—vivid dreams occur for a purpose guided by Self. To indulge in vivid dreams just for their sake is to entertain the ego and stray from one's path. There is no 'better' reality than where you are right now and you must align yourself with this heaven on earth. If I'm told to physically travel to a certain place, I do so. If I'm told to astrally travel to a certain place, I do so. To travel in any way for ego's sake is to ignore your purpose. All things in life have Ultimate purpose and this must be respected.

Sometime very gifted spiritual students will see you and have a great deal of trouble being in this reality—they simply love to fly off to other worlds and it becomes addictive. Remind them of their purpose here on earth and that they are simply not *seeing* the exquisite beauty of this reality—they are truly missing out!

Vivid dreams can occur through 'daydreaming' or during wake times while doing something mundane or repetitive, just before falling asleep, in meditation or just upon waking. These visions at first are very brief flashes but are very real and vivid. As one masters focus and releases fear, these visions can be sustained and even the ability to be transported to their actual location can be achieved through intense focus. We are unlimited beings and time and space cannot limit our purpose here.

These astral travels may seem to have no meaning in the sense that you are just 'visiting' or 'looking around' with seemingly no particular aim or objective in mind. You can sometimes confuse a symbolic vision, revelation or inspiration for astral travel, leading to frustration as you search to 'understand' or make sense of what you've just seen. I once was looking for a new house in reality. In the following days I had several 'visions' of different houses. At first, I was confused thinking the house I had seen in the vision was the one I was to purchase. After I saw the second, a different house, I knew I was simply 'looking around'. Interestingly, these were actual houses I had seen before. Because we can literally translocate, my mind was going where I was thinking. It had no real meaning—I was just viewing remotely.

During meditation, I had a vivid dream of flying toward lush, green mountains near the ocean. The Self was imprinting a strong visual memory and a passion for me of what could be in my future. These types of dreams only usually occur during sleep and we rarely remember them. Through practice meditation, we can remember our dreams effectively and achieve very clear and vivid messaging through them.

Manipulation of the dream

We have all heard the notion that we are living in a dream. You are the dreamer and the dreamed but you have forgotten this. If you are the dreamer, you control the dream and this is what you and your patients ultimately must practice as this realization (even if only in a small part of one's life), is the key to healing. First change perspective, then reality will change by that inertia. If you change the settings or props in the dreams (perspective), it follows that your reality or dream (life) will then also be different. All this you can do at will. Your sleeping dreams are interesting because they actually offer a glimpse into reality, bubbling up from the subconscious mind to remind you that you are the dreamer and you must change the dream before it consumes you and you are living in a nightmare.

The tangibles of everyday life seem to stump and stop us from constantly seeing this perspective from that of the dreamer. With practice, even a trip to the bank or changing a diaper can be seen as a dream. Have fun playing with this! You can imagine any day you like and how it could be and watch it unfold that way. Although you can't create in someone else's reality (dream), you can often influence them in a positive way. If you know you cannot be harmed, that it's only a dream, what would you do? Live that and your life will be paradise.

Why is it that some individuals can train themselves to feel no pain, bleed or suffer? Why is it that some people can move objects around easily as through telekinesis? Or levitation? Or telepathy? Or simply by disappearing? There have been many such unexplained so-called paranormal events throughout history. It's as simple as a change in perspective—realizing that you are the dreamer in the dream and the dream is yours to dream up literally anything you like within it. Don't be fooled by illusions of limitation. Anyone who's dreamt knows they can fly.

Alternate Realities

There is nothing that lies beyond this reality.
*It's just that you don't see, as of yet, all of **this** reality.*

Power Spots

Nothing major has to be adopted for a change in perspective. However, at times, and if permanent change is requested, you must sometimes assume a completely different location and surrounding to help you literally launch out of old ways of being.

We are all aware of times when we have visited a place that felt 'surreal' as if we could have easily seen other realities and done extraordinary things within that location. Most of the time, these places are in nature.

Visiting the remote area of Haida Gwaii, my partner and I experienced something of this type of major reality shift. The old growth forests have a timeless feeling, almost like time doesn't exist for them. The whole island felt this way—cut off from the rest of so-called reality, creating another reality entirely of its own. Sitting in the forest, one could 'feel' the giant, ancient trees and their wisdom, as if they were speaking to us. Here, the existence of fairies and other mythical creatures did not seem at all far-fetched.

Stone circles, certain land formations such as mountains or deserts, water and rivers, valleys, hills and mountains can all signify power spots. A power spot elicits a certain surreal feeling within you—it is a place of significance for you and this feeling must not be denied. Aside from being just nostalgia or 'liking' a place, a power spot may have no real esthetic beauty at all (although, they often do). What matters is the energy around the spot and its draw for you as a healer. They are places of healing, of intense energy and of limitlessness. A healer must always choose the correct power spot within which to heal—even within a city, town or dwelling. The place must wholeheartedly feel right and speak to you. Then, your presence and love for the place will increase its power, augmenting your ability to heal and stay present. A healer cannot afford to reside in anything that distracts from his focus.

When you are 'finished' with the power place, it's time to move on. Often we are taught that to be comfortable and successful, we must simply buy a nice house in nice surroundings, with a nice car, with our possessions and family and die in front of our TV set some day. This is not conducive to growth and change as all things are dynamic. This does

167

not on the other hand mean we are restless either, never reaching satisfaction or feeling at home. However, we must at all times listen to inner imperatives of whether to stay in one spot, leave or simply vacate for a while. Remember, your outer world reflects your inner and as you change, so it changes. It is not uncommon for students to change locations many times due to inner change.

Many people flock to 'holy sites' or 'sacred sites' to feel presence and change reality. Not only do the places themselves hold physical properties that are similar such as remoteness, uniqueness and certain physical electromagnetisms, vibrations or 'vortices' but they are viewed by the collective as 'special' or 'gateways' and then therefore *become* so since we create our own realities through our perceptions.

These spots can greatly affect one's perceptions in general and help to tear away unwanted fears and stuck perceptions of reality. Use them as tools to take a new perspective 'back home with you'. It's not to be left there at that location but energetically spread out so that all of humanity can eventually see their own limitlessness. Staying in these places for some is necessary. However, beware of the need to *escape* by hiding and becoming the recluse or hermit within them or 'finding other kindred spirits' that will 'understand you' amidst these places. Follow only your own inner imperatives. In these times, healers are not to hide away from the rest of the world or to add yet another label by joining and identifying only with spiritual groups but to bring their wisdom and learning outward and into the world in a gentle way. Take your retreats as necessary for resetting, prayer, meditation and the release of limitations but always return to the world still in it but not of it. You can go to the grocery store while seeing limitlessness and potential in all you meet. Use every opportunity as a meditation for you—the picking and choosing of fruit and food as sacred, the connection with the people you meet and even the building that houses this abundance as sacred. You can still be 'real' and not 'out there' with this endeavor. Just choose to see everything with joy, humor, ease and sacredness as it truly is—like a child. As this presence infiltrates the rest of the world, we will soon forget it was any other way.

Entities

When you first begin healing work, many things will be a mystery and many things you will learn from. When I first began, I was very frightened of 'other worlds and realms', 'ghosts' and the 'unseen', especially being so logically and formally educated. I never thought I'd eventually get used to it! As you work on constantly staying present and focused, your clarity increases and the boundaries defining this world and others (or rather, other *possibilities*), fades. You become lighter, lucid and able to communicate on subtle levels. We all have these gifts and it is in no way 'special'. They only need to be tuned and allowed for.

Entities, shadows, ghosts or spirits as they are sometimes labeled are commonplace and nothing to be feared as they are illusory and have no power over you or anyone else for that matter. As your clarity increases, you will feel them and even see them if you choose. You are all-powerful and nothing can harm you except any fear you allow to overtake you. Mastery with entities takes time and practice. As for all things, accept the fear you may feel in their presence but do not allow it to overtake you—simply observe. Go into meditation and ask what the purpose for you feeling or seeing them is—ask them 'what they want'.

Entities can present in many forms. Sometimes it's a chill, a touch or simply a knowing. Sometimes it's visual such as shadows or movement out of the corner of your eye, lights, auras or coloured orbs. They can sometimes come as sounds, voices or ringing in the ears. They can even elicit certain odours or smells. Animals and small children will often sense their presence as well and may talk about them. Entities may also have a liking or an aversion to specific areas.

The spirit can also be a visitor to support you from another realm such as a relative or angel or it can be a fear. Depending on your disposition or tendencies toward the positive or negative, those types of entities will be around you. Always ask Yourself through meditation or focus what the entity wants of you. An entity can be positive and beneficial and trying to give you a message, an intuition or even a life-changing inspiration. If the entity appears 'dark' in vision or feeling to you, it usually is. They may hang around in specific areas or follow you around. They cannot 'do' anything to you and are usually hanging around simply because no one has asked them to leave. You have not addressed the underlying fears that have *attracted them to you in the first place*—don't forget that you create your entire reality. Take responsibility—they are here for a reason. Clear yourself of fear through awareness of why you are fearful or help the entity leave through loving prayer.

An entity can exist in a particular location due to a past event or emotion that occurred at that particular location. The vibration can stay there and linger and be picked up by those who are more sensitive and open. Sometimes, a patient can 'linger' past their visit if you share fears, some healing needs to be finished or they are just lost souls.

An entity can also sit with or within a patient, almost imperceptibly at times, only to be revealed when the patient is ready for their release. We have classically called this 'possession' but it's simply a memory that has not been removed from the person—a trauma, event, person etc. whose vibration is still very real and present to that patient on a soul level. In this manner, they are not being fully present as they are literally dragging their past along and all its baggage with them. I have even seen physical dis-ease in patients be entirely related to someone else's issue. Your knowledge of this stagnation in a patient can be just a feeling, a knowing or other cues aforementioned.

No entity can exist in the presence of love and light as it is too bright for it and it will either go to the Source automatically (vibrate with the light) or it will scurry back to its dark hiding place (vibrate with the dark), usually back with its owner. If you have some fears that are similar to it, it will linger in your presence. Rituals help such as smudging or clearing of some kind. Thank the entity as it is there to remind you there is something you need to deal with. Go into meditation to go directly to the Source and deal with the soul itself, talking with it and 'clearing it of fear'—as you also clear yourself at the same time. Sometimes you may feel a chill run through you—this is simply fear leaving *you* (which can happen any time you release fear, not just in the presence of entities). As you do this for yourself, you also do it for the 'owner' of the fear, dead or alive, near or far.

Essentially, a negative entity is a 'dis-ease' in another realm that can make itself manifest physically within this one. It can be born of a thought, a feeling or anything negative and fearful. It settles into the physical body and is made real. Once this occurs, the body simply acts as a host for the mind's fears—often appearing physically as parasites or lingering infections—any chronic dis-ease can be due to an entity. The only true and permanent cure is the healing of the mind of its fears. Once all fears are removed and healed (seen from their proper perspective), there can exist no dis-ease.

Entities that exist within a person are literally like parasites whether they appear as actual parasites or not. They are extremely common and can be revealed anywhere on one's journey. Our 'possessions' can seem so natural as to go undetected until we reach the deepest parts of ourselves. One's parents almost always exist within us to a degree—we pick up their tendencies and behaviors that become physically reflected in our DNA. It can take years of self-reflection to even recognize this type of 'possession' and through awareness it can be released. Tendencies from past lives can also show up in the same manner and because we are so used to them, can elude both patient and healer. One must have the ultimate goal of releasing all attachments to all things and people across time to truly become Ourselves.

'Poltergeists'

Anyone can move objects (telekinesis) as this is just another limitless gift we have forgotten (like levitating and astral travel). No one from another realm can move objects around—only you can do that in the land of the living! It's an exciting thing when people are doing this because it means they are opening up to their spiritual gifts and potentials. All too often however, they fall prey to the common and false philosophy that it's somehow evil and not within their control.

I knew a young man whose coffee maker would start and have coffee ready for him every morning! Why would this be something to be afraid of?! Like radio waves, the mind is very powerful and sends out strong and very real energetic and vibratory messages to everything around it—a coffee maker is no exception as it will respond just like anything else to life force. I can call my partner into the room or have him call me on the phone with my mind which works the same way.

These things are commonplace and are not honored and used properly when they are made out to be rare, a freak show or something to be feared. We also never believed we'd fly airplanes and now huge pieces of metal are up in the sky! If everyone believed that no one could swim, we'd think it was really out there if someone came along and did the backstroke in front of us.

When you understand what these things are and when they become commonplace, the fear around them dissolves.

I find it interesting that poltergeist activity seems to occur more so around young teenagers. At this point in their development, they are experiencing huge shifts in consciousness and vibration, not to mention changes in hormones. They are also often quite angry. Anger is fear in action. It is a motivator with a strong energy that can literally move objects if focused. Of course, most of these teenagers are not aware that this phenomenon is actually of their own making and they tend to 'freak' themselves out. (Perhaps this explains their collective obsession with horror movies as a way to explain these occurrences to themselves).

Remaining unaffected (neither fearful nor fascinated) while any 'paranormal' event is told to you is key. Show the patient a different perspective and all fear is dissolved. Once we learn to consciously harness these abilities we become masters of the physical world. The dreamer of the dream is limitless.

'Extraterrestrials'

E.T.'s are entities from other realms or 'planets'. When I was pregnant with my third child, I kept having vivid dreams and waking visions about perpetual machines, pyramids, numbered sequences and coordinates and felt I was clearly 'downloading' instructions for something important but for which we have no present day reference for here on earth. I felt as though I were being relayed complex information from another world or dimension and it felt vital that I record it somewhere within myself. Although I've had this experience, I've had no conscious personal contact with an actual extraterrestrial myself. It seems that most people that have, however, describe that they are peaceful and relay the message of world peace.

Many people describe 'orbs of light' and then seeing an E.T. Entities come in all shapes, sizes, forms and energetic vibrations of light and darkness – perhaps E.T.'s are simply a variation on this theme.

We must remember however, that we are created in the image of the Divine Self and there is nothing and no being that trumps that. We are literally Masters of the Universe and therefore, have nothing to fear and need not pursue 'dominance' because of this, over anyone or anything. Our power, we must respect.

Animal messages

Although anything in life can provide us with a message (numbers, 'coincidences', people, objects etc.) animals deserve special mention as they are so alive, prevalent in nature and efficient in their messaging to us. Most people never stop to really listen to the coyotes that howl at certain times or wonder why they keep hitting deer on the road. Traditional native cultures had a clear understanding of animal symbols, spirits and guides. They knew they were highly intelligent creatures here to guide us, warn us and provide symbols and omens to us. When you start opening yourself up to this world, a whole new world literally becomes available to you—the animal or totem realm.

I have many animal stories but here, I'll relay just a few for example. When I first bought my ranch, I kept seeing owls. Ever since I had bought the place, my right eye had been red and irritated. I could not see something, that much I knew, but I was not ready at that moment to understand what it meant. One day, I saw a great horned owl up close. His yellow eyes stared right into my soul and he was not afraid. He kept winking his right eye at me which I understood as a sign or omen right away. Then, I saw his aura emanating out from him like ripples on a pond—a beautiful wave of peaceful energy. I then felt peaceful myself and thanked him. That winter, it finally came to me (after the assistance of owl) that I needed to move from my house to the ranch. My eye then stopped bothering me at that realization.

At my office in town, my office manager and I kept seeing crows. We knew they were the messengers from the spirit world and because crows are so good at communicating, they were there to tell us something (crows are not always relaying messages about death). One day, a friend of mine said she saw two crows noisily fighting over the rooftop of the office but then they flew off together in harmony. I knew this was an omen and I felt uneasy. The very next day, a conflict arose in my life that affected my soul deeply. It resolved itself but left me entirely changed for the better as old fears were finally released.

Animals, like anything else in life, are here to teach us and bring messages or omens to us. Nothing is ever 'bad'—all is here for our learning. Animals are not just here to balance nature and the ecosystems and to provide us with food. They are integral parts of Ourselves and our collective Selves. Like children, nothing goes unnoticed with them and they are highly reflective of what's going on with us. Pay attention to the signs and know they are always more than coincidental.

Past, Present and Future

You cannot gather the past or the future but you can gather the present.
You can only gather what's here.

The past

Past lives is really a technically inaccurate term as there really is no such thing as the past—it does not exist. Only the present exists. The past can be perceived like a continuation of an eternal film or movie that the soul is playing over and over in different realms at the same time. The soul can be in many so-called places and many so-called times at once, learning different things and playing out different roles but it's all happening 'now'. For example, if a spirit/entity is seen from another realm, it means there is still fear for that person in the realm they are in now—the film is simply playing this negative feedback loop over and over again. When a spirit goes back to the Source, *it goes back to its owner in present time*, with that fear eliminated from them. In this manner, we can go back to all our 'past lives' and clean up all our fears so we aren't 'haunting' anyone anymore or ourselves for that matter, with fear (in some circles this is called 'soul retrieval').

If there are past life issues, deal with them like you would any other never-well-since trigger and move on. The semantics over what is a past life, is it real or not etc. are not relevant for the purposes of healing. What is relevant is the *symbolism* that past lives (i.e. a particular past life and/or its events) represent for the person healing *now*. Oftentimes upon hearing even a small detail about a past life, the patient will start healing around that issue. It's irrelevant *how* healing is accomplished but perception changes are relevant for healing to occur and we use what is necessary to change the mind. Don't get caught up in fascination with past lives—all that's important is the present.

In many cases I have found patients coming to me that don't know why they are so sad, angry, irritated, have certain symptoms that seem inexplicable or just can't seem to heal no matter what they've tried. These cases are unique in that they often involve past life traumas or karma that has been unresolved. Go into meditation and ask for guidance. Visions are helpful to understand what is ailing the patient in these cases. When I first started practicing, I would be nervous about relaying a scene or 'past life' to the patient as it seemed somewhat outlandish and I wasn't sure what their response would be. However, time and time again, my visions would prove correct. The patient would have an emotional breakthrough, 'get all over body shivers', tell me they have an inexplicable attraction to that part of the world or that era or that object etc. or they would simply heal. As 'outlandish' as clairvoyance can seem, take a risk and speak the truth.

The logistics of explaining past lives can be difficult for healers, especially for those patients with religious backgrounds. You can use many techniques to explain it that help make them more comfortable with the idea, especially if there are inexplicable reasons for the illness. The idea of cellular memory or ancestral DNA passing on certain tendencies or traits is helpful in these cases. You can also describe the concept of the Holy Spirit (intuition) as working through you or just receiving messages from the Divine. Otherwise, simply state it could be from the past or DNA and with confidence, carry on with the healing. One can simplify while remaining truthful. We are not here to challenge people's beliefs but to relay the truth as it's told to us. *The healer has no beliefs at all* which makes her completely open and non-judgmental to any and all beliefs.

The present

The present is all that exists. It is your only vantage point from where you can heal and act. All healing takes place in an instant—the instant that's been chosen for it by the patient. In the present, you can set up this instant for them by showing them their potential with unwavering will and faith. Through focus (presence), you are aligning yourself with the present in which all things occur and in doing so, you manifest the very thing you desire. Only by being present can the manifestations of healing become real.

Practice being present every moment through gently focusing on the patient. The patient is the most important thing in the world at that moment and the only thing in it and requires your utmost attention. With this, all answers will easily come to you and all healing come cleanly through you—this will become effortless.

When we are fully present, we can know everything we need to know because *we are not distracted from things that are not here*. When we are present, we can clearly see what *is* here—we can clearly see the truth. We can clearly see reality.

The future

During meditation, you will sometimes be shown a 'potentiality'— not the actual future per se as it's not set in stone. If you are shown this, ask what you are to do about it and how you can change it if it appears negative.

I once had a patient who wanted desperately to move overseas. I restrained from telling her the truth that she wasn't ready yet. Then I had a vision that occurred during meditation where she and her family all died in a car crash. At the time, I did not know what to do with this information and was angry it was given to me as I felt it was very negative. I spoke to her later and finally told her the truth that she may not be ready to move at this moment in time. She was very angry at this truth but I could not withhold it from her. A few years later, she finally did move and she subsequently thanked me for the help I'd given her and her family in the past. All of a sudden it dawned on me that the message I'd given her not to move at that time had saved her life!

Do not be frightened of the message. At the same time know that no message is mundane. Ask what can be done and new potentialities will open up. Many people are given premonitions but very few act upon them. All messages given to us are important and must be acted upon. Only through positive intention can we intervene and change the course. This is a power of the healer.

The potentiality of the future is simply 'possibility' and as the above example has shown, can be changed. Future is really just patterning that may continue based on the patterns of today. Our intentions set up the future but don't bother worrying about it—you'll never get to the future anyway because you can only ever be in the present!

Mental and Emotional Challenges

I will do whatever it takes to have you remember Who You Really Are.
Suffering therefore, is My ally.

There are many symptoms that can arise during the clearing and releasing of fears on the spiritual path. None of these are necessary to endure but they are common. Non-resistance (allowing or full surrender) is the key to having no occurrence at all. Here are some of the more common ones:

Lack of Courage

It takes great courage and personal power to embark on one's spiritual journey let alone become a master healer. When I first started speaking the words of my Higher Self, I scared myself with the wisdom that came through me and the energy that was transferred to patients from Me. Sometimes, I didn't understand the messages or the energies being relayed. However, the power of the healing was so strong, it kept my faith high and therefore, I could also pass this onto the patient even though we both didn't understand at times. We knew on a deeper level something good was going on. Most people are very receptive when they come to truly heal and are also ready so there's no conflict or issues, even if full *mind* understanding is not there.

At the beginning, I had to resist the temptation to mince words or even 'translate' the message or change it in some way so as to make it easier to understand. This only serves to muddle things and make things even more confusing. I felt I was 'channeling' yet I still felt like myself. I felt so different and clear yet the same somehow. Words would come out of my mouth without any premeditation, speaking truths. I could no longer deny their power.

Although these days, anything goes and you can say and do as you wish, within reason, there is still the mind's fear of being ostracized, of ridicule or of simply being misunderstood. You must work at eliminating these things as being your concern. You must in essence, give up your allegiance to the cares of this world.

The mind at first can become somewhat paranoid or suspicious of others and what 'they're thinking'. This changes over time as you not only get used to this new state of being but care less about other's fleeting and random thoughts.

It takes courage not to shut down this process—we all have

177

moments of great clarity (this can frighten us at first). Know this is your true state of Being and Your greatness is at hand. Old ways of being and behaviors (your 'personality') are simply old habits, contrived by societal expectations, training and limits—your past history—your past 'story'. Recreate yourself anew each moment *as you choose* and your magnificence can only shine through from then on.

Courage is what's required to complete one's journey and to begin it. This is why most people never embark on this path because the courage that's required is paramount. We do not understand where to get this courage so we simply continue old behaviors—seemingly safe and familiar yet unsatisfactory.

Courage comes from sharing with the Divine—with others. It comes from the faith that our futures are secure and that we are strong. We can only develop faith by knowing we are supported—that life is supported—that life has a vested interest in life—in *abundant* life. Life wants us to live and be whole—to be One. If we align ourselves with this, we thrive. Only our own choice to malign causes otherwise. When we share fully of ourselves, the Divine or True Self responds in kind, providing for our every need. Remember it's not little you that does it all—Big You does. 'Borrow' all the courage you need from Your Higher Self.

Fear

When you feel fear (which always feels the same), practice simply observing it and how it feels; how the body responds and what you're thinking at the time. Soon, fear will not seem so scary to you anymore—it will just be a lower vibration—a 'shaking' that you're picking up and nothing more. When you become aware of this about fear, you then master it and can then control it by being fearless of it. Fear, like everything else, is temporary, fleeting and illusionary. Don't take fear so seriously and it won't enter into you and become part of you. Watch it, learn from it and then let it go for both you and your patients.

Sometimes when a patient would first walk in, I would feel fear. At first thinking it was my own 'nervousness', I muddled through without any real resolution of the fear. As I advanced on the spiritual path, I realized I was simply picking up a lower vibration from the patient that I also shared somewhere within myself. I started to just observe the fear and get along with the healing as though fear was not an obstacle—it would get taken care of because I was observing it and not going into it. As the visit would roll along, the fear would dissipate until both myself and the patient, had resolved the fear. This is healing—this is a miracle.

178

Self-importance

Essentially, whether or not trauma was experienced, true forgiveness ultimately is the giving up one's concept of oneself and therefore, our self-importance. Our self-concept is mind-created. It is the sum total of all our experiences, traumas, learnings, upbringing, peer, parental, cultural, societal and religious influences, as well as many others. This mind-constructed self believes it is the 'real me' and has been so well trained that it forgets it's true Self and even harshly 'disciplines' the true Self and 'keeps it in line' with all the rules it has learned.

When I was allowing my true Self to emerge and become Me once again (as it was when I was a small child), my 'self-concept self' (trained ego) would chastise and discipline the true Self, telling it this and that was wrong or unprofessional or inappropriate and regularly apply guilt while the true Self would laugh and shrug its shoulders as these issues were not important to it. For example, my true Self wanted to grow her hair and dye it with blonde streaks. My ego was appalled by this and scolded the true Self for being unprofessional and that I also couldn't dye my hair because it was 'unnatural' and against the 'rules' of my profession. It took some time, clearing and courage to finally give in to the true Self and allow for this. A lot of guilt and fear arose during this time even though it was only hair! I may not keep my hair this way forever. The true Self will decide. But by surrendering to Its desires (and all Its desires are *always* there for teaching purposes, even if we don't understand them), I was able release even more of my old self-concepts, allowing for their death and the rebirth of my true Self.

Self-pity

Along with self-importance, self-pity is arguably the greatest obstacle on the spiritual path. We are constantly and unconsciously feeling sorry for ourselves at every moment and at every turn. This stops us in so many, many ways.

We are lazy because we feel sorry for ourselves: 'I shouldn't have to work' or 'this is too hard'. Work is a pleasure that has been lost. To toil and work is good for the body—the body is made to work and stays healthy this way yet we prefer to be sedentary and a few times a year, or go to a gym occasionally to appease our sense of guilt.

We get angry because we feel sorry for ourselves: 'How dare someone speak to me like that? How dare someone do that to me? You must do as I say! etc.'

We are sad because we feel sorry for ourselves: 'How could this happen to me? Why is life so unfair? etc.

179

We feel sorry for others or circumstances in our lives without realizing again, we are feeling sorry for ourselves: 'Why is this happening to me (or them)' we ask, 'why can't I (or they) . . .' or 'it's such as shame that . . .'

We don't need anger to get out of self-pity—we need awareness—just the pure fact that we are being so pitiful at a certain moment.

We control our lives due to self-pity: 'People won't like me unless I have a clean house—what would they think . . .', 'my kids don't respect me or listen to me . . .', 'I can't take this anymore, it's just too much responsibility', 'I've had such a bad day, I'm going to eat that junk food or drink that alcohol . . .'.

Oftentimes, self-pity will manifest in addictions, depressions, anger and actual physical ailments. We actually use these addictions, emotions or physical ailments to aid and abet with our self-pity, fueling it and 'proving' it to ourselves how bad it really is for us. Self-pity is a seething, quiet, acceptable, even honourable way to martyr oneself and create attention for oneself in very subtle ways, even if we are physically alone in the world. Others will say, 'look how hard he works and yet he just can't seem to make it . . .', 'see how sweet she is yet she still can't find a mate . . .', 'it's no wonder he can't get along with anyone or be successful—that tragedy ruined him . . .' None of these things define us yet we allow them to. It creates a subtle way of remaining part of the pack.

Healers must be especially careful of the desire to sigh and feel as though they are 'different' than others, outcasts of society and misunderstood, pioneers of new ways of thinking, that are shouldering all the responsibility for the collective good. We are no such thing. We are simply here to fulfill a purpose from a very practical sense just as everyone else is their own way. When one no longer has self-pity, enlightenment is reached and one 'cares' not (invests no emotion or pity) for anything nor anyone, including oneself. A great freedom overcomes us at this point as one literally has no more cares in this world. We are not *meant* to care. We teach ourselves to and in fact, it's honoured to 'care' in our society. Do we 'care' so much about our parents that we become them? Do we 'care' so much about our children that they become us? Do not confuse 'caring' with compassion—the unobstructed focus on unconditional yet *unaffected* love.

We are taught self-pity as it is an integral part of how we function socially. Essentially, we act like children that have never grown up. We are still pouting, crying, having tantrums, not sharing, teasing, whining and speaking out of turn. When we grow up to realize we no longer need self-pity to function, we become truly enlightened—we grow up to become true adults.

At every turn, be aware of self-pity. Practice observing it in daily life and how you interact with others and with yourself. Watch how insipid it is and how it creeps in constantly. Shine the light of awareness on self-pity and it too will become nothing more than a past memory for you.

Self-blame

Self-blame is really just self-pity reflected outward! The benefit to lack of pity is also lack of blame. This does not mean we become irresponsible—it means we actually become fully responsible but the responsibility is no longer placed on our small self—it is now in the hands of God. Self-blame is a sneaky way for the ego to remain in power. It keeps telling us we're no good anyway so why bother—we can never do anything but fail. This becomes a vicious cycle of self-pity that feeds the ego and keeps us from peace. We continually judge what we think is winning or losing or good or bad, creating immense suffering. Often, my greatest lessons and greatest wisdom have come from so-called mistakes. For these I have learned to be grateful.

Self-blame often comes up for the healer in the face of a misdiagnosis, an unhealed patient, or a misunderstanding. It is prudent to always check oneself and bring awareness to any situation—we must of course make sure we correct any 'mistakes' we may make. However, the Universe has its own timing for healing and we may or may not even be the healer for that person, the person may not be ready to heal, we may have issues ourselves around the subject and therefore can't see clearly or simply a mis-communication has arisen. As long as the healer's intent is loving, we can rest in peace.

Concern with appearance

We are taught to look good at all costs physically, emotionally, professionally, mentally etc. We are not taught to allow Higher Self to shine through and to be childlike. We become layered with many things, all designed to make us at least look good on the outside. It is one thing to look after oneself and take care as you would your own child and quite another to hide yourself or pride yourself in any way. We fall prey to this especially as makeup, hair, clothing, vehicles, possessions, houses and even the appearance of our partners and children, become all important. The question now lies in not so much how good we look but what we are told from Within is right for us at the time. There is a vast difference and a great freedom gained from owning one's appearance as a choice—as a manifestation of Higher Self, outward. As you allow inner beauty to shine forth, your appearance also changes and, becoming so 'naked', you also start to see more beauty in others as superficial layers of 'beauty' are torn away from yourself.

My obsession with physical appearance started to fall away when I cut off my hair and stopped dyeing it. It took great courage to do this as a female's appearance takes such an unhealthy prominence in our world. I also wore no makeup at all at times and dressed as I chose. My daughter taught me a valuable lesson one day. Using moderation as a guide in our lives, I gave her a little eye shadow and lip balm to play with when she was 6. She wore lots of it to school one day and I questioned her. "I'm just playing mummy—it's ok". *It's ok to play and have fun* with outer appearance as long as that's the goal—not the fear of what others will think or to please them!

Now, I wear what I choose but only to my soul's direction and guidance—sparkles and all! The comfort and freedom this has leant me has provided me with more joy than I could imagine. I have also helped set the pattern to my girls to also choose for themselves without fear or guilt. A thing must only ever feel right at the time—this is your only guide.

When buying a new house or car, you must ask yourself, is this truly my heart's desire what I'm choosing here? Am I choosing what others may approve of or what they think is best for me? Is this really for me? Is the timing right? Do I have passion for it? We must not compromise either—we are not meant in any way to live in poverty or lack. We must certainly learn however, to live with *appropriateness*—for Ourselves.

When I bought my first house, I waited a long time to find the right one. One day, it came and I just knew it was the one. Joy filled my heart as I entered it and I knew it was home. It needed a lot of work and was small but it sat perfectly with my soul. Another house would have been a compromise—even a million dollar one. Recognize abundance when it comes knocking and *know what abundance looks like*—abundance comes through the feeling of joy and it may be unexpected. The joyful child within you loves it!

If things aren't 'happening for us', we tend to fall at this point into either accepting the incorrectness of our focus or to force a manifestation about. One cannot force passion. The forcing only brings us suffering but also lessons to boot. Become a master at this by continuing the practice of feeling awareness around any decision you make. When it is your soul's desire, the manifestation will fall into place quite easily, and without much effort. It simply must be completely right in all ways and its manifestation can't help but be brought about easily because it's from the Highest Will.

Elitism

Perhaps one of the most subtle and overlooked tendencies, spiritual elitism is quite common and can ravage the most kind-hearted of us. Not only do we secretly criticize and look down upon others and their activities, but we become very harsh and hard on ourselves. The wisdom that we have acquired, becoming increasingly sensitive to other's energies and the power of knowing and connection with Higher Self can lead to this subtle judgment and criticism of others. Certain behaviors and preferences such as some lifestyles, ways of eating, spiritual paths or 'ways', environmentalism, spiritual groups or even clothing can be seen as 'better than', even if it's subconscious. Extremes of any nature are unnatural and unnecessary. Be constantly flexible. For example, you may find being a vegetarian works for you most of the time but always honor and eat any food given to you out of love. You may abstain from using alcohol to keep yourself clear however you may find occasion when it's even in your Highest Good to have a drink. As you practice flexibility and extreme non-judgment, elitism falls away and peace enters. Small self does not get to choose—only the present moment can choose for us and we must become at Its mercy for peace to occur.

This concept can be particularly difficult because being spiritual is often associated with being 'good' and doing only what's perceived as good things. It is also seen as anti-establishment and the following of certain rules to demonstrate that goodness. It also encourages the joining of groups or at least group *concepts* that seem to 'support' spirituality and goodness. Good is often seen for example, as giving all our money away (or having none to begin with or doing work only for free), or it may be seen as having a certain appearance. The truth is, if you do all things through the advice of your joyful spirit, It will choose correctly for you, for the world and for the earth.

Tools

At first, to the 'spiritual novice', the tools of spirituality are attractive because they can be used to represent the limitlessness of one's perceptions and abilities which in and of itself is fine. We can certainly (and so we must), learn from and use these tools as necessary. These things all can be used as needed and in the correct situations but often, people become obsessed with the tool alone. Don't get caught up in the tools you use or worse, become frightened of your own power and of 'the unknown'. All things are known to Self and power is yours through inheritance from your Higher Self.

Some people also only swear by or use certain tools, unwilling to use others. We must release judgment of one tool over another simply because it has worked in the past or we are used to it. We are not here to be comfortable but to accept. Sometimes you may be called upon to use tools your mind does not initially agree with. Work through this prejudice so you may do what's best for yourself and the patient.

Eventually, all tools fall away for the healer and only Divine connection is necessary for healing.

The Darkness

One must understand darkness to understand light. Darkness is not 'bad' in and of itself, simply a polarity. During meditation, it came to me that darkness is the ally of God. Initially, I didn't understand the concept until I realized that all things are created by the Divine according to the Master Plan, including darkness. There can be no light without darkness and vice versa. Each gives birth to the other—the true yin and yang of life. Darkness is a *tool* to bring one to the light—a necessary ally of creation. In this way, we can perceive the ego or 'child of darkness' as also the ally of the Divine. In this way, the child comes to know itself. Shying away from what it is not and becoming what It Is.

There is no 'evil' in the darkness of space—it is the substrate from which stars are born.

Altruism

Although some people are naturally altruistic, most are not. We are trained in our society to be selfish and look out for number one. We are not well trained to give. Most of us will give in emergencies or if we really have to we'll 'do the right thing' but we are not used to daily acts of kindness and generosity. This is a tricky point for the student as we must be careful not to become impoverished, thinking this is true altruism, but to give when *commanded* to and how we are commanded to. Once again, listening and following inner Self is key here. True living cannot occur without both giving and receiving. A delicate balance must be played between the two and only Divine influence can provide this for us. We can't possibly 'logically think' our way to this balance—it must come naturally, without thought.

Altruism is the peace of mind that comes through sharing—with all of life. You can't help but be altruistic when you are One with God. This doesn't mean you give up your life as you know it, become a hermit, give away all your possessions etc. It means something unique to *you*. Perhaps you have created something wonderful for all to share, taught something, helped to heal someone, given something or simply stayed in your power. There is no rulebook that states what you must do. The answer as always, lies Within you. Do not judge your giving or your receiving—it all balances out in the end. The most important barometer for you is how you feel inside—what your inner state of being is.

Highs and Lows

It is common to experience states of joy, bliss or 'satori' as well as states of depression. As you accept both unconditionally as being neither preferable nor repulsive, you will be at peace. Peace does not lie in a state of bliss or depression but in the center. At the center lies stillness and non-judgment—pure contentment. Many on the spiritual path mistake satori for this state of contentment. Satori is simply a temporary state that one may experience and can come in many forms as teachings and wisdom are revealed to you along the way. Your system has to get used to this new vibratory state and incorporate it into daily life. This satori or 'high' is invariably followed by the normalcy of life settling in again. This in itself is not troublesome for most but after reaching this new threshold, some pine for it like a drug, sometimes until their demise.

Seek not the extremes of highs or lows. Seek the stillness of acceptance of all that is.

Mania

During heightened awareness it's common, especially for those of us with a more emotional nature, to become 'high'. We get off on life and its beauty and the love that's all around us. We feel and are limitless and have no fear. How can you need anything else?! However, this can lead to hyperactivity, including excessive talking and very little need for sleep or food and eventually, a crash in energy and/or depression. With breath and practice, one can channel all this energy and utilize it properly and creatively. We have limitless and immense access to power and we must learn to use it wisely. We are here to create so we must create using an energetic outlet. Some choose art, some choose writing, others choose healing, others like to exercise and master the physical etc. It matters not where your outlet lies but that you use this gift of energy appropriately and in a timely fashion.

A so-called heightened state must not be judged—it is not better or worse than any other state. When you truly look at it, being hyper is not peace or joy, nor is being emotional. These things you do not really want nor need. The goal is to *keep and conserve* energy and utilize it only as commanded from Within.

Depression

Many students and healers come to me saying they feel depressed and lost when they are not in higher states of awareness or consciousness and want to be there all the time. They get upset when they have to deal with everyday life and its normalcy. Self will not always have us enter into a higher state as it may not be required at that moment—when you're busy driving a car you need to be present while driving, not having visions! What will be required of us at all times is to be present and focused on what's right in front of us. There is no other reality than this!

Just as there is a time to create and heal, there is a time for rest and solitude. You can still be joyful and at peace but just because you're not singing or creating that art piece, does not mean you are not still connected. Normal states of awareness do not mean you are not connected. As long as you are present, a state of contentment settles in. Keep the ego's need to be frantic and emotional in check—it sees the high as the only way to go. Again, do not judge normal states of awareness as being better or worse than any other state. Washing the laundry or driving can be just as satisfying when you are truly present with it. Practice being present and contentment is your reward as you learn to balance all things and become unaffected by any state or feeling.

Knowing everything, knowing nothing

There will be times on your journey when you feel you know nothing. And other times when you feel you know everything. Neither is relevant and all is fleeting, just like all thoughts are. Swells of the ocean are meaningless too, as are the dips. Dive deeper than your thoughts into the stillness and depths of Yourself that provide you with the template for all that is. Only this can give you peace.

Many times as I sit to write or teach or heal, my mind may interfere and say you know this or that or you do not. But all the while, as I dive deeper into Me, I find the words just come from Me, the writing just happens from Me, without any thought from me at all. It even amazes me to see this almost 'automatic' knowing come from Me and spill out into my life. This awesomeness of Who We Really Are is difficult for our small minds to believe! "I wrote that?", "I said that?", "I did that"?—it comes out in any skill we may possess. Accept this as being You—as the *real* You. However, do not attempt to do this with the mind—it will

186

remain in disbelief. Do this as you would remember an old friend. Someone whom you'd long forgotten and are just getting used to having in your life again. Over time, the mind will get used to the fact that the old friend is really back home again.

Moodiness

Every healer has different tendencies depending on his/her personality, upbringing, social situations, race, culture or gender. A healer could be very present, pleasant or powerful in one situation and downright depressed, angry or rude in another, depending on the triggers and fears that still remain for them. Recognizing one's triggers and fears is first in the release of mood swings. Many healers literally feel out of their element when they are not doing their life purpose or their life's work and are doing more seemingly mundane tasks like taking the kids to school, shopping or driving a car. Although a healer can never go back in terms of his/her awareness, they can certainly go out of presence and become 'possessed by the mind' again with its constant chatter, worries, fears and useless meanderings. This can lead the healer into great frustration as they feel they should 'know better' and *should* be able to be at peace any time they choose. Being patient is an understatement here as it can take a lifetime to master presence and ease in all social situations. The one thing you must remember is that you have asked to be present at all times and this prayer *must* be answered simply because it was asked in earnest. Be patient of both the process and the time it takes for it to be answered. A useful practice is to act or pretend that you are in your power when you feel you are not. This will trick the mind into allowing you to become present—to become Who You Really Are.

Loss of motivation

I was always a very active person and I always had a goal of some kind. First, it was to do well in school, then in university, then as a naturopathic doctor, then as a parent etc. However, somewhere along my spiritual path, I lost motivation to succeed 'in this world'. My egoic drive simply wasn't there anymore. Whereas before I was driven by the desire to do well, to gain material wealth, to gain respect (and I used emotions such as anger to drive this), I felt I had no interest at all in the cares of this world. It brought on a sort of depression, although, I knew better than to be *actually* depressed at that point on my path—I just couldn't pinpoint what was wrong. I knew that anger only depleted me of energy and I could no longer muster anger or emotions to drive me forward. This was entirely new territory. I had known no other way to move forward in life than what my ego had provided. Many days, I found it difficult to even get out of bed because I had no drive. I had it all, things were going well, but I'd lost my passion. I no longer understood my purpose—at least my ego didn't. My partner put it very succinctly one day. "Your ego no longer is your reason for living—it's no longer your drive. You have surrendered your will to your Higher Self but you aren't aligning that will with Its passion." It was a case of mistaken will. I felt that because I felt no passion that there wasn't any! Whereas I'd placed passion with my ego all my life, I had surrendered myself to my Higher Self and I needed to face a passion that was somewhat foreign to me. At first, it felt like I was being controlled or had surrendered to a 'parent' that constantly told me what to do. At first, I'd felt I'd given up my freedom. Gradually, over time, I came to know this new Me and It's passions and desires. What's funny is that without the stress, It could get me to where I really wanted to be in the first place without all the expectations or cares we usually associate with so-called success. The fact that it didn't matter to me was now a great asset. This unaffectedness became my freedom.

Uncontrollable emotions

As emotions are understood and released when consciousness changes, these revelations can lead to an uncontrollable release of emotions that have literally been 'pent up' for lifetimes. This type of release albeit uncontrollable, is accompanied by a sort of relief as the Higher Self understands the purpose of it. Although it may seem spontaneous, it usually occurs due to a trigger of some sort at the time of release, whether one is aware of it or not. The emotional release allows for a new set point in the conscious mind to process and perceive differently than it had previously.

A movie I once saw displays emotion and release very clearly. Although the camel in the film was not conscious nor aware in human terms, it exhibited some fascinating behaviour. The camel had a difficult labour with her first offspring and subsequently rejected her baby camel. It refused to nurse its offspring regardless of its owner's attempts—until a ritual was done in which a Mongolian violin was played to it while the baby attempted to suckle. After a while, the mother camel wept! Tears were running down her face and she succumbed to the baby, feeding it.

---

[11] *The Story of the Weeping Camel.* DVD. Directed by Byambasuren Davaa and Luigi Falorni. MGM, 2005.

In this awesome display, we witnessed something of a miracle as the mind/habits of the mother changed, creating emotional release and subsequent changes in behaviour.[11]

Spontaneous emotion

As you begin to be more and more present, flowing with every moment and event in your life, you also become increasingly subject to the tide of emotions. Fear, joy, crying, laughter, anger, irritation, yelling etc. can all change in a matter of moments, depending on the vibration of both your surroundings, from others and due to your natural tendencies and sensitivities. Simply work at observing these fluctuations as they too are temporary. The more unaffected and witnessing you are to the emotions and feelings, the faster they pass. Discipline and awareness is required to stay in stillness. Allow yourself to be in the moment or to be the observer as inner imperatives guide you from moment to moment. Sometimes we are called to act and be a part of emotion and the goings on of life and other times, to be still and an observant witness only of emotion. It is neither prudent nor safe to resist or augment any inner imperatives, no matter how 'challenging' emotionally they may be. There are no 'good' or 'bad' emotions as small children teach us so well—this you must know in earnest to be free of emotional turmoil.

As you become more at ease and surrender to any emotion or feeling, they start to level out and stillness is the replacement as indulgences and/or resistance to emotions are left behind.

Desire for attention

When someone seems to be listening to us, even when we are present, the ego loves this attention. Watch this closely as often only a few choice words, phrases, stories or parables are necessary during a visit with a patient. The ego will tend to want this attention—to linger and drag out the message and milk it for all it's worth. Keep the message loving, truthful, concise and precise. This takes practice so be kind to yourself. Often a patient will give very clear body language messages that they have had enough or are done for the day. They may fidget in the chair, start to get up or get their things, start looking at their watch or lose consistent eye contact with you. Sometimes, you may just feel a certain energetic change and a sense of finality. Sometimes I would just have nothing more to say and my body would literally stand up. Listen and follow. This can be particularly challenging with spiritual students as they show a keen interest and they can feel a soul connection with You.

189

This will please your ego and its desire for attention, fame and power. Recognize your longing for these things as simply misplaced longing for connection with God—our only special relationship. It's a good thing when a student no longer needs you. Celebrate in their accomplishment.

The outsider
As one begins to see the world differently and behave differently toward it, one can begin to feel different than others. You will at times feel that you simply don't fit in. Almost everyone, save those in certain very close knit cultural communities, will experience this feeling.

With certain first nations cultures for example, healing practices of medicine men and women although seemingly strange and incomprehensible to Western thinking, are revered and respected within their communities as necessary, important and powerful. They remain unquestioned for the most part, holding the medicine person within a certain status and in this way, insulating them from ostracism. Whole cultures are based around shamanism as it is interwoven into the culture itself and therefore, becoming an important and intricate part of it. Some on the journey will be drawn into these cultures because to their acceptance of the healer. Although very helpful as a learning tool, caution is warranted not to get caught up in the culture *itself* or the rituals it uses as the end all be all. As mentioned, all definitions and labels must eventually fall away to be free.

In Western culture, feeling like an outsider as a healer can be particularly difficult as we have no context within which to place true healing that is 'acceptable' to society. For the most part, healing in this manner is still seen at worst as witchcraft and at best as flaky. Healing within Western society requires a different sort of courage as there are no cultural safety nets to catch us. It is important however at the same time, not to heed to cultural norms of any kind and practice becoming unaffected altogether by the opinions of Western culture. Only by this approach may we change this perception of 'healer as outsider' as well. We *all* must ultimately become healers for the survival of our very Selves.

The lonely road
Most find the spiritual path somewhat lonely. Not that you are particularly disliked or persecuted but because no one else seems to truly understand the journey or level of consciousness that has become You—as you become more childlike and see the world differently. The spirit that sees all starts to gain in strength and presence and the old way

of thinking about the world and people simply no longer fits—you can't go back. Some friendships fall away, sometimes even long-term relationships with partners and family, new locations or career occur, differing perceptions due to satori and enlightening experiences arrive. All these changes can leave one feeling in a bit of a void and departed from the world. This is normal and it does pass as you get 'used' to how others perceive you and to new states of perception. Like anything else, the more it's resisted and 'self-pitied', the longer it takes to overcome. As you leave the cares of this world behind, you must go through releasing your old ways, people, things and occupations as necessary and guided from Within. With this comes periods of loneliness and isolation. Once you are more used to your Self, you are usually able to integrate yourself back into society with a new outlook, even better than before. You become wide, open, carefree and as joyous as a child with nothing to lose or hide. With this, you ironically become more attractive and liked by others and they will seek your counsel and want to be with you just for the love you exude. You will eventually simply not care for compliments or insults and so you're free—for the first time. You no longer care if people 'understand' you as you sometimes don't even understand Yourself! What you have done is become completely present, going from moment to moment with joy. You become more connected than ever with experiences becoming more meaningful and fulfilling on all levels. Loneliness then becomes something of the past—just another old fear.

The split personality

Unless you are fully enlightened (at One/present all the time), you divide your attention between listening to Self/God and listening to self/ego/animal. Almost everyone has at least two 'personalities' that they portray to the world, some of us more. An easy example is the you at your life's work and the you at home. One is usually more formal, and one more relaxed or casual. We also have different personalities depending on who we are with—we act differently around friends, acquaintances, family, storekeepers, salespeople, animals, sick people, on vacation, toward people of other race, religion or economic status—the list goes on. We adjust ourselves, ever so subtly, to these different people, environments and situations, usually to please others or to follow social rules. Contrary to sweeping popular belief, this is not normal. When you are always Yourself, you are always the same regardless in the sense that and you are always peaceful and full of joy. With the exception of young children and animals, most of us never act

191

the same way or feel the same way in these varied situations. It's not to say we don't vary our speech or affect according to the situation or to who we're interacting with. We simply stay the same *inside*—confident, peaceful and unaffected.

Often, how we portray ourselves is heavily ingrained and literally sits in our DNA. For example, our parents are our examples of what it means to be a parent and so we unconsciously follow their lead, even adopting their behaviors, appearances and health conditions. I speak mostly of parents because they usually have had the greatest influence on us. Top this all off with the *belief* that it's just your DNA and that you can't do anything about it, and you literally *become* your parents. Conventionally, we chalk this all up to genetics but I ask you to look at yourself when you're in a scenario where you have no previous notions or experience—like visiting a country your parents have never been to or engaging with people or in activities your parents never did. You may find yourself not knowing how to be or act and so you make up your own way which you may find quite pleasant, enlightening and freeing.

The most striking example for me was the way I was in the domestic setting versus my practice. Since I had no previous example from which to draw for the healing setting, I was free to be as I chose. It was quite a different matter with my family life as my memories of family and parenting were many and they easily influenced me. What is really interesting is how even my physical body literally changed while in one of the two different situations or 'personalities'. When I was 'a parent', I found I had certain health issues and emotions would arise more easily. However, when I was *present* in the practice, there were no such ailments. My blood pressure would rise as a parent and be normal as a healer. My back would hurt as a parent and would leave as a healer. Nothing seemed to stress me as a healer, everything did as a parent. I had to find some way to change my perspective of parenting *and* being a partner—to remain present in the domestic setting and to literally remake myself and my perceptions of domestic life apart from what I'd learned in my past.

All this being said, we must never blame or place responsibility on anyone or any setting. We have simply learned from it. Others in the same family may have very different perceptions and memories. Our parents have learned from their ancestors and evolved and so will our children from us. Such is the honour we give our parents—for birthing us into this wonderful world and being catalysts for our evolution and growth.

The memory of the past (family, house, physical surroundings, sounds, smells, feelings) keeps stimulating the same part of the brain that is used to perceiving in this same manner and then creating the outer experience—this has been termed the holographic model[12]. Another perspective has not been allowed because the old memories keep interfering. *Realizing* there is interference to begin with is the first step. Then one must practice looking at the situation from a different angle or perspective every time until one gets used to a new way of thinking and being. This is why props help. Using feng shui, moving location, changing clothing, changing décor, having different people around etc. help because the background doesn't quite meld or jibe with the old memory. It's easy to become stuck in the old dream but if someone or thing new comes along into the dream, your perception has a chance to change. Something different than what you remember is now present, shattering the habitual illusion. Meditating in a cave in a mountain does something like this because most people have not lived in a cave before and it has no outer world reminders for us and therefore, the mind can gain any perspective it likes. Change your inner world through awareness and change your outer world as a tool to help with the shift.

Commitment to Self

Retraining and reawakening the mind takes practice. And just like learning any new skill, takes time, patience and diligence. At first, you may go in and out of being 'at One' or present which will frustrate you. The mind clings strongly to its old ways. The change may be so gradual that you hardly notice it yet others around you clearly see it. You may find it harder to change in some areas of your life than others depending on the habits ingrained therein. We are suckers for habit and the mind loves repetition. I would find myself so powerful one moment and then irritated and frustrated the next. Triggers must be overcome and this is conquered through practice. Think of it this way. If I told you after all these years that you could literally walk on water, you'd not only find it hard to believe, but you'd have to rewire your entire brain neural networks just to have faith that the concept is possible! Once this is accomplished, to actually walk on water takes the ingredients for healing which is ***will, faith, compassion and self-worth***, and a lot of practice. We are never really practicing physically (although the body does respond and tone accordingly); we are always firstly and most

---

12 Talbot, Michael. *The Holographic Universe.* New York: HarperCollins Publishers, 1992.

importantly, *practicing changing the mind*. New neural pathways must be created in the brain and body and used in order for the mind to remain in a certain perception. Not only must we discover our abilities but we must continue practicing them in order to keep our brains firing along those new pathways. It's never enough just to imagine. We must literally *live in that imagination* in order to create a new world for ourselves.

Flashbacks and memory clearing

With changes in one's vibrational frequency and consciousness, old memories, suppressed and repressed fears, guilt, hurt, unresolved issues etc. can arise. They are usually accompanied by emotional upheaval and physical symptoms such as stomach cramping, fever and/or chills, anxiety or guilt and shame. Although these memories and flashbacks can be somewhat like 'delirium' in nature, you will usually be consciously aware of what's taking place and what you are clearing out of your system to some degree. Certain triggers in your life may bring a state like this about such as moving, leaving relationships of any kind, loss or gain of any kind no matter how seemingly 'minor', change in career or lifestyle, trauma, healing from a healer etc. Many of these states can pass quickly within 24 hours if one uses releasing techniques and lets go of resistance. Intense prayer and meditation, solitude, journaling, therapy, baths, sauna, fasting etc. and assistance from other healers are all beneficial during this time. Use tools as you are intuitively guided.

The logical mind

We live in a world that worships thought and thinking, logic and constant questioning and above all, the scientific method. The mind's original purpose is as a useful tool—for things like math equations—but we allow it to run amok with random 'logical' thoughts that are limited in their scope and nature. This insanity with logic becomes a horrible obsession to 'know', even as a spiritual student and healer. Going on pure faith allows for the true miracles of life to shine through to us. The word 'faith' brings up connotations of belief and religious doctrine but it could not be further from these things. Faith is something primal, real and guttural. It is a knowing beyond the mind and into the soul. It is the truth and can be shared. It cannot be as frail as a belief because it surpasses all time and space and comes from the infinite. It is not trendy nor is it passing. It has no agenda and belongs to no group or thing. It simply is.

Trying to understand it all with the mind dulls it all, making it mundane, controlled, and less powerful. All too often the mind finds 'an answer' or something is 'proved' only to be shattered by a different answer or proof later. Some studies show caffeine protects the liver and in others, it damages the heart. Something is always trumping something else to no end. Time and time again we see that what's good for some is not good for others. Some patients test well with caffeine or garlic, others do not. The current collective consciousness around a thing seems to determine whether a thing is 'good' or 'bad' for us at any given moment.

Only intuition can guide us appropriately. We must go Within to find the true answers for ourselves *at that moment* because like all things in life as we change, so do the things we are affected by. We cannot make logical or hold down what is dynamic and constantly changing.

The mind is a useful tool but it too must be utilized properly. We are educated to become 'master minds' when the mind cannot be the master at all! Only the Self can fulfill this role.

Not all things will you understand, nor do you really *want* to understand them. Simply trust they are the way they are. True spiritual understanding may come to you at some point as a revelation but never try to *force* understanding—you end up straining yourself without results. True understanding (revelation) is beyond the mind and is given to you as you are ready—no sooner, no later. Until then, trust all is well, enjoy life and have fun. You can do nothing until then anyway. The mind then simply becomes a servant of the heart or Self—of faith. You can spend years pontificating to the mind and calculating, researching and reading but you will never come closer to Self/God without faith which is beyond mind. When you feel yourself getting caught up in this, breathe, put it all down and go Within. All answers lie within you now and always. No one else knows better than You—you are *never* left without instructions—you merely need to listen.

Lingering fear

Sometimes fear doesn't seem to be leaving during a visit. You cannot practice in this state. Almost always, awareness that it's not 'yours', breathing and releasing it to God, will end it. If not, you must excuse yourself to clear. You can use nature and step outside for a moment or use other methods that work for you. If you cannot clear, and the fear is too strong, you must ask the patient to come back another time as the energy is not right. You are not obligated to 'push through' the visit. Neither of you will benefit. If the patient is open, share this awareness with them so that it's 'out in the air'. Usually the patient has triggered something serious within you that must be released and more often than not, the fear will dissipate over the course of the visit/interaction. Regardless, simply clear it through awareness and get help as needed.

Who am I?

Most people from your past will have great difficulty seeing you as different from what they remember you as. This can be particularly difficult for family as it can be challenging to see one's children or siblings any differently than what we are used to. As you evolve on the spiritual path, you change in many profound ways that can be confusing to all those around you, including yourself. People are used to seeing us, treating us and behaving around us in ways they are comfortable with, regardless of whether they are so-called right or wrong. The moment you present to them the real You, their minds do not recognize you and their egos can feel unsafe. You challenge them to reveal their own true Selves. Unless they are open and willing to perceive their world and life differently or through the present moment, they will only be able to see you as 'not fitting' into their perceptions and expectations of you based on your and their past and what is seen as currently 'right'. Remember this and be compassionate toward them. Stay in your power, answer to no one except Yourself, set boundaries and release taking their perceptions of You personally. It takes great courage and diligence to stay in your power around those who do not see or recognize You (and Themselves) as powerful. They will remind you of your past self which can have the strong effect of bringing you back into that old self again. Be an observer of your own tendencies to sway from your power and to lovingly forgive yourself for doing so.

At this point as a spiritual student, you may tend to isolate yourself away from others that are not able to remind you of Your power and help you to maintain it. You may tend to push away or resist others which can seem very hurtful to family and friends. Eventually you will understand that nothing is 'wrong' and no one needs to change to 'help you' or to suit you. When you need no more reminding of Who You Are and you can maintain that power with any person or situation, you are ready to be in this world again and be lovingly compassionate to all those around you.

Confidence

You will start to appear both very wise and arrogant at the same time. The ego mistakes spiritual confidence for arrogance. Arrogance has no room here as it comes from fear and pride. Point this out to yourself and patients as necessary only. Do not be afraid of your own confidence—it has no room for uncertainty. Arrogance begs for proof, confidence begs for nothing. Confidence is the Isness of Truth.

Joy

As you become more and more present, joy will rise and well up inside you more often. Do not suppress this and share with those around you if you are feeling joyful. They will pick it up too. To some, you may actually appear 'brighter' or 'lighter' as joy flows through you. You may also notice this in others who are joyful or present—they appear somehow brighter in appearance and feeling.

Do not suppress spiritual excitement as the soul loves joy and plays with it. Allow yourself to express pleasure and joy at seeing Yourself in others and seeing their beauty. You are allowed to be childlike. We are often taught that a teacher must be serious but you are the opposite—life is a joyful game within a dream for you. Be honest and express your true feelings toward people always—without expectation of anything—even of mere acknowledgment in return.

A wise young man came to see me and told me he was in love with a woman and he was going to tell her so. He did so only to have her laugh in his face. He returned to our next visit happy. I asked him why he was happy and he said "It didn't matter to me how she felt in return—I told her!" Just be happy you expressed your joy and loved others for *yourself*, not for them. In this way, you have truly lived without fear and loved the most important person in your life—You.

We've all had the feeling of joy come to us—that upwelling of feeling that comes from the heart and makes us smile. But this too, comes and goes with the fluctuations of life. Contentment lies in the centre of our dips and crests. Peace is not indulging in any emotion or feeling but sitting in the middle place of the acceptance of what is.

In traditional Chinese medicine, excess joy is a dis-ease. The heart simply can't handle the rush of it over time. I once read about someone who wrote a book about joy and sought joy constantly, thinking that was enlightenment. The person died of a heart attack soon after the book was written.

Love for animals, plants and objects

This can occur suddenly or gradually or almost as a kind of childhood remembrance as you start to see all things, including nature, animals and innate objects in a very different way. You may find yourself 'communicating' with the cat in ways you never had before, as she literally connects with you on a soul level. You may find close and loving connections to things like your desk, your house, and your car as they also are in your life to serve you out of love. This is normal and part of your evolution of awakening to see the life force and love in all that exists.

Animals and plants can become not only your companions and literally relay messages of spiritual importance to you but provide you with unconditional love and support along your journey. In this way, they are healers themselves—they are ever present and set a pattern for us to follow.

Compassion fatigue

Healers in particular can experience difficulties in dealing with the constant demands placed on them for compassion. Anyone though, can feel this after a lifetime of 'looking after everyone'. There comes a time when true 'burnout' with respect to this can occur. Those of us who are in helping situations often simply feel tired or ready to quit without knowing that we are burned out from putting out. I remember reading about an elder healer who slept and napped throughout the day when dealing with clients. Then, she would take off for long periods and no one knew where she was. At first, it irritated me and I thought her lazy. Now I understand fully why she napped and got away!

Sometimes, even extended breaks or sabbaticals are necessary if this is occurring. A career change may also be in order. It's ok not to spend your whole life 'helping' in this respect. Even if being a helper is your purpose, there are many different and creative ways in which you can contribute. Give yourself permission to have a stress-free life.

Aversion to being in public

The need for solace and solitude can be profound at times as the spirit craves stillness. Although solace is required frequently throughout your journey (to cleanse, clear and reset), and you must listen to when and where to seek solitude, you must release the need to become a hermit. Only by being *in* the world can you come to release all fears regarding it, rise beyond it, learn what you need to from it and love it. Do not force yourself either way but listen to your inner imperatives at any given moment. Balance is key while healing, with periods of work and periods of retreat to recharge. Nature and solitude are the best way to achieve this balance.

Before going out of your space and into the world at large, you must practice 'protecting yourself' by allowing Higher Power to emanate Its light in and from you. This is the way to prevent lower vibrations from entering your vessel and creating turmoil.

Loving everyone

As healers, we work on 'loving everyone unconditionally'. This is true in the spiritual—we see their beauty and their potential. However, this doesn't mean we allow toxic people or situations into our lives because we are working on the guise of being compassionate or loving everyone. Sometimes, others will simply be incompatible with us and that's ok.

I always felt I had to acknowledge and give at least some energetic attention to those who do not like me. I felt it was my duty to actively show them love even if they were 'throwing rocks' in return. My partner helped change my mind after I continually was caught in the 'line of fire' doing this. With respect to this type of situation he said "I'm polite but I don't bother giving to those I can't share with. In fact, I usually wait for them to actively engage with me first. I just don't care. Not in any dis-compassionate or ill-intentioned way—I can still see their innate beauty but my attention is elsewhere because I can't share with that person. There's no use in wasting my energy and causing myself pain."

The accumulation and use of power

The accumulation of power is made by:

Will
(Com)Passion/Inspiration
Faith
Self-Worth

The accumulation of power is really the same as prayer. If there is something you desire to make manifest or occur, even something requiring great feats, these things must be present for it to occur. Humans are capable of performing many great feats beyond our so-called natural abilities. During times of great stress, we can lift cars, run great distances, leap tall structures, overcome insurmountable obstacles etc. We have power at our disposal and can use it as needed to do whatever we need to. This is done by changing our 'tune' or vibration. The will to get the thing done, the passion and inspiration (the use of breath and breathing to help bring in the power from the Divine), the faith it can be done and the knowing that we are worthy to receive it.

199

This must all be aligned in order to manifest our desires.

In the practice of bending or moving objects, one must focus on the object and our intention for it whether we want it to come closer to us or for it to bend etc. Then with the use of deep, powerful breath from the soul, the thing can be made manifest. The key is to let go of control and expectation of outcome and simply allow this power to work through you as though you were simply Its channel. As with all things, this takes practice.

Paranoia and suspicion

Once you start to gain clarity, you also become clairvoyant and can literally 'tune in' to anything and anyone around you, both positive and negative. At first this can be overwhelming as you know/feel what others' energies and fears are. You must go at it slowly and learn to shut it on and off at will. If people are not asking for help, it is simply not our business to be 'tuning in' to their energies and it will only distract us and bring us into lower states of consciousness and pain. This can lead to the aversion of being in public. However, we must still be in this world, without getting caught up in it. The more you are with other people, the easier it will be for you to relate to them. When you are at ease with yourself entirely, you will be so with them. You can only learn this through the aware practice of it. Observe how uncomfortable you are with certain people, your body language and theirs, your speech and your thoughts. Look at this gently and without judgment and you will quickly correct it. Eventually you will find yourself being more like a child who just doesn't care what others think! You will look, do and say what you please with love and enthusiasm. You can even be funny and humorous while you're sending a healing message. You can be likeable but unattached.

Periods of paranoia and suspicion we all have. We are just good at suppressing them. The healer will eventually have to encounter his true fears and this can be a trial. However, like all things, it too passes and new wisdom and revelations surface. If the goal is to release all fear, all fears must be faced. In the end, nothing is as frightening as we *think*.

Turmoil

As revelation and certain karmic events trigger increased levels of awareness, a once previously 'happy' or content state, turns into its opposite, sometimes for long periods of time. Old thoughts surface as a literal 'life review' comes up to reassess and re-evaluate every thought and previous action since our last elevation of consciousness. What was once perceived as OK or even as appropriate behavior, is now questioned and re-evaluated. This can bring about great agitation, anxiety, guilt, depression, fatigue and other symptoms as you literally rewire your brain and body to suit a new consciousness. Old patterns may seem irritating to you as well as old habits or ways of being and seeing. Solitude is usually necessary during these times to adjust to the shift and clear out any fears.

Control

Fear of loss of control is a paradox. The whole point of the journey is to surrender control to Self which seems to the ego, as the loss of it. The battle that ensues can be extremely frustrating and confusing. Often what Self intuits as correct to do or say, ego may not like let alone understand. Sometimes the ego may be attracted to things but Self is not commanding these things to Itself so their manifestation is fraught with difficulty. Relinquishing control requires patience as the healer sits and waits, sometimes for years, for certain things to become manifest. Other times, relinquishing control requires acting very quickly before the ego or mind has a chance to jump in and convince us otherwise. In a way, it's like a child that is looked after, with our 'Parent' (Self) knowing what's best for us. We must give up our tantrums and allow the Parent to lovingly guide us. In this way, what's best for us actually does and can occur. If that Self is Who We Really Are, then we are ultimately *gaining* control.

Giving up control and therefore, gaining it is perhaps the most challenging aspect of the journey.

Decision making

Making decisions can become very difficult for the aware student. In the past, we were simply taught to decide on one thing or another, depending on what our mind thinks of it, depending on logic or what others do. When one enters the spiritual journey, logic although still present, takes a back seat to wisdom, to Self. Listening and hearing wisdom then becomes the new challenge in decision making. This can become quite frustrating for the student as they struggle between choosing what the mind thinks and what wisdom is telling us. It is no longer a case of black and white calculation and speculation. It becomes deeper, etheric, meaningful and dire. We can no longer make snap decisions and say 'oh well' if things don't turn out, leaving it to luck and fate. We know we are creators and these excuses cannot apply to us any longer. Therefore, decisions become much more dire and serious, even small ones. We must sit upon a decision now until we are sure and clear of our message, sometimes for long periods of time, before we can take action and make the decision. Once the decision is made however, we must stay with it and live in the present. We cannot afford to question the decision. As with most things, this requires practice and the willingness to make 'mistakes'.

Oftentimes, our Self will present the answer right away with something that *feels* right but we shut it out with logic, worry and fear, entertaining endless possibilities and scenarios and 'what ifs', rather than focusing on the true answer for us. Eventually, this fear of making mistakes over a 'wrong decision' falls away as we practice listening to Self.

The pride of wisdom

Wisdom will come naturally to you as you stay present and it is very powerful, peaceful and all-knowing. Others may marvel at it. Others will want to be in your presence because of it and even love you because of it. Remember that you re to be present all the time, without preference for any person, place or thing to be present with—it matters not to you. If you find yourself drawn to being with particular people because they appear to marvel at your knowledge, you have gone into ego and pride. This type of pride can be very sneaky as it appears to be just the sharing of spiritual wisdom but there is an underlying agenda for you in sharing it. Usually, the other person is marveling at you but not truly listening, healing or even wanting to learn. In cases of spiritual teaching and healing, the sharing is natural and Divine, regardless of where you either of you are on the spiritual path—you are both in meditation, you are both present.

Remember that it is never 'you' that is relaying wisdom and power—it is always Self.

Seeking approval

The mind seeks approval and has an insatiable desire to know and understand everything. When it cannot understand, it suffers angst and agitation. It will then go into either blame or denial to justify its lack of understanding. Seeking approval outside of you is a product of seeking it from the mind/ego—an impossible task because it's not from there. We become upset when we don't achieve approval from others which is really an attempt to achieve their understanding. However, understanding cannot be achieved without communication and communication cannot occur without sharing and sharing is a choice.

I once had a patient who came to see me that was very religious. He came to me covered from head to toe in psoriasis and having the appearance of a burn victim. He had been to see everyone. I told him that in spite of what he may want, I could not throw more remedies at him. What came to me was a 'past life' or ancestral issue around burning that had not been resolved and that he must address it if he wanted to heal permanently. Aghast at my suggestion, he defended his religious beliefs to me adamantly and frantically. I understood the difficulty this placed him in and with compassion, told him that he must look deeper—to find a way to heal. He naturally did not return. Upset at myself for a time at what I was told to tell him—that I had not pleased him—I realized that he would never forget what I told him and that someday, perhaps even this lifetime, he would pick up the healing of those words and use them to heal himself—the seed had been planted and I had done what had been commanded of me to do.

As a healer, we can feel 'uncomfortable' as we relay the truth to those who appear not to be 'ready' for it but as we are commanded by Higher Self to do so. This can place the ego and its desire to be liked, in an awkward position. Those we are relaying the Truth to may look at us askance, doubt us, fear us, ridicule us or call us insane or worse. The issue lies in the misinterpretation that love (approval) is outside of oneself and is exclusive to people or their reactions toward us. Love is not something that's gotten or had or even sought—it simply is and is always. Love cannot be a 'there' or a 'that' but must be everywhere. Only those that can see love will reflect this back to us. Others cannot and cannot be *expected* to as they are not able to do so yet. Trust if they are brought to you, they are ready in some way. You are not in control of the message or the healing—it simply comes through you in whatever manner. The message is not faulty, only the *interpretation* of it at the time by either you or the patient.

So, how does one interact with those that are unwilling and unable to hear or see us? Through the observation and coolness of the Witness. Seeking and approval are no longer sought after as the realization that others cannot provide love becomes apparent. They can only reflect it according to their free will and ability to see beauty and love themselves. Give gratitude for the beauty you see in them, but do not ask for this recognition in return and your soul will be at peace.

Here is where nature provides us with solace. Nature constantly provides the reflection of love and is therefore satisfactory and a catalyst to peace. No other medium can provide in such a way so consistently as it is love and Isness incarnate. It reflects eternal stillness, dynamism and love that few humans have ever experienced let alone can reflect. Nature is ultimately enlightened and enlightening due to its still, uncaring and unaffected nature at any loss or gain. Our exclusion of nature in our modern lives, has reflected our all-encompassing need to escape the reality which the ego abhors. The ego has no control of nature—nature controls it—a truth it hates as control is its goal. The release of control is unsettling to the ego as now it is vulnerable and 'in danger'. The conundrum is that vulnerability lends to peace and stillness, which is *beyond* control. The sadness of the soul is upon the leaking out of its power for the appreciation and pleasing of others. It then finds this loss of control increases as this appreciation (like a dangling carrot) is never reached. That hurt is then seen as undesirable, and cannot be seen in its correct way as simply inapplicable at that time or space or with that person or thing. It's misinterpreted to mean 'danger'.

Sometimes a patient would come in and my affect would be a certain way. At times I would treat a patient purely in the physical for the moment—as if it were chosen for me and I went through those motions accordingly. Other times, I would be taken over by the speaking of deep truths that again, were apparently beyond my control, whether the patient seemingly was 'ready' for them or not. An underlying fear that 'the timing was wrong' would come up from the ego which was really a disguise for the need to be liked if the truth were spoken. This was really a problem in loving and accepting the Self and then in turn, others, due to the fact that I was holding back the truth. I had misinterpreted love for *like*—others can do nothing but love me as they *are* love. Whether they liked me at the moment or not were subject to their egoic will and was fickle, coming and going and entirely irrelevant. I had to trust that it was okay and to extend gratitude to others for just being the way they were in the stillness of that love beyond their ability or not to like me.

Life's eternal mysteries are beyond us, extending into the bottomless genius of the Universe. For mind to interpret or even to understand them takes away from that limitlessness, to have it stagnate in limitation. Life does not exist in limitation.

One must plant a seed but that seed may lay dormant while other seeds beside it grow. It still must be planted as it will grow sometime. Without a planter of seeds, there can be no garden. If you are asked to plant, be the planter!

Looking outside Oneself

As mentioned, seek assistance and information as you are intuited. Sometimes you don't have enough information to make a proper decision. Sometimes you have fears that need to be cleared first. Other times, you need to utilize someone else's expertise or gain another perspective. Sometimes you simply don't have the tools that someone can lend you, tell you about or help you with. However, concerning decisions and any spiritual questions, a healer truly has all the answers Within Himself. He knows the answer even before he asks it. He can talk to others and even share his questions with them but never with the expectation of result or even response. The healer cannot look for answers outside of himself or he has given away his power. I can engage in discourse around a subject of inquiry with another but through the discourse itself, I will arrive at the conclusion or the 'knowing' that is already Within me. The other person only acts as a catalyst and it is not from them that the answer comes. Sometimes through talking, it allows one to listen to Oneself. This also holds true of another person or patient. They do not find the answer from you as a healer per se but from the discourse with you, they arrive at it themselves. In this way, they always ultimately heal themselves.

It is all too easy for us to seek assistance again and again until we lose all sense of confidence and look to oracles, other people, tools etc. to tell us what is. This is a dangerous path to self-doubt and disempowerment. Get assistance from others in the sense of sharing as intuited but know that all answers ultimately exist Within you.

Becoming unaffected

One must become flexible (the opposite of stubborn) to be unaffected. One must allow for life to be managed not on a micro level but on a macro one—through the Universe. Trust that all things are managed by the Universe and need no 'managing' from you. Releasing our tendencies toward righteousness allows for flexibility and unaffectedness. We have faith that all is managed and managed well, beyond our understanding. This is not to say we do not act, say or do what is best for us from Inner knowing—we must continually go with the flow of life. This is also not to say that we lay down and allow others or our own egos to walk over us in a sort of numbness or indifference either. Command comes from an inward space with full faith and the allowing of what is simply 'correct' for us.

To become unaffected, one must no longer 'care'. Caring requires concern for yourself and others which cannot be if we are to be at peace. This does not mean we are unloving or uncompassionate but we cannot for ourselves or others afford to waste life force energy on caring. To be unaffected is to be unattached. Healer dona Mercedes articulates it well

". . . [healers] have very little attachment to [their] parents or children. Yet, they love them with all their might but only when they are facing them, never when they turn their backs."[13] In other words, love what's in front of you because only that which is here right now is real.

Judgment and good vs. bad

To release all judgment, one must see that there is no such thing as good or bad in any real or meaningful sense. There can only be correct and incorrect or even more accurately, ripe and unripe as ancient texts have described it. In the original Aramaic language, things were described as simply either ripe or unripe, not in the stricter terms of good or bad. This changes our view of good and bad drastically. Ripe and unripe simply point to improper timing or appropriateness rather than to anything moral or amoral. It may be appropriate or ripe to defend oneself in a battle but inappropriate or unripe to attack another out of vengeance. Neil Douglas-Klotz has an excellent discussion of this concept in his audio series, Original Prayer[14].

Most people already know what they're doing wrong (unripe)—they need help knowing what to do *right (or ripe)*!

What we are really looking for is release of judgment and the allowance of true discernment between what is ripe and what is unripe. With this perception, not only can we be kind and gentle to ourselves for our perceived mistakes, we can release the vicious cycle of guilt and allow for what's ripe and unripe to teach us. With unaffectedness, we can truly learn this discernment and become masters of choosing ripeness every moment.

Sympathy

Compassion is our nature, being sympathetic is not. Sympathy comes from the desire to be liked and to share in the pain of another. We are to be supportive while knowing that it's okay—that whatever is happening with others (and ourselves) is just okay. We must become agreeable to what is happening whether the mind 'agrees' with it or not.

---

[13] Donner-Grau, Florinda. *The Witch's Dream*. USA, Simon and Schuster, Inc. 1985:74.

[14] Douglas-Klotz, Neil. *Original Prayer*. (audio CD course) Boulder, Colorado: Sounds True. 2000.

This is the allowing.

Impatience

Since we are little we are told to 'be patient', without knowing what patience really means. We think it means waiting and we hate that. Mostly because we learn to hate being present where we are right now. Everything needs to be done yesterday and then when yesterday comes, we're on to the next object of our impatience. But patience actually means to be still—to be—now.

Once when I was a young waterski instructor working at a resort, I had the privilege of working with people from all walks of life that wanted to ski, including those with physical and mental challenges. With one such guy, I knew it would be very difficult (and my mind thought impossible) for him to actually ski. He was very excited but after a few tries, it was clear he was not going to ski that day. I became impatient with the kid and my irritation started to rise. Then, like some kind of soft wind, I just accepted that I might be doing this over and over all day long. A sort of peace came over me—an acceptance. I kept calm, even—tempered and continued helping him with a smile. He was a determined little guy and as long as he was, I would keep going. I must have realized somewhere in me that it didn't matter. The next moment wasn't going to be any better than this. He was learning and enjoying it and so could I if I chose. Cold and tired, we had one more try ahead of us. This time, he did it and even stayed up for a minute. My patience had paid off with the grand prize of his absolute joy!

Impatience doesn't leave us once we embark on the spiritual path. In fact in some ways, it can get worse after we've 'tasted' enlightenment or presence. We yearn for it and fail to realize its right here all along. There is no future. The whole point is to accept whatever is going on right now—the so-called good, bad and ugly. It does no good to force enlightenment upon ourselves or others—it belies the whole point of it. Go through and process what you need to, learn and clear and gain awareness along the way. Place Ultimate trust in Self that this will and is occurring for you and with this, Oneness is inevitable.

This stillness brings with it the patience that we actually *are*.

Doubt

One of the greatest of all impediments is doubt. Doubt takes diligence and commitment to overcome as it will creep into consciousness if not checked. In the practice setting, it's often instigated by patients themselves who are sitting in doubt. Be mindful of it and do not allow it to distract you. All healing occurs in faith without doubt. Quiet the mind and ask for answers if in doubt and clarity will come to you. When doubt would enter for me, I would simply ask Higher Self to come and take over for me—to do the healing *for me*. Because I knew all things I ask for are answered, this faith alone would allow for the healing.

Sometimes during a visit, my mind would enter and question, doubt and stray toward this possibility and that. We tend to want to go back to old behaviors and logical explanations that we are comfortable with. I then had to listen very carefully to the voice underlying my mind that would speak softly but with sureness of what the issue was or where to find it. This takes practice mostly in the listening and the following of your 'gut instinct'.

Sometimes great changes or miracles in one's life can instantly overcome doubt, allowing for enlightenment. More often, doubt must be slowly weakened with diligence, commitment to Self and the proving of one's faith as you see the outcome of your trust time and time again occur in Your favor.

Worthlessness

As all thoughts are meaningless, worthlessness is also meaningless. There is no such thing and we must turn our thoughts to nature to show us this. No animal or plant deems itself more or less worthy than another, more or less guilty than another. They take their place in life—their only job. We feel as healers to be worthy, we must either teach or learn. We must be *doing something worthwhile*. If we have not *contributed*, we are worthless. There is no teaching or learning, only remembering and this remembering is not done by you but by Self. Staying present in the traffic jam is no more or less valuable. Even not being present has no value nor is any worse than being present. Acceptance that you are worthy by your very nature and mere existence is required to eliminate infectious thoughts of worthlessness. Be diligent and apply acceptance—to the good, bad and ugly—to everything to truly know your worth. It is not up to you to decide whether you are worthy or not. It has already *been* decided for you and the ramblings of your mind make no difference whatsoever as to the facts at hand that you cannot be anything *but* worthy or you would not exist. Know your significance.

Guilt

Guilt cannot exist in this moment. Guilt is a product of thinking on the past and since the past does not exist, it is illusory. We are taught to feel guilt and remorse, that somehow these feelings will change things and cease the repetition of doing things incorrectly. However, guilt only breeds more guilt. All that's needed is a recognition that we could have chosen differently—chosen with Self as our guide. You can only choose according to where your mind is at the time. We cannot be punished for this choosing due to the fact that that was simply where we were at the time. This ability to choose with Self takes a lifetime to master and like children learning, we must be kind and patient. A child cannot learn through guilt but she can learn by seeing the correctness of her actions—by learning to choose correctly or with ripeness.

Anxiety

At times anxiety will arise, sometimes seemingly out of the blue. However, there will always be a trigger. Anxiety and even panic can occur when the ego is being challenged. When the mind is called upon to literally change its way of thinking/perceiving.

I once had nearly six months of anxiety triggered by 'conflictual' events. This anxiety and the habitual worry that went with it however, were far from foreign to me. I'd been this way for years just without the intensity of anxiety and panic. Over those months, I literally forced to retrain my mind because my symptoms were so acute. My spirit was calling me to finally release my fears of conflict and issues with poor self-worth. The only message I received from Self was 'stand up My child'. I thought the suffering would never end.

Then, late one night, I woke up once again in a panic and went outside, now almost used to this angst. But, something in me had changed. I sat down and looked at the stars and said to my fears with full confidence, 'you may try to scare me and try to get me but you will never succeed in taking me. My commitment is to God.'

I didn't have anxiety like that again. I'd finally stood up for myself.

Time and time again, I see this same scenario with people to the point where they're on medication, drugs or alcohol to control their anxiety. We only need to stand up for ourselves and choose what we will accept in our lives. God/Self cannot do this for us no matter how much we plead. It's up to us.

Physical Challenges

Your body is always a servant of its master.
Know which master you are serving.

Below are some of the more common physical symptoms and signs that can arise on the spiritual path. These symptoms will not usually be long-lived and tend to leave as quickly as they arrive. Always however, go Within to ask for their origin and for appropriate treatment and assistance for them as necessary. Pathologic symptoms must be treated appropriately through correct means.

As with all symptoms, non-resistance is key to healing.

Chills

A wise healer once told me chills happen 'when someone's dying'. Confused at first, I later came to realize that part of *me* (my fears) were dying. In the process of releasing attachments and old fears, the body may chill, sometimes to the extreme of shaking and sometimes for days. It's interesting to note that when one feels a presence or entity, chills often occur as this too is fear releasing. Release resistance, rest, breathe and bring awareness to them and the chills will dissipate. Use tools and releasing techniques as necessary.

Shaking and tremors

Similar to chills, vibrations are simply increasing in the body and old fears must be released. Sometimes they can be mistaken for hypoglycemic episodes. Shaking or tremors can occur after meditation or spiritual revelation or simply due to readiness of the soul to evolve. The mind can also become extremely agitated (sometimes to the point of anxiety, panic and confusion) during these episodes due to changes in brain and nervous system chemistry. Higher intakes of calcium (and its cofactors such as magnesium) and plenty of water help to ease the strain this adjustment can take on the body and nervous system. Release resistance, rest and bring awareness to these changes and the body and mind will calm and settle.

Anxiety and heart palpitations

It's quite common to experience heart palpitations while under duress which is often the case when fears are surfacing and need to be faced, dealt with and cleared. They will usually dissipate upon the addressing of any issue that has been suppressed and through calming exercises such as breathing and meditation. If needed, seek help to clear any blocks or resistance. Witnessing the anxiety can help as well. Prayer, journaling, bathing, sweating, aromatherapy and alternating hot and cold showers are excellent relievers.

Lightheadedness

As new spiritual truths take over, the head can feel light and you may feel physically lighter or 'floaty'. Sometimes the dizziness can last for extended periods or come and go. Spend time alone to process and ground yourself. Nature helps with this. Due to lack of groundedness, one can get injured in these states so it is wise to refrain from doing much (risky) activity. Driving, cutting vegetables, sky diving etc. may have to wait.

Illness

Usually these occur as colds, sinusitis, flu's, diarrhea and vomiting, stomach cramping, aches and pains etc. Pent up resistance, fears and emotions will often manifest as colds and flu's (crying/sadness/despair). Stomach issues can be due to relationship and emotional release. Aches and pains are almost always due to resistance. The less you resist, the less fierce any of these will be. If you do get ill, treat yourself as you would any other illness with rest, contemplation, meditation, support and with any remedies that may assist you. Simple awareness and rest is helpful. Some illnesses can be so extreme they can leave you feeling like you're literally dying—and you are—rather your ego or old concept of self is. This can occur in stages and you may have several 'illnesses' along your path. Spiritual sickness can lead to physical illness if left 'untreated'. Seek assistance as necessary, while trying to avoid suppression which can worsen symptoms.

Stomach aching

As negative energetic cords or attachments are released from others, especially close family and friends, aching around the navel region can occur. These cords are 'heavy' and 'thick' and based in dependency or attachment. As these cords are released, new positive cords can replace them—lighter, brighter, more flexible cords. This change marks a change from dependency to self-love.

As this transition occurs, anything from mild stomach aching to severe cramping and diarrhea can arise. This can sometimes feel like you've done a hundred sit-ups! This can last anywhere from a few hours to a few days. You are simply releasing from the navel or relationship chakra. You can hold your belly to ease this, sending yourself healing energy. Release resistance and increase awareness and you will have an easier time of it.

Youthening

When you are truly present, your physical appearance will be youthful, eventually creating real physical changes such as darkening of the hair, loss of wrinkles, healthy skin, improved physical flexibility and stamina etc. Aches and pains cease during full presence as well as any health issues. Your eyes will also feel and appear brighter to you and others as the light of Self shines through them. Some babies and small children will stare at you. Some people will become intensely attracted to you, both men and women and even want to touch you or do nice things for you. To others, you will be almost invisible as Your light is not recognizable to them if they are not able to vibrate within that frequency at that time.

Pulling of the third eye

When intuition is being resisted, you may feel a pressure or pulling just between the eyes at the third eye location. Sometimes it can turn into pain with any active resistance to it. Relax, be silent and close your eyes and allow visions or messages to come to you and the pulling will release.

Eye irritation

Usually this happens when there is some truth we are not allowing ourselves to look at. It is almost always subconscious. Eye soreness, irritation, itching or burning can come and go according to where the mind is at that particular moment. For example, if a person is focused and present on the task at hand, they will not experience the pain or irritation. If they are grappling with some important life decision and not able to 'see' the truth, the eye irritation will begin again. Simply being aware that this represents the fact that you are not seeing the truth is very helpful in guiding you in the right direction. The body never lies. Use the body to your advantage and as a tool to help you on your journey.

Even if you are aware that you are not seeing some truth, you may not yet be able to address it. You may simply not be ready or you are pushing too hard to find out. Be patient and ask Self to help you and release any fears that are blocking you from seeing. There are times when this will come easily and others when it will take great pain in other aspects of one's life until this truth can be seen. As usual, it all depends on levels of resistance.

The reflection of pain in others

Sometimes, the mind suppresses pain subconsciously. Although this cannot be sustained for long as 'something has to break', it can lead to reflection, usually temporarily, in another outlet—others. Those closest to us are usually the ones targeted. Although neither you nor the target may be conscious of it, emotional symptoms representing inner turmoil or even physical issues can turn up in children, partners, family, friends, and even in animals and inanimate objects. Pay attention. Nothing is coincidental. Although we do not want to analyze each and every situation, we must at least be open to the truth as it presents itself to us in its many forms—either in us or through others.

My first two children when they were born would develop an 'eye infection' soon after birth. Even my new puppy would develop them. Of course, I did everything I could as a mother but nothing would relieve it until I addressed the truth—taking responsibility for myself and my own issues. They were showing me yet another truth that I needed to see.

Ear pain

This one is also literal and can simply be not listening to the truth from Within. The side of the body and ear affected can also have significance to you. Sometimes patients would tell me that someone was always nattering at them about something, be it a partner, child or friend and would report a seemingly unrelated symptom—ear issues. Meditation and going Within to listen, points to the nature of the pain.

Sometimes after or during meditation, high pitch sounds or ringing will be heard. This tinnitus does not last long nor come very often. It is the brain adjusting to new vibrational frequencies and 'downloading' new information. If it happens more often, it can be pathologic so seek appropriate assistance.

Itching, Rashes and Hives

Suppressed anger and irritation is often released through eczemas, rashing and/or hives. On my first trip to Maui, I had released a lot of anger and past suppressions. I woke up in the middle of the night with the fronts of my legs hived out and itching terribly. My mind ran over many things at first—sand mites, bedbugs, mosquitoes etc. but I knew better. I itched and itched until I got on the plane to go home. Then, as fast as they appeared, they left!

Another incident occurred after a healing session with another healer. I had carried a lot of tension in my hips for many years and she had released some during the session. The next day, I had hived out all over the right hip. I then had days of inexplicable all over body itching. It too left with an ensuing change in consciousness. I had released yet another layer of anger and irritation.

Yawning

You're not being boring if people yawn in your presence! I once had a patient who told me she stopped seeing a counselor because all she did was yawn in her presence and felt she wasn't getting anything out of the visit! Little did she know this counselor was helping her *awaken*. Even animals will yawn if your presence is clearing to them (or vice versa). For open patients, you can inform them of the 'side effects' of this type of healing. For others, simply observe them. You may also feel like yawning in others' presence as they too help you to clear. In some cases, it can be for the whole visit. It's a good sign that things are healing. Explain it to others as you are guided and just allow it.

Feeling others' pain

You may be so sensitive you pick up on the patients' actual pains. Do not mistake them for your own. Bring awareness to the pain and release it back to them with your breath. Upon realizing and/or relaying this information to yourself and the patient, the pain will dissipate as they now (consciously or otherwise) take ownership of their pain and allow for its resolution.

It's not yours to carry and you won't get further 'clarity' by feeling their pain or continually focusing on it. The patient must be responsible for their pain in order to move beyond it. Move into just knowing (claircognizance) which is just as available to you, without going out of your power and health. You cannot help them heal when you are in this state as you have gone out of the present and are vibrating at a fear frequency or at the same frequency as the patients' issue. Only a *higher* healing frequency can change this fear frequency and allow for healing. Breathe and release it back to God with love to reset yourself. If you find the pain is particularly stubborn, leave the room and clear yourself.

Changes in speech

It can be quite disconcerting to release all labels, your past and who you thought you were. You are literally left asking the question, 'who Am I if I'm not who I thought I was?' Your ego may find ways to make this shift more comfortable for you by assuming yet another 'personality' known as the Self. This new Self personality may show up during healing, meditation or other interactions so as to make it 'easier' for your ego to assume this new role and feel comfortable in it at first. Changes in speech and affect occur as if you were 'channeling'. You are simply channeling another aspect of you—the Higher aspect or True Self which can connect to anything or anyone at any time. As time goes on and as you accept that this is actually Who You Are and Who you've been all along and Who you always will be, the ego backs down to make room for this more confident, wise, all-knowing and present You until it becomes you completely. This can take time to integrate.

Speech may naturally change only in terms of inflection, clarity and enunciation but appears to be very different to your usual way of communicating. You may find your speech is much more concise, efficient, to the point, clear, calm and passionate. The speech may also be slower, more reflective with pauses before answering or mid-sentence as information is literally 'transmitted' from Self. Sometimes words will not seem to fit well together or to make sense but communication is limited by speech and it may only *seem* confusing to you. You may also find yourself laughing or find something humorous at times when you 'normally' wouldn't have in the past. You may find yourself using emphasis while using certain gestures of the hands, the eyes and head or with sounds and breath. All the senses seem to be wide open and you will use them to their fullest. In this way, this behavior can seem almost primordial or instinctual in nature at times but be assured you are simply finally using your senses as they were intended to be used.

When I first started experiencing this way of perceiving, my ego's perception of Self was that of a wise and haughty bird 'sniffing' around the patient to gain insight! You may find you need to tilt and turn the head to gain a different perspective or shift the eyes to gain a different focus. You may use or widen the nostrils to 'smell' the patient or increase your sensory awareness of them overall. Your eyes will focus on the patient's soul and look deep into them with gentle intensity and will. You may also naturally start to do unconscious hand movements to help move energy and emphasize life force energy (this is what Reiki and Reiki symbols are based on which we all innately know how to use). Use the hands as a tool to focus and channel loving energy toward the patient in direct gestures as you are guided, for more aware patients. None of these things require any thought and come about automatically and naturally.

As I became more practiced in this, my gestures calmed and I became less affected by ego's perceptions and fears. I still, however, notice subtle but a distinct change in my voice inflection and my affect during heightened states of awareness.

Clothing and colors

Tight clothing, especially around the neck can become suddenly uncomfortable. Turtlenecks can be cut along the side seam to ease this. Wool can also create 'hot flashes' and feelings of discomfort. Some types of metal and jewelry will also irritate you—do not ignore these signs. You may be drawn to more vibrant colors (try wearing clothing colours that enhance your chakra strengths/numbers or help heal any chakra weaknesses) and white clothing as well as to simpler more basic and freeing outfits and hairstyles. You may also lose the need to dye your hair, wear makeup or conform to other social appearance trends. There will still be a drive to dress nicely and care for yourself but obsessions with age and beauty fall away as your brilliant inner beauty simply shines forth to stun all around you, including yourself. The obsession to shop falls away and shopping only as intuited arises for things necessary for the spirit and body.

I used to shop and buy many items of clothing and shoes to make myself feel better—temporarily. As my consciousness increased, I found I no longer cared as much. Once I had the intuition to buy red shoes. For the first time ever, I went to a store, found the red shoes and left— without even looking elsewhere or buying anything else. I had left with the satisfaction of buying what I needed only. I had satisfied my soul by staying on purpose and conserving energy. The red shoes served me well to help ground me and to express fun and femininity in my life—they served a higher purpose than as just another pair of shoes.

This is not to say that you don't do or buy what your heart desires! Continue to express your unique childlike Self with joy—there is no right or wrong way to do this. If you want to wear something funky, do it! If you have no other agenda than just to have fun, then express your joy.

When you are present and on purpose, your soul is already content and no longer seeks love and fulfillment outside itself in shopping, appearance etc. It just doesn't care anymore what others think so you're free to express yourself as you wish.

Food

It is not helpful to judge others and see certain ways of eating as better or 'righteous' in any way. It is simply an inner imperative for some and not for others. Others may achieve their enlightenment through other means. It only matters what is correct for You to consume.

As you clean your mind, your diet will also clean up significantly. Many spiritual students choose veganism, vegetarianism, raw food diets, reduced-calorie diets, juicing or regular fasting. You may even develop an aversion to meat after being an avid meat-eater. Listen only to your own inner imperatives and not to others' versions of what you must do on your spiritual journey. You may not be ready for certain food changes and must not push yourself as you can create more suffering than is necessary for yourself. However, so-called 'poisons' such as alcohol, drugs, tobacco, coffee, sugar, white flour, white salt, fried foods, processed and fast foods naturally tend to be replaced by a more natural and whole food diet conducive to a higher vibrating vessel. It's OK to eat other foods on occasion as inflexibility is also dangerous. When offered food by others as a loving gesture, eat it if you are in your power—it's coming from love even if it's a fatty fried burger or store-bought cookies. That love will be amplified when your consume it and keep you safe, allowing all toxins to be released with safety. Apply life force energy to the food through your breath and intent and all impurities will be removed before eating anything. Do not underestimate the power of life force to eliminate all mind-concepts of toxicity. This is part of the gratitude prayer over food.

There are so many guides to food that it can be overwhelming. Your only and best guide is Yourself. What you eat becomes you—literally. Your life force becomes entwined with the life force of the animal or plant that you have consumed. Eating therefore is a very spiritual act. The energies accumulated from eating these things sit with us and changes us. If I eat elk, I become elk and elk becomes me. This is why animals and plants will lay down their lives for us so they can become a part of us energetically. This is why we must love, respect, honour and give thanks to food each time we consume it. It is about giving and receiving.

Fasting

Food is such a focus in our society that it has taken too much space in our consciousness. Food has now become socially acceptable 'consumerism'. Food is simply part of our lives, not all of it. We spend inordinate amounts of time growing, buying, preparing and eating food—mostly to excess.

Fasting or dieting can be a helpful tool like any other and must be heeded if you are told to so do by Higher Self. However, fasting rarely needs to be done on a regular basis or in a ritualistic fashion for long-term as this can lead to other extremes and even eating disorders if one is not Self-guided. Many on the spiritual journey are drawn to strict diets as a way to achieve higher levels of consciousness because eating well conserves energy. When we're not spending all our energy assimilating, digesting and removing toxins, we can use this energy to be focused and still. Food and the discipline in eating a certain way are simply used as a 'way' to enlightenment. This can be very helpful to engage in at first but it must not become an obsession and a 'rule'. All rules must be broken (as you are ready) for you to be truly free. Without preference or judgment, you will learn to eat as you are told to by Higher Self—what, how much and when. Simply listen to inner imperatives and food will no longer be such a focus.

When I was doing a raw food cleanse, I found that my need to eat was very little. The fresh, alive food had such high energy (life force or prana) that I found myself without much of an appetite and had lots of energy. Some gurus attest that our bodies can assimilate prana from breath, without the need for food at all. Until the time when we have evolved ourselves to this point and can remain fully healthy this way, eating cleanly can help cleanse and purify the soul and conserve energy.

Through fasting or changing the diet for spiritual reasons you can learn that:

- that food and survival are two different things
- that food and weight are two different things
- that food is no substitute for fulfilling yourself with Self love
- certain foods trigger fears and fasting off those foods can help with fear release
- certain foods enhance connection to Self

Weight

Because weight issues are so predominant in our society it deserves special mention here. I will pose that weight and food are not the same issues.

There are of course physical issues that create weight issues such as poor diet, lack of exercise, stress, thyroid issues, allergies etc. However, when all those physical issues have been addressed, there are still people that have weight issues. I have seen many patients who cannot lose weight at all even after extensive physical treatment and they don't overeat, they exercise and have very healthy diets. Others overeat, don't eat well, don't exercise and don't gain weight at all! Most of our research says this is due to metabolism or genetics however, when I go into meditation on the subject, the person in question is actually creating the weight issue due to some fear or trigger. Yes, our bodies are made to be a certain way due to our very structure but there is some aspect of the mind that contributes heavily to how and what we 'carry'. Although there are many triggers that can cause weight issues, the most common is the need for protection. Having trouble losing weight is almost always a protection issue or not feeling safe. Weight subconsciously provides a barrier or 'armor'. I've had many patients come and say they want to lose weight desperately but their soul adamantly says something different. That weight is serving a 'purpose' and until they face those fears, that weight will stay on. For myself, I noticed that my weight, especially around the belly (navel or *relationship* chakra) would increase when I felt unsafe and would decrease when I was carefree—without any change in diet or exercise.

Although I've seen patients eat anything they want and not gain weight, those people simply don't use weight as a protection—they may use other bodily symptoms or signs to express this fear. They may also believe that their bodies process food without an issue and so no weight stays on them. (They do however, suffer from other health ailments that a poor diet will create).

When patients are losing weight, we often see them do well at the beginning but once significant weight starts to come off, they get scared. It's important to counsel them at this point around facing their true fears regarding the weight or they invariably put the weight back on or simply can't lose anymore. It's important they understand they are in control of their weight on a mind-body level. As one 'tones the mind', the body will follow.

Sleeping

There are so many thoughts on how much sleep we need and what is best for proper sleep. As with everything else, no rules apply here either. You must sleep as much or as little as is required. Those who meditate for many hours a day may need little sleep as they are already refreshed fully during meditation. We often require 8 hours because we do not get into a deep state of rest or consciousness (deep sleep) until a few hours after closing our eyes. With training, this state can be entered into rapidly without the need for hours in restless sleep states. Meditation helps immensely with this to train the brain into deeper states.

Your sleeping space must also be conducive to spiritual rest and peace. If you are living with a family or even in apartment buildings, the energetic 'commotion' does not cease at night. As you are ready, it is helpful to have your own sleeping or meditation space so that you may reset your energies, clear them and allow for peaceful and psychically undisturbed sleep.

The direction and placement of one's bed, the color and cleanliness of the bedclothes and room and objects within it, sleep and wake times, alarms, reading materials, activities before bed, décor etc. must all be conducive to your inner guidance. Meditate upon their placement and remove any unwanted objects to be recycled, given away or destroyed. Everything has a vibration that affects you. Be sure the effects are as positive as you can make them.

It used to irritate me if I was awoken during the night. We are taught that it's good if we sleep through the entire night. My children taught me otherwise! Now, if I awaken, I know it's for a reason. I go Within to ask what is to be done about it. If I'm agitated, I clear or get up or even go outside to ground myself. Sometimes, my dreams have given me guidance or a revelation and I must write it down or meditate upon them. Day or night, 'awakening' is a good thing!

'Areas of weakness'

In healing yourself and others, all 'areas of weakness' must be targeted and weeded out. For some areas, this can take time and immense patience as it represents some stubbornness toward change. It usually affects some particular part or parts of the body and can come and go. Some of us have tendencies toward chronic back pain or stomach upset or colds etc. Find out what it is in your subconscious that's resisting and work at weeding it out. It can take time and revelation for it to heal fully. Sometimes, you may fall back into old tendencies that will bring it back. Apply love, patience and diligence. You are not weak, you are learning.

For me, my area of weakness was my back. My particular issue had changed over the years in terms of what was affecting the base chakra. It had been money issues in the past, mental strain and concerns over student poverty, insecurities of various kinds as a young adult and the last issue being insecurity over my role as a new mother and my ability to cope and do well by my children. Finally, it rested upon the immense weight of responsibility I assumed as mother, wife and healer. Many of these 'fears and ideas' I realized much later, were products of my upbringing and societal notions and were not 'my own' per se. The pain would come and go depending on the amount of 'strain' and responsibility, both mental and emotional, I allowed into my life as I tried to please or 'look good' while my Self was going in quite another direction. Nothing could palliate it and some days I suffered immensely to the point where I couldn't walk. Great learning and mastery occurred due to this as I practiced the act of surrender. After many years of suffering, I finally surrendered to Myself. Back pain only returned after that whenever I temporarily 'forgot' or was not present with Self. I had to be willing and ready to give it all up—all my previous notions of how and what my life would be and literally 'go with the flow' while pursuing my passions and destiny without care for worldly expectations and conformation.

A friend of mine was on an ominous path to self-destruction when he was younger. He asked God to change his life so he could pursue his destiny. Later, he developed severe knee pain and could no longer work or do the destructive things he had in the past. As painful as his knees still are to him, he is now on his path as a healer, helping others and himself. Although the results of his prayers were unexpected, he said without his knee problems, he would be dead. His area of weakness became his strength allowing him to pursue his path, be a healer and to remain here on earth.

Use these bodily signals as tools and as feedback. The less you resist, the easier it is for you. The first step is to just *recognize* that you are resisting. If you ask for its relief, it *must* come to you.

The 'Death' of the Healer

All too soon, life seems to lead us to death yet all too often we've missed this One precious moment.

Reincarnation

Most of life is doing the same things over and over— life is extremely repetitive. Wake up, go to bathroom, brush teeth, take a shower, get dressed, eat breakfast, wash dishes, go to work, eat lunch, back to work, go home, eat dinner, entertain oneself, go to bed and repeat. I watched myself almost go crazy as a mother doing the same tasks daily. Doing a never ending stream of laundry and dishes, meals and cleaning. I liked it when I could have (what I thought) was variety in my day. I was always looking for something 'exciting' or 'different' to do each day. Strangely, that constant 'reincarnation' I pursued daily allowed me a freedom in the end. Every day I would complain and every day it was the same. How was I going to get out of it? I left to go to work but there were mundane things there too. I traveled but after a while that didn't fulfill me either. It was all the same, over and over. I finally realized there was no escape. I went through a period of depression and some days couldn't even get out of bed because I only had to look forward to doing the 'same things over and over again'. I got lazier and lazier and sadder and sadder. I did my best but I was grumpy most of the time. Then, after about a year, something changed. It wasn't overnight but I started to accept my 'lot' as I first put it. I started to enjoy my kids more and made time in my day for them. I started to be fine with the chores as they needed doing. What mattered was not what I was doing but how I was *feeling*—inside!

All I had to do was change my mind to be free. I realized this moment too, will pass. Soon, sooner than I think, my kids will be all gone from home. Soon, as in all things in life, change comes. Soon, life will take on a different meaning. All too soon. If I were to have no regrets, if I were to know I am present, if I were to live—to be alive—in this moment just as it is—dirty laundry, diapers and all—I could reconcile my life. I could find peace. And, that peace would remain even after this moment has passed and a new moment arrives.

As master Eckhart Tolle tells us, reincarnation does not just occur

---

[15] Tolle, Eckhart. *Living a Life of Inner Peace.* New World Library; unabridged edition, audiobook CD, August 30, 2004 lecture.

once in a lifetime—it occurs constantly when we are not in this moment[15]. It's not the outer world or the act that makes a difference at all. It's our inner state of being that does. Acceptance is the only way out.

Eternal Life

'Energy cannot be created or destroyed, it can only be changed from one form to another.'
Albert Einstein

This means literally, that you can never die because you were never born! You can only change from one form to another. This is the Isness of You. Death then, is merely an illusion. The only true 'death' is death of the old self. The only true birth is 'rebirth' of the Self.

When we speak about eternal life, most of us believe in an afterlife of some sort – that life goes on after we die while the physical body is laid to rest. I find it interesting that even in spiritual discussion, we don't really consider 'immortality' as an option. The whole subject itself seems to place even the most aware of us on edge because we have not considered this possibility— this limitless option—this power.

We are limitless beings and there is no limitation as to when we pass from this world in physical form. As you become master of the dream, you master all aspects of the dream. We cannot afford to pretend this is not our birthright. All things are possible, all things attainable—by anyone. The pattern and example has been set for us by the masters that have come before us. Their true message was only to show us that we, being the same, can and will do anything.

This being said, it must not become one's 'goal' alone to 'live forever' or to only strive to 'look young'—it must become a *side effect* of living at One with Self just as physical wealth becomes a side effect when one is connected to Self. Karma and Self ultimately determine our 'fate' in this respect. If we do pass on, it is prudent to do so in peace and clear as many fears and issues from this life as possible so that any reincarnation that follows will also be peaceful. Longevity of one's life and existence here on earth must be determined by the Self, not by the timeline set by the mind. Life is already eternal and was before you were born and will continue to be.

In Toltec wisdom, death (and life) is the great Eagle. It consumes all of life and it is ruthless. At death, it consumes your body and all your wisdom, it eats and takes for Itself. It has no mercy except if you have forgiven yourself and see yourself as the Eagle Itself. Then, it will spit you out because it does not eat Itself. You get to 'keep' your awareness beyond this reality. Then, you will have mastered this life to become the

Eagle—a living God/Goddess[16].

To be consumed by the Eagle is not our true fate unless we deem ourselves worthless or we simply don't care. To know ourselves to be the same and to have been created in the same image as the Eagle is to know the truth of our power. Then, there is only one death—of the old egoic self—and the rebirth of Who You Really Are—Who can never die.

Death as a 'choice'

As difficult a concept as it may seem, death too, is a choice—either conscious or unconscious. How one dies and 'where' one goes after death can be chosen by the Self. If energy just changes from one form to another, it follows that the energy we are as the Self also has infinite possibilities before it, behind it and in how it desires to present Itself. Because most of us believe either secularly or religiously, that death 'is the end of the physical body', we rarely if ever entertain the fact that it may be possible to change into some *other* form after 'death' or even to delay it. What one thinks, attracts the thing one is thinking about. If one believes in reincarnation, reincarnation occurs. If one believes in the spirit world, one exists 'there'; if one believes in 'heaven' one goes 'there'. In atheism, one becomes 'nothingness'. We are the dreamers and creators of our reality in every way and our transformation from this life form is no exception.

Aging

According to ancient religious texts, humans used to be capable of living hundreds of years—living 800-1000 years was not uncommon[17]. This is because we lived in paradise as gods and goddesses—our thoughts and minds pure and pristine, our food, air and water Divinely pure and fully sustaining and our lifestyles conducive to health, simplicity, ease, peace, love and happiness. Somewhere along the line, our Divine origins were forgotten and all the benefits along with it. We have truly fallen from Grace in the sense that we've forgotten Who We Really Are.

---

[16] Castaneda, Carlos. *The Eagle's Gift*. New York: Washington Square Press. 1981:172-174.

[17] Genesis 6:4-32.

Today, especially in the Western world, there are those that are living longer and longer. Most people over the age of 100 (statistics show their numbers are increasing rapidly[18]) say the same thing—they are simply happy to be alive. Many places called 'blue zones' where people are living longer than average show people living quite stress-free lives, eating closer to the land, and having strong, close social communities[19].

As more and more people live beyond the age of 100, more people will believe it's possible and then it can become a possibility in our collective consciousness. According to science, the body (all the cells) regenerates itself completely every 7 years— so why do we have to age and die?! The answer is easy. Time does not age us. We are joyless and feel we have no control over aging or our destinies. Age does not cause death—despair does.

Aging is due to the *belief* in aging, feelings of weakness and incapability as one ages, and feeling unworthy of youth and vitality. I find it interesting that we are 'fighting' aging more than ever now—a reaction to what we know somewhere inside us, is out of alignment with what is true. Our methods may be perhaps faulty but our deepest intents, pure. Religion and society will tell us the desire to remain youthful is lustful and unrealistic but we are merely attempting to remember our Divine nature.

To be youthful in all respects one must have purity of mind, have full presence and live without fear—one must be fully enlightened. This is the return to our Divine origin and the fountain of youth lives here within our God-like Selves. Youth can't help but be with us because we become youth itself—light. Age is merely a perception. One must first shift one's perception and youthfulness will shine from Within.

Burning from within

There are many accounts of enlightened masters 'burning from

---

[18] Desjardins, Bertrand and Robert Bourbeau. *The emergence of supercentenarians in Canada.* Supercentenarians, Demographic Research Monographs, DOI 10.1007/978-3-642-11520-2_4, © Springer-Verlag Berlin Heidelberg 2010.

[19] Buettner, Dan. *The Blue Zones: Lessons for Living Longer From the People Who've Lived the Longest.* Washington: National Geographic Society. 2008.

within' at the point of 'death'. They simply vanish! Don Juan gives us a beautiful explanation of this type of transformation:

> *'By becoming familiar with the rolling force [death] through mastery of intent, the new seers, at a given moment, open their own cocoons [energy fields] and the force floods them rather than rolling them up like a curled-up sowbug. The final result is their total and instantaneous disintegration.* [20]

The vibrational frequency of consciousness increases to such a point that they literally become light itself as all the molecules of the physical transform from matter into 'waves' of energy. This too, is in alignment with our understanding of quantum physics[21].

Fear of death

Death is usually the most common fear. But it's really the fear of the unknown. Death, being an illusion, is also unknown and we don't like to be out of control. This fear then brings with it impatience. With the illusory end of you comes the end of so-called time and that creates impatience. We must get things done before our time is up! We must accomplish this or that. We must rush here or there and accumulate more and more. Impatience leads to more pain as we are running too far ahead into the future and away from now. Ironically, when there is stillness in the moment, there is no time and no impatience and so, no fear of death. That's how you overcome it—then you have all the time in the world!

Death is where all fears lead to. If there were no death, we would have no fears at all. We think we know death but we're not too sure. No one's lived to tell! Every healer must face his fears of death at some point along the path. What seems to be facing our fears is really just facing death. When I did this myself, I came to realize that after days in fear, anything, even death, was better than this suffering! A favorite exercise once taught to me at a retreat is to go deeper or beyond whatever fear you're experiencing; 'mining down' through the fear.[22] Ask

---

[20] Castaneda, Carlos. *The Fire from Within*. New York:Washington Square Press 1984:227.

[21] *What the Bleep Do we Know!?* DVD. Directed by Mark Vicente, Betsy Chasse and William Arntz. Captured Light Distribution & Lord of the Wind Films, 2004.

Yourself what's below anxiety. Uncertainty. What's under uncertainty? Annoyance. And below that? Pain. And below that? Nothing. And below that? Stillness . . . All things eventually lead to stillness—the ultimate substrate from which all arises.

Death as an opportunity

Rather than an ending, even physical death, if it's chosen, is an opportunity to elevate one's consciousness and surrender to God—to Self. You have only mastered life and gone Home to God when you have surrendered yourself and realize that you are God/Universe/Oneness Yourself—as you merge little self with Big Self. Life force cannot be exclusive of its maker.

We often think salvation will happen automatically at death but this doesn't necessarily happen without a certain level of consciousness and surrender—at a certain vibration. Physical death itself is no salvation—only consciousness is. Do not wait for physical death to do all the work for you—it may not be the tool for you. Death can only serve as an *opportunity* (as any life change can be) to change consciousness.

---

[22] Jaxon-Bear, Eil. *The Enneagram Retreat.* Maui, HI. February 2010.

The Rebirth of the Healer

As you are born, so you will die.
Be born unto Me and you cannot die.

Rebirth

Rebirth is simply releasing one's past or story. Once you have done this, you start to question who you are. This can bring on great fears and doubt as you question what was once your entire being and existence. Observe these fears as you go through this massive change and actually become Who You Really Are. You are not your so-called personality and past, your tendencies and habits. These things fall away into memories as your true Self shines through for all to see. Do not fear these changes. They are normal and necessary on your journey. You have literally saved yourself meaning there is no more 'death' for you. The real death (the illusion of a self with a history and personality) has already occurred. Now it's just a matter of getting *used* to the 'new' or real Self and incorporating it into your life (which can also take some time so be patient with this as well). You need to relearn how to relate to others, how to speak and communicate from a different/higher place, how to keep old residual egoic tendencies/habits in check, how to incorporate your awareness into daily life and what you're meant to be doing with your life now (true purpose).

As a newborn baby takes a while to adjust to life here, so do you. You are no longer dreaming. You are the dreamer.

Birth of the Child

As old self falls away, one's childlike Self emerges into the open for all to see. This child has always been there and for some, has been more suppressed than for others. The child is the playfulness, the fun, the innocence and the simple wisdom of us. She chooses what her heart desires without guilt, says what she needs to without guilt, wears what she would if she were a child bereft of society's influences. Everything is seen through childlike eyes with innocence and beauty. She loves herself and she loves others unabashedly, showing them fully. She also cares not what others think and stands up for herself. She loves nature again and every day is a new, exciting adventure. She rejoices and laughs at the smallest things, clapping her hands or singing and dancing with joy if she feels moved to. She talks to whom she desires spreading her love all around.

She plays with life again.

Satori

When I first fully connected with my Higher Self, I was a passenger in the truck with my family, driving in very dangerous, icy conditions. I felt very large—larger than life. I somehow consumed the whole vehicle yet I didn't feel heavy. I had no thoughts, only stillness in mind. Even though the kids occasionally got upset, I remained as calm and unaffected as could be without an ounce of effort of my behalf. I was both object and subject. The children responded to me like putty in my hands and through my loving kindness, bent easily to My gentle Will. As I looked out the window at the very 'stormy' scene, all I could see was beauty and marveled at the snow, ice and darkness. I even felt I could part the road with my mind if I chose to and I knew we were ultimately safe. I was fearless for the first time in my life. Nothing mattered. I had become powerful.

This feeling lasted for a few days and then I was seemingly 'back' to my old self although I knew my life was changed forever because of this 'satori'. I became depressed and yearned for this feeling for more than a year. It was a state that I could not forget and pined for with all my being like a drug. Finally, the pining waned and I realized that the satori had not left me—I was simply getting *used* to it and releasing fears I could no longer live with.

Although not everyone has a story of a satori or state of 'enlightenment', they can occur to anyone and do not 'leave'. If I took myself as a child and put her into the 'me' of now, she would be in a state of bliss due to the change in her vibration and perception. I'm simply used to it now.

It took me years to incorporate this new vibration/rebirth into my life so that I was living that way with more and more comfort, every day. I had surrendered my old self and was now resting in and remembering the light of Self—my true Self.

Once I connected with my Higher Self and realized Who I Really Am, gradually, my old personality and all its fears, ideas and issues, fell away. I no longer was moved by what I was before and felt very different in a very good way. I simply disassociated from my previous 'life' or past and became my true Self. This process took time and some suffering as some things were stubborn to release. Old residuals still do arise but they are accepted and surrendered to become more and more fleeting as times passes. Most of us go through 'a slow death'.

It took me a long time to accept this Self as being the real 'me' and to accept it. I would slip from time to time back into my old personality but as time went on, it would happen less and less. I simply had no desire to be the old way with all the old fears. It was too tiring and too fake. There were still some things my soul was learning but it was done with much more peace and ease. I had so much control, confidence and power when connected with my Self that it soon became my new norm.

It takes great courage to do this and it may seem strange to you and to others at first as it literally changes your world. Anyone can do and have this—it is not special and it is not difficult—it simply must be your will to do so.

Each person's journey is unique. Rarely, some awaken or rebirth quickly, usually after near-death experiences, completely leaving egoic self forever.

All this being said, do not be concerned if you have not experienced 'satori'—it is not necessary and only occurs if significant leaps are made in consciousness *all at once*. Changes in consciousness more often than not occur in a slow, steady and sure progression in nearly imperceptible increments. It is much safer and more practical to tune a guitar string slowly than to quickly tune it to another key.

The power of vibration

Life force is simply vibration. All things exist due to this force and everything is made different and unique simply due to a difference in vibration. We are singing, just singing slightly different tunes. A healer in any field is able to tune into and 'sing' different tunes or vibrations depending on what he/she chooses to tune into. This gives us the natural ability to change our vibration into that of a tree, another person, an object, a place etc. In this way, we become limitless in our ability to transform ourselves into new things, in becoming one with these things, in attract them to us or changing things in any manner of ways. Until we all realize this ultimate truth and the simplicity of it, we are stuck in the darkness of the same tune played over and over.

The face of 'God'

As this is such an inexplicable topic, I will only relay to you my own story. Remember it as such—unique to me—your experience may be different. If you don't see the face of 'God', it really doesn't mean anything. This story is only an example of our True Beingness. Being a very visual person, I had simply come face to face with my own soul. You will see 'God' in many people and things—the face of God becomes Universal and all-encompassing occurring at any time with and through anything.

One night, I had the most exquisite dream of my entire life. The dream was vivid and real. I was sitting in the front row of an audience waiting for the speaker to appear. I looked up to see the most beautiful, radiant, peaceful individual I had ever seen. I could not discern if it was male or female and nor did it matter. S/He had dark, short hair (which I also had at the time), brilliant blue eyes and was dressed all in white. I recognized him/her immediately and ran up to embrace him/her. S/He welcomed me with the sweetest embrace and I was at Home. For all of life I did not want to leave His/Her presence and stayed in that warm feeling for a long while. Upon semi-waking, I started to question who this was—was it a guide? A spirit? A man? A woman? God? Me . . . ? All these and everything—I knew I had seen the 'face of God'.

The Stillness of the Healer

*You have been struggling against the flow of the river all along, yet the river still
takes you onward.
When you finally surrender, you realize that you are you, the boat, the river
and the flow itself—and you have been all along.*

What is enlightenment?

Enlightenment is a term tossed around quite a bit in spiritual
discourse and needs some clarification here. It literally means to *become
light*. To become light, we must become one with Self, Who is the light
and Who comes from light. We must remember this is Who We Really
Are. When there is light, there is no darkness or fear left. When we are
fully present (enlightened), we are fully in this reality and then there is no
judgment and therefore, no fear. We all have moments of
enlightenment. To sustain it and make it our true identity is to be fully
enlightened.

Enlightenment as a choice

Because we are creatures of free will, enlightenment or being
present is a choice. There is a notion by students that enlightenment
'overtakes' us by some other force outside of us and nothing is ever the
same again—that we just have to keep meditating and being 'good' and
eventually, we will be 'rewarded' karmically by enlightenment.
Enlightenment is a choice each and every moment of your life. To be
present takes great discipline, commitment and surrender. As one would
practice any art, enlightenment is no different. To become a master, you
must practice it until you become it—and you must really desire it.

A karate master no longer practices karate—he *is* karate.

Enlightenment as karma

Enlightenment is also karmic in the sense that although is it
essentially a choice on some level, one must also be 'ready' or prepared
for awakening into this reality. As others around us awaken and as
global awareness increases in general, it assists us in our own awakening
since we are part of the whole or collective consciousness. In this sense,
we can interpret karma as timing. Some of us must suffer enough
before we can possibly awaken.

The surrender of self and Self made manifest

The surrender of the self/ego can be a speedy thing, usually after some drastic life altering event but more commonly, it is a slow and steady process. This is the wedding procession of self to Self.

The practice of acceptance is key to the full manifestation of surrender. Everything must be accepted and therefore, have its release from judgment. Suffering lies in the *meaning* of things—in the judgment of things. As acceptance enters fully, suffering ceases and health begins in all respects.

Once the soul begins its rebirth and release of attachments, fears and past personal history, reconnection with Self begins. The vision of parent and child comes to mind. The parent is the Self—the true Self within all of us—the Allness and Isness of us. It is not a fantasy or a lovely spiritual notion that's never able to be reached—it is real and as tangible as you are right now. This Self is Who You Really Are.

We all have moments when Self takes over and we become that Self—when we fall completely in love like we never have before—with Ourselves. This power is Who You Are at your very essence. And for this connection to be realized, the recognition of yourself as This must be made. Your mission on earth is to make Self manifest. To real-ize (or 'to make real') that this as Who You Really Are and live that truth fully in all Its glory.

When we surrender finally to the Parent/the Self, we surrender our lives to It. We surrender all small agendas or ideas of who we think we are or may have once been and place our lives fully in Its hands. This can only be done willingly on our part and we must be ready. We must be finished with pain. Honestly ask yourself if you have had enough pain.

As Self gently filters down into one's entire life eventually becoming One with all of it, small self's old agendas, tendencies, goals and wants become weak and bereft of pull or passion. An ultimate acceptance enters of whatever is happening and whatever comes one's way. There is no longer any importance placed on this or that or whether one has this or that. Things are still loved, still appreciated but nothing outside oneself provides for anything satisfying any longer—the Self is already manifest and at peace, needing nothing more. As Self becomes manifest, the ego usually puts out a massive struggle at first with the previously mentioned conditions and 'side effects' coming in various ways to try to stop it. When full surrender has been made, struggle ceases and the ego is 'tamed' as submissive to the Self—at its full command. After starting to surrender, the ego will not 'like' or be pleased with the commands of the Self—to go to this place, to say this, to live here, to buy or not buy that. In fact, the ego may feel quite out of control at this point. It will however, no longer put out active resistance but a withered sense of displeasure. As the will follows It's commands, our lives are no longer our own—It's will becomes fully ours. Our agendas all become the Self's agenda—doing simply because we must. The ego may still feel 'shafted' at this point that it's no longer being listened to and angry at not getting what it 'wants' but there is no power to its whining any longer. The healer then feels almost exhausted by the fight of the ego and by releasing ever milder states of resistance, allows and prepares for its final release into Oneness with Self. When the time comes, the mind is fully taken over and there is no resistance left. The world is now a different place altogether—seemingly the same yet so different as sight is full and perception, healed. The world is now entirely the healer's domain— where creation and limitlessness are natural to her. It becomes heaven on earth where anything and everything is possible.

Our interests at this point become 'global' in nature. Whatever we do now is for humanity and the common good. Altruism becomes a focus along with the Big Picture. In this, we must place trust that Self knows and guides us automatically toward what We truly desire—for all of us. We must fully accept our present circumstances and life which really means to be fully present with it. It doesn't mean we are despairing or give up, that we do not have aspirations or inspirations or that somehow our life has ended. It means we surrender to the present and allow Self to do It's Will in us and through us—to continue to create.

The ego's final distraction

This last distraction can be very sly and go almost unnoticed even by seasoned spiritual students and healers—until the very end. The mind will use spiritual discourse instead of everyday discourse, to trick oneself out of the present. It will think on this or that spiritual subject. It will ask many questions with respect to the spiritual, it will try to fathom or 'figure out' the personal past; it will also try to foresee the future and look for symbolism. (This is not to say that Spirit doesn't speak to us in these ways—it's just that we allow the mind to enter and judge or analyze). Just because the subject of the discourse has changed, doesn't mean much. You are still engaging in a battle with the mind using a slightly different playing field.

At this point in my journey, I realized this would be a never-ending discourse. I would always want to know more, even if the subject was spiritual, and it would only lead me to more suffering and more questions. Some part of me enjoyed this discourse and wanted to keep it going. Another part of me wasn't interested and just wanted to enjoy life and keep walking forward. I really had to stop and ask what it was that I truly wanted. Did I really want silence? Was I really done with pain?

At this point, I engaged in a conversation with Self and asked all my questions until I truly felt exhausted of them. I asked and asked. I opened it all up in my journal and the answers were insightful and came pouring out. Truths were revealed and knowing entered. This is a very powerful point on the spiritual path. Some never leave it, becoming oracles and spending a lifetime in questioning and answering. There is nothing wrong with this—it can provide great insight and deep understanding but it will not make you peaceful or fulfill you unless you are *living* these truths.

Even with all this, I knew I was not living in the present—I was not *tasting* enlightenment. I knew what that kind of silence was and this was not it. I was still engaging in mind, only on a different level this time. I asked how I should communicate with others then if I was no longer to ask questions. You will provide the space, Self said. They ask the question to Me of which you are the vessel. The question and then the answer become irrelevant to you. You are simply the channel.

I understood then what I was doing. I was focusing my attention on the questions and answers themselves and not on the present moment! It was like looking at the inside of a channel or tube but not *being* the tube!

Full surrender, full enlightenment meant being—just being alive.

Honour the discourse when it arrives. But eventually, this too falls away. The present—the flow of the Universe—will guide your every move and your need to know everything will fall away too as you surrender fully to It. Ironically, all will be revealed to you in the present moment—you will 'know' everything on a 'need to know' basis.

The ego's final battle

Once our abusive love affair with pain is over and we prepare for our full surrender to Self, the ego pulls out all the stops. All our remaining fears surface to look at us finally in the eye. This point can be particularly shocking as many of the fears that you either did not know existed or thought you had dealt with somewhere along the path, surface with a vengeance. Chills, illness, emotional turmoil and great fear and paranoia can surface at this point with some intensity. One now has to face the fear of death. The ego is no longer going to be the boss and it knows it. It is a battle to the death—the death of egoic control of the mind.

One eventually no longer has any control over what is said or what one does—there are simply no thoughts—only the voice of God.

What becomes of the ego?

The ego's original purpose is to provide us with drive and motivation. However, for most of us, this drive becomes driven by fear a lot of the time and only sometimes by love. The ego gains a lust for power over the mind and tries to drive it rather than Self or the flow of the Universe, being at the helm. The ego does not die at the point of surrender but becomes the *servant* to its true master, the Self. Self's drives now become the ego's drives. The ego willingly gives back to the Self this servitude and in return, the Self loves it unconditionally. The ego may still request this or that but the Self tempers its request and makes them Its own. At this point, the ego becomes 'indifferent' to what the drive or motivation is and goes where it's told to flow out of loving service.

The final surrender

With final surrender, Self takes over and we *become* Self all the time and in all ways—we literally become a different person; a person with no fear, full confidence, faith, love, knowing and limitlessness. Our lives are no longer our own (or our ego's) as they were before. They are always guided by the Self and no matter how 'odd', different or challenging the guidance from Self may seem, it is followed without fear into ultimate freedom.

We do not know where our lives are bound, nor do we want to know as life is meant to be a joyful and creative adventure. We only truly want what's best for us, not necessarily what we want, and that is what's provided with full surrender. What's best for us we cannot fathom as God/Universe wants it all for us and has no limits. Only our self-imposed limitations keep us in the bounds of mediocrity and without the full experience of true joy.

With this willingness, the parent then carries the child across its previously made boundaries of fear and safety and we enter into a new place of consciousness with boundless possibilities and potentials waiting for us. With time and increasing comfort in this new way of being, we gradually grow up to become Self fully—God made manifest. Self is nameless, sexless, and boundless. Self is joy, love and eternal energy. Self is One with All and is All. Self becomes fully manifest through this being. She comes down into us—Earth is now Her heaven.

Stillness
The ocean has waves and the waves come and go. They change; some are big and scary, some are small and pleasurable. Under the waves is the deep, stillness of the ocean, unaffected by the waves of the surface. Fear will always be present. So will joy. Enlightenment is everything and nothing. Underlying all the 'things' that make up the Universe lies the unspeakable—stillness or nothingness, the blueprint from which all things arise—the ocean of the Universe. This is the cloth from which Self creates forevermore and it is the cloth to which we return. Go deeper than anything, even joy, and you will find it there as it always has been there. You will simply recognize it now and seek no more for pleasure, happiness or pain. *Contentment* is the acceptance of all the 'waves' and true peace lies within this awareness. Accept All That Is for nothing can shake this Stillness. Carry on with life and truly live it now without judgment; to live with childlike abandon, playfulness, laughter and joy. To take nothing seriously or personally, even fear and death; to be the dreamer of the dream and realize the joke of it all. To sit in the only place you belong, amongst it all

in the Stillness . . .

237

BIBLIOGRAPHY AND
SUGGESTED TOOLS

Andrews, Ted. *Animal Speak*. St. Paul, Minnesota: Llewellyn Publications. 2003.

Anugama. *Shamanic Dream*. (audio CD) USA: Open Sky Music. 2002.

Buddhist Monks of Maitri Vihar Monastery. *Tibetan Mantras & Chants*. (audio CD) Sounds of the World. 2005.

Buettner, Dan. *The Blue Zones: Lessons for Living Longer From the People Who've Lived the Longest*. Washington: National Geographic Society. 2008.

Carson, David and Jamie Sams. *Medicine Cards*. New York: St. Martin's Press. 1999.

Castaneda, Carlos. *The Art of Dreaming*. New York: HarperPerennial Publishing. 1994.

Castaneda, Carlos. *The Eagle's Gift*. New York: Washington Square Press. 1981.

Castaneda, Carlos. *The Fire from Within*. New York: Washington Square Press. 1984.

Castaneda, Carlos. *The Power of Silence*. New York: Washington Square Press. 1991.

Centerpointe Research Institute. *The Holosync Solution: Awakening Prologue*. (audio CD course) Beaverton, Oregon: 2005.

Coelho, Paulo. *The Alchemist*. New York: HarperCollins Publishers. 1998.

Desjardins, Bertrand and Robert Bourbeau. *The emergence of supercentenarians in Canada*. Supercentenarians, Demographic Research Monographs, DOI 10.1007/978-3-642-11520-2_4, © Springer-Verlag Berlin Heidelberg 2010.

Diamond, John, M.D. *Life Energy*. St. Paul, Minnesota: Paragon House. 1985.

Donner-Grau, Florinda. *The Witch's Dream*. USA: Simon and Schuster, Inc. 1985.

Doige, Norman, M.D. *The Brain That Changes Itself: Stories of Personal Triumph From the Frontiers of Brain Science*. Penguin Books Ltd. 2007.

Douglas-Klotz, Neil. *Original Prayer*. (audio CD course) Boulder, Colorado: Sounds True. 2000.

Emoto, Masuru. *The Hidden Messages in Water*. Hillsboro, Oregon:

Beyond Words Publishing. 2004.

Foundation for Inner Peace. *A Course in Miracles: Combined Volume.* Mill Valley, California: Foundation for Inner Peace. 1992.

Gordon, Richard. *Quantum-Touch: The Power to Heal.* Berkeley, California: North Atlantic Books. 2002.

Gordon, Richard. *The Quantum-Touch Video Workshop.* (DVD) Kapaa, Hawaii: 2004.

Hawkins, David, M.D., Ph.D. *Power vs. Force.* Carlsbad, California: Hay House, Inc. 2004.

Hay, Louise L. *You Can Heal Your Life.* Carlsbad, California: Hay House, Inc. 2002.

Jaxon-Bear, Eli. *The Enneagram Retreat.* Maui, HI. February 2010.

Kornfield, Jack. *After the Ecstasy, the Laundry.* New York: Bantam Books. 2001.

Long, Max Freedom. *The Secret Science Behind Miracles.* Wildside Press. 2009.

Long, Max Freedom. *The Secret Science At Work: New Light On Prayer.* Los Angeles, California: Huna Research Publications. 1953.

MacLeod, Ainslie. *The Instruction.* Living the Life Your Soul Intended. Boulder, Colorado: Sounds True, Inc. 2009.

Megré, Vladimir. *Anastasia.* Kahului, HI: Ringing Cedars Press; 2nd ed. 2008.

Millman, Dan. *The Life You Were Born To Live.* Tiburon and Novato, California: H J Kramer and New World Library. 1993.

Millman, Dan. *Way of the Peaceful Warrior.* Tiburon and Novato, California: H J Kramer and New World Library. 2000.

Off the Map. DVD. Directed by Campbell Scott. Sony Pictures, 2005.

Peaceful Warrior. DVD. Directed by Victor Salva. Lionsgate, 2007.

Sankey, Mikio, Ph.D., L.Ac. *Esoteric Acupuncture: Gateway to Expanded Healing.* Volume 1. Inglewood, California: Mountain Castle Publishing. 1999.

Shakespeare, William. *Romeo and Juliet.* Act 2, scene 2. line 184-185.

Spalding, Baird T. *Life and Teachings of the Masters of the Far East, 6 volume set.* Marina del Rey, California: DeVorss & Company. 1986.

Talbot, Michael. *The Holographic Universe.* New York: HarperCollins Publishers. 1992.

The Secret. DVD. Directed by Drew Hariot. Prime Time Productions, 2006.

The Story of the Weeping Camel. DVD. Directed by Byambasuren Davaa and Luigi Falorni. MGM, 2005.

Tolle, Eckhart. *Living a Life of Inner Peace.* New World Library; unabridged edition, audiobook CD, August 30, 2004 lecture.

Tolle, Eckhart. *The Power of Now.* Novato, California and Vancouver, Canada: New World Library and Namaste Publishing. 2004.

Truman, Karol K. *Feelings Buried Alive Never Die.* Olympus Publishing Company; 4th revised edition. 1991.

Virtue, Doreen, Ph.D. *Archangel Oracle Cards.* Carlsbad, California: Hay House. 2004.

Virtue, Doreen, Ph.D. *Goddess Guidance Oracle Cards.* Carlsbad, California: Hay House. 2004.

Walsch, Neale Donald. *Conversations with God: An Uncommon Dialogue, Book 1.* New York: G.P. Putnam's Sons. 1995.

What the Bleep Do we Know!? DVD. Directed by Mark Vicente Betsy Chasse and William Arntz. Captured Light Distribution & Lord of the Wind Films, 2004.

17938556R00137

Made in the USA
Charleston, SC
07 March 2013